Adolf Hausrath

A History of New Testament Times

Adolf Hausrath

A History of New Testament Times

ISBN/EAN: 9783743399624

Manufactured in Europe, USA, Canada, Australia, Japa

Cover: Foto ©Lupo / pixelio.de

Manufactured and distributed by brebook publishing software (www.brebook.com)

Adolf Hausrath

A History of New Testament Times

Prospectus of the
THEOLOGICAL TRANSLATION FUND.

As it is important that the best results of recent theological investigations on the Continent, conducted without reference to doctrinal considerations, and with the sole purpose of arriving at truth, should be placed within the reach of English readers, it is proposed to collect, by Subscriptions and Donations, a Fund which shall be employed for the promotion of this object. A good deal has been already effected in the way of translating foreign theological literature, a series of works from the pens of Hengstenberg, Haevernick, Delitzsch, Keil, and others of the same school, having of late years been published in English; but—as the names of the authors just mentioned will at once suggest to those who are conversant with the subject—the tendency of these works is for the most part conservative. It is a theological literature of a more independent character, less biassed by dogmatical prepossessions, a literature which is represented by such works as those of Ewald, Hupfeld, F. C. Baur, Zeller, Rothe, Keim, Schrader, Hausrath, Nöldeke, Pfleiderer, &c., in Germany, and by those of Kuenen, Scholten, and others, in Holland, that it is desirable to render accessible to English readers who are not familiar with the languages of the Continent. The demand for works of this description is not as yet so widely extended among either the clergy or the laity of Great Britain as to render it practicable for publishers to bring them out in any considerable numbers at their own risk. And for this reason the publication of treatises of this description can only be secured by obtaining the co-operation of the friends of free and unbiassed theological inquiry.

It is hoped that at least such a number of Subscribers of *One Guinea Annually* may be obtained as may render it practicable for the Publishers, as soon as the scheme is fairly set on foot, to bring out every year *three 8vo volumes*, which each Subscriber of the above amount would be entitled to receive gratis. But as it will be necessary to obtain, and to remunerate, the services of a responsible Editor, and in general, if not invariably, to pay the translators, it would conduce materially to the speedy success of the design, if free donations were also made to the Fund; or if contributors were to subscribe for more than one copy of the works to be published.

If you approve of this scheme, you are requested to communicate with Messrs. Williams and Norgate, 14, Henrietta Street, Covent Garden, London, and to state whether you are willing to subscribe; and if you are disposed to assist further, what would be the amount of your donation, or the number of additional copies of the publications which you would take.

We are, your obedient servants,

JOHN TULLOCH,	H. J. S. SMITH,
H. B. WILSON,	H. SIDGWICK,
B. JOWETT,	JAMES HEYWOOD,
A. P. STANLEY,	C. KEGAN PAUL,
W. G. CLARK,	J. ALLANSON PICTON,
S. DAVIDSON,	ROBT. WALLACE,
JAMES MARTINEAU,	LEWIS CAMPBELL,
JOHN CAIRD,	RUSSELL MARTINEAU,
EDWARD CAIRD,	T. K. CHEYNE,
JAMES DONALDSON,	J. MUIR.

A Committee selected from the signataries of the original Prospectus agreed upon the works to commence the series. Of these, the following were published in

The *First* Year (1873): 3 vols., 21s.

1. KEIM (TH.), HISTORY OF JESUS OF NAZARA. Considered in its connection with the National Life of Israel, and related in detail. Second Edition, re-translated by Arthur Ransom. Vol. I. Introduction; Survey of Sources; Sacred and Political Groundwork; Religious Groundwork.
2. BAUR (F. C.), PAUL, THE APOSTLE OF JESUS CHRIST, his Life and Work, his Epistles and Doctrine. A Contribution to a Critical History of Primitive Christianity. Second Edition, by Rev. Allan Menzies. Vol. I.
3. KUENEN (A.), THE RELIGION OF ISRAEL TO THE FALL OF THE JEWISH STATE. Translated by A. H. May. Vol. I.

The *Second* Year (1874): 3 vols., 21s.

4. KUENEN's RELIGION OF ISRAEL. Vol. II. Translated by A. H. May.
5. BLEEK's LECTURES ON THE APOCALYPSE. Edited by the Rev. Dr. S. Davidson.
6. BAUR's PAUL; the second and concluding volume. Translated by the Rev. Allan Menzies.

The *Third* Year (1875): 3 vols., 21s.

7. KUENEN's RELIGION OF ISRAEL; the third and concluding volume.
8. ZELLER, THE ACTS OF THE APOSTLES CRITICALLY EXAMINED. To which is prefixed, Overbeck's Introduction from De Wette's Handbook, translated by Joseph Dare, B.A. Vol. I.
9. EWALD's COMMENTARY ON THE PROPHETS OF THE OLD TESTAMENT. Translated by the Rev. J. Frederick Smith. Vol. I. General Introduction; Yoel, Amos, Hosea, and Zakharya 9—11.

The *Fourth* Year (1876): 3 vols., 21s.

10. ZELLER's ACTS OF THE APOSTLES. Vol. II. and last.
11. KEIM's HISTORY OF JESUS OF NAZARA. Vol. II. Translated by the Rev. E. M. Geldart. The Sacred Youth; Self-recognition; Decision.
12. EWALD's PROPHETS OF THE OLD TESTAMENT. Vol. II. Yesaya, Obadya, Mikha.

The *Fifth* Year (1877): 3 vols., 21s.

13. PAULINISM: a Contribution to the History of Primitive Christian
15. Theology. By Professor O. Pfleiderer, of Jena. Translated by E. Peters. 2 vols.
14. KEIM's HISTORY OF JESUS OF NAZARA. Translated by A. Ransom. Vol. III. The First Preaching; the Works of Jesus; the Disciples; and the Apostolic Mission.

The *Sixth* Year (1878): 3 vols., 21s.

16. BAUR's (F. C.), CHURCH HISTORY OF THE FIRST THREE CENTURIES. Translated from the third German Edition. Edited by the Rev. Allan Menzies (in 2 vols.). Vol. I.
17. HAUSRATH's HISTORY OF THE NEW TESTAMENT TIMES. The Time of Jesus. Translated by the Revds. C. T. Poynting and P. Quenzer (in 2 vols.). Vol. I.
18. EWALD's COMMENTARY ON THE PROPHETS OF THE OLD TESTAMENT. Translated by the Rev. J. Frederick Smith. Vol. III. Nahum, Ssephanya, Habaqquq, Zakharya 12—14, Yeremya.

The *Seventh* Year (1879): 3 vols., 21s.
19. KEIM'S HISTORY OF JESUS OF NAZARA. Vol. IV. The Galilean Storms; Signs of the approaching Fall; Recognition of the Messiah.
20. BAUR'S CHURCH HISTORY. Vol. II. and last.
21. EWALD'S COMMENTARY ON THE PROPHETS. Vol. IV. Hezeqiel, Yesaya xl.—lxvi.

The *Eighth* Year (1880): 3 vols., 21s.
22. HAUSRATH'S NEW TESTAMENT TIMES. The Time of Jesus. Vol. II. and last.
23. EWALD'S COMMENTARY ON THE PSALMS. Translated by the Rev.
24. E. Johnson, M.A. 2 vols.

The *Ninth* Year (1881): 3 vols., 21s.
25. KEIM'S HISTORY OF JESUS OF NAZARA. Vol. V. The Messianic Progress to Jerusalem.
26. EWALD'S COMMENTARY ON THE PROPHETS. Vol. V. and last. Haggai, Zakharya, Malaki, Yona, Barukh, Daniel.
27. A PROTESTANT COMMENTARY ON THE BOOKS OF THE NEW TESTAMENT: with General and Special Introductions. Edited by Professors P. W. Schmidt and F. von Holzendorff. Translated from the Third German Edition by the Rev. F. H. Jones, B.A. (in 3 vols.). Vol. I. Matthew to Acts.

The *Tenth* Year (1882): 3 vols., 21s.
28. EWALD'S COMMENTARY ON THE BOOK OF JOB. Translated by the Rev. J. Frederick Smith (in 1 vol.).
29. PROTESTANT COMMENTARY. Vol. II. The Pauline Epistles to Galatians.
30. KEIM'S HISTORY OF JESUS OF NAZARA. Vol. VI. and last.

The *Eleventh Year* (1883-84): 3 vols., 21s.
31. PROTESTANT COMMENTARY. Vol. III. and last.
32. REVILLE (Professor ALB., D.D.) PROLEGOMENA OF THE HISTORY OF RELIGIONS. Translated by A. S. Squire. With an Introduction by Professor Max Müller.
33. SCHRADER (Professor E., D.D.) THE CUNEIFORM INSCRIPTIONS AND THE OLD TESTAMENT. Translated by Professor Owen C. Whitehouse. Vol. I. Map.

The *Twelfth* Year (1885-86):
34. PFLEIDERER (Professor O.) THE PHILOSOPHY OF RELIGION ON THE BASIS OF ITS HISTORY. Translated by the Rev. Alex. Stewart and the Rev. Allan Menzies. Vol. I. Spinoza to Schleiermacher.

Beyond these, the following Works are in the hands of Translators, and will be included in the next years' Subscriptions:

SCHRADER (Professor E.) THE OLD TESTAMENT AND CUNEIFORM INSCRIPTIONS. Vol. II.
PFLEIDERER'S PHILOSOPHY OF RELIGION. Translated by the Rev. Alexander Stewart, of Dundee, and the Rev. Allan Menzies Vols. II.—IV.

CONTENTS OF THE
THEOLOGICAL TRANSLATION FUND LIBRARY.

A Selection of Six or more volumes may be had on direct application to the Publishers, at 7s. per volume.

1. **Baur (F. C.) Church History of the First Three** Centuries. Translated from the Third German Edition. Edited by the Rev. Allan Menzies. 2 vols. 8vo. 21s.

2. **Baur (F. C.) Paul, the Apostle of Jesus Christ, his** Life and Work, his Epistles and Doctrine. A Contribution to a Critical History of Primitive Christianity. Second Edition. By the Rev. Allan Menzies. 2 vols. 21s.

3. **Bleek's Lectures on the Apocalypse.** Edited by the Rev. Dr. S. Davidson. 10s. 6d.

4. **Ewald (H.) Commentary on the Prophets of the** Old Testament. Vol. I. Yoel, Amos, Hosea, Zakharya, c. 9—12. Vol. II. Yesaya, Obadya, Mikha. Vol. III. Nahum, Ssephanya, Habaqquq, Zakharya, c. 12—14, Yeremya. Vol. IV. Hezeqiel, Yesaya, c. 40—66. Vol. V. Anonymous Pieces, Haggai, Zakharya, Malaki, Yona, Barukh, Daniel, Index. Translated by the Rev. J. Frederick Smith. 5 vols. 8vo. Each 10s. 6d.

5. **Ewald (H.) Commentary on the Psalms.** Translated by the Rev. E. Johnson, M.A. 2 vols. 8vo. Each 10s. 6d.

6. **Ewald (H.) Commentary on the Book of Job,** with Translation by Professor H. Ewald. Translated from the German by the Rev. J. Frederick Smith. 1 vol. 8vo. 10s. 6d.

7. **Hausrath (Professor A.) History of the New Testament** Times. The Time of Jesus. By Dr. A. Hausrath, Professor of Theology, Heidelberg. Translated, with the Author's sanction, from the Second German Edition, by the Revs. C. T. Poynting and P. Quenzer. 2 vols. 8vo. 21s.

8. **Keim (Th.) History of Jesus of Nazara.** Considered in its connection with the National Life of Israel, and related in detail. Vol. I. Survey of Sources, Paul, Gospels, the Sacred Groundwork. Vol. II. The Sacred Youth, Self-recognition, and Decision. Vol. III. The Galilean Springtime. Vol. IV. The Galilean Storms, Recognition of the Messiah. Vol. V. The Messianic Progress to Jerusalem, the Decisive Struggle, the Farewell, the Last Supper. Vol. VI. The Messianic Death, Burial and Resurrection, the Messianic Place in History. Translated by Arthur Ransom and the Rev. E. M. Geldart. 6 vols. 8vo. Each 10s. 6d.

9. **Kuenen (A.) The Religion of Israel to the Fall of** the Jewish State. Translated by A. H. May. 3 vols. 8vo. 31s. 6d.

10. **Pfleiderer (Professor O.) Paulinism**: a Contribution to the History of Primitive Christian Theology. Translated by E. Peters. 2 vols. 21s.

11. **Pfleiderer (Professor O.) The Philosophy of Religion** on the Basis of its History. I. History of the Philosophy of Religion from Spinoza to the present Day. Vol. I. Spinoza to Schleiermacher. Translated by the Rev. Allan Menzies and the Rev. Alex. Stewart, of Dundee. 10s. 6d. (Vol. II. in the Press.)

12. **Protestant Commentary on the New Testament;** with General and Special Introductions to the Books, by Lipsius, Holsten, Lang, Pfleiderer, Holtzmann, Hilgenfeld, and others. Vol. I. Introduction, the Gospels, the Acts. Vol. II. Epistles to the Romans, Corinthians, Galatians. Vol. III. Ephesians, Philippians, Colossians, Thessalonians, Pastoral Epistles, Revelations. Translated by the Rev. F. H. Jones. 3 vols. 8vo. 31s. 6d.

13. **Reville (Rev. Dr.) Prolegomena of the History of** Religion, with Introduction by Professor Max Müller. 10s. 6d.

14. **Schrader (Professor E.) The Old Testament and** the Cuneiform Inscriptions. Translated by the Rev. Owen C. Whitehouse. (In 2 vols.) Vol. I. Map. 10s. 6d. (Vol. II. in the Press.)

15. **Zeller (E.) The Acts of the Apostles Critically** Examined. To which is prefixed Overbeck's Introduction from De Wette's Handbook. Translated by Joseph Dare. 2 vols. 8vo. 21s.

The price of the Works to Subscribers, 7s. per vol.

Works in the Press:

Pfleiderer (Professor O.) The Philosophy of Religion. Translated by the Rev. Alexander Stewart, of Dundee, and the Rev. Allan Menzies. Vols. II.—IV.

Schrader's Old Testament and Cuneiform Inscriptions, Vol. II.

All new Subscribers may purchase any of the previous volumes at 7s. instead of 10s. 6d. per volume. A selection of six or more volumes may also be had at the Subscriber's price, or 7s. per volume, upon direct application to the Publishers.

THE HIBBERT LECTURES.

1886.—**Professor J. Rhys. Lectures on the Origin and** Growth of Religion as illustrated in Celtic Heathendom. 8vo, cloth. 10s. 6d.

1885.—**Professor O. Pfleiderer. Lectures on the Influence** of the Apostle Paul on the Development of Christianity. Translated by the Rev. J. F. Smith. 8vo, cloth. 10s. 6d.

1884.—**Professor Albert Reville. Lectures on the Ancient** Religions of Mexico and Peru. 8vo, cloth. 10s. 6d.

1883.—**The Rev. Charles Beard. Lectures on the Reformation** of the Sixteenth Century in its Relation to Modern Thought and Knowledge. 8vo, cloth. 10s. 6d. (Cheap Edition, 4s. 6d.)

1882.—**Professor Kuenen. Lectures on National Religions** and Universal Religions. 8vo, cloth. 10s. 6d.

1881.—**T. W. Rhys Davids. Lectures on the Origin and** Growth of Religion as illustrated by some Points in the History of Indian Buddhism. 8vo, cloth. 10s. 6d.

1880.—**M. Ernest Renan. On the Influence of the Institutions,** Thought and Culture of Rome on Christianity, and the Development of the Catholic Church. Translated by the Rev. Charles Beard. 8vo, cloth. 10s. 6d. (Cheap Edition, 2s. 6d.)

1879.—**P. Le Page Renouf. Lectures on the Origin and** Growth of Religion as illustrated by the Religion of Ancient Egypt. Second Edition. 8vo, cloth. 10s. 6d.

1878.—**Professor Max Müller. Lectures on the Origin** and Growth of Religion as illustrated by the Religions of India. 8vo, cloth. 10s. 6d.

Works published by the Hibbert Trustees.

Illustrations of the History of Medieval Thought in the Departments of Theology and Ecclesiastical Politics. By REGINALD LANE POOLE, M.A., Balliol College, Oxford, Ph.D. Leipzig. 8vo, cloth. 10s. 6d.

The Objectivity of Truth. By GEORGE J. STOKES, B.A., Senior Moderator and Gold Medallist, Trinity College, Dublin; late Hibbert Travelling Scholar. 8vo, cloth. 5s.

An Essay on Assyriology. By GEORGE EVANS, M.A., Hibbert Fellow. With an Assyrian Tablet in Cuneiform Type. 8vo, cloth. 5s.

The Development from Kant to Hegel, with Chapters on the Philosophy of Religion. By ANDREW SETH, Assistant to the Professor of Logic and Metaphysics, Edinburgh University. 8vo, cloth. 5s.

Kantian Ethics and the Ethics of Evolution. A Critical Study by J. GOULD SCHURMAN, M.A., D.Sc., Professor of Logic and Metaphysics in Acadia College, Nova Scotia. 8vo, cloth. 5s.

The Resurrection of Jesus Christ. An Essay, in Three Chapters. By REGINALD W. MACAN, Christ Church, Oxford. 8vo, cloth. 5s.

The Ecclesiastical Institutions of Holland, treated with Special Reference to the Position and Prospects of the Modern School of Theology. By the Rev. P. H. WICKSTEED, M.A. 8vo. 1s.

WILLIAMS AND NORGATE,
14, HENRIETTA STREET, COVENT GARDEN, LONDON;
AND 20, SOUTH FREDERICK STREET, EDINBURGH.

A HISTORY

OF THE

NEW TESTAMENT TIMES.

BY

DR. A. HAUSRATH,

ORDINARY PROFESSOR OF THEOLOGY IN THE UNIVERSITY OF HEIDELBERG.

THE TIME OF JESUS.
VOL. II.

TRANSLATED, WITH THE AUTHOR'S SANCTION, FROM THE THIRD GERMAN EDITION, BY

CHARLES T. POYNTING, B.A., & PHILIP QUENZER.

WILLIAMS AND NORGATE,
14, HENRIETTA STREET, COVENT GARDEN, LONDON;
AND 20, SOUTH FREDERICK STREET, EDINBURGH.
1880.

BS
1938
H28

LONDON:
PRINTED BY C. GREEN AND SON,
178, STRAND.

CONTENTS.

Fifth Division.

HEROD [*continued*].

	PAGE
10. The Augustan Age in Judæa	3
11. Herod and Augustus	10
12. Jewish Politics	21
13. New Family Disputes	29
14. The End	41
15. The Inheritance	52

Sixth Division.

THE HISTORICAL RELATIONS OF THE LIFE OF JESUS.

1. The Lords of the Land	61
2. The Incorporation of Judæa into the Province of Syria	72
3. The Procuratorial Administration	83
4. The Jordan Baptism	93
5. The Gerizim Expedition	123
6. Jesus appears in Capernaum	128
7. The New Preaching of the Kingdom	142
8. External Points of Contact	156
9. The First Messianic Community	169

		PAGE
10.	The Kingdom, and those to whom it was proclaimed	189
11.	Moments in the Contest	213
12.	Jesus and the Messianic Idea	222
13.	The Passover of Death	252

Fifth Division.

HEROD.
[Continued.]

HEROD.

10. THE AUGUSTAN AGE IN JUDÆA.

THE great changes in the organization of the empire which Augustus undertook upon his return to Rome in the autumn of the year 29 B.C., did not at first affect Judæa, since this country retained its sovereignty. The more did the people feel the greater activity in trade and commerce, which soon showed itself under the protection of monarchy. In the East, the industries of the Hellenists especially received a fresh impulse, but the mercantile Jews also honoured in Augustus the patron of their business. Streets and public buildings became the chief objects of attention to the administration; and as Augustus himself, for the purpose, laid most serious contributions upon the public treasury, so also did he demand from his friends and connections similar exertions for this end. Among the rulers who courted the favour of Rome, a genuine rivalry sprang up to attract attention by erecting buildings, laying out roads, improving streets, making aqueducts and canals, enlarging harbours, and similar works of public utility, which was the more profitable since the chief minister of state, Agrippa, almost surpassed his master and friend in this passion for building.

A further merit of this new era was its cultivation of poetry and art. Since it was not possible for oratory to exercise its noblest task in the Forum, all talent embraced the literary career. The rostra having been deserted, there followed the age of the ode, the epic, the elegy, the lyric, and especially the stage. The theatres, the circus, the prize games of the chariot-races and singing were everywhere cultivated in order to make the people forget public life. Here, too, the ambition of the lesser princes urged them to keep up with their master.

Herod took hold of this tendency of the day as zealously as though attention to the public welfare and cultivation of the fine arts had always been his chief delight. And yet nothing was really farther from his nature. It was not owing to Hellenic inclinations, but because he was a son of Edom, that he was ever a stranger to the Jews; yet he did not therefore, with his untamed savagery of temperament, approach any the nearer to Western civilization. His personal inclinations were far more those of an Oriental despot, than of a statesman earnestly desirous of advancing the work of civilization. We should look in vain for any manifestations of such a tendency in Herod during the time of Antonius. He had caroused with Antonius,[1] zealously guarded his harem, drilled soldiers and extorted money; but of any interest in art during the whole of the first half of his reign, not a trace is to be found. Here, however, he coincided with the feelings of his people. The Semite is a man without any sense for art, otherwise his laws would never have forbidden him to make images and symbols. He can live without painting a picture, or carving a statue, or stamping a coin, and want of taste is one of the characteristics of the Semitic peculiarity.[2] But since the times demanded it, the shrewd Jewish king affected a taste for such works of peace also, and the first proof of it was his taking part in that servile display in which the Oriental kings combined, to complete the temple of the Olympian Jupiter at Athens at their own expense, and dedicate it to Augustus.[3] But he soon paraded the colours of the new times in Palestine itself.

The indiscreet and overbearing manner in which he violated the most pious feelings of the Rabbis in doing this, displays

---

[1] Antiq. xv. 3, 8. [2] Compare Hepworth Dixon's "The Holy Land," II. p. 41.
[3] Sueton. Octav. 60; Bell. Jud. i. 21, 11.

less of any interest in art than that bitter exasperation with Phariseeism, which devises how it may be most thoroughly avenged upon its opponent. Herod, upon the accession of the emperor, had demanded that an oath of allegiance should be taken to the latter and to himself; but this oath the Pharisees had refused to take. More than six thousand remained unsworn. He could not do more than punish them by fines; but the money was promptly raised for those who so well understood how to devour widows' houses, and even the king's own family made contributions.[1] Enraged did the king stand opposed to his people. In all the passions which had raged within him during these latter years, in the perception that he was hopelessly at enmity with the best of his subjects, in the aimlessness of his own will, in which every nobler purpose was effaced, did the little that had been yet pure and true in him seem destroyed. Even his administration, the clever moves of which had at an earlier date demanded the admiration of the Roman statesmen, bore at this period for some time the mark of Cain—that hatred of man which is especially fond of doing what is most objectionable to one's own people. Deification of force, and contempt for the idealistic tendencies of public life, seemed the only maxims of his government,—maxims which were never more out of place than among a nation accustomed to regard the whole of life, down to the minutest detail, from a transcendental point of view.

Thus his first enactment, in which he sought the approbation rather of Rome than of his own nation, was the introduction of the games of Actium. After his victory over Antonius, Augustus had re-established the ancient games of Apollo at Actium. Their celebration took place for the first time in the year 28 B.C., and it was accepted as a mark of loyalty to observe this festival, so important for the royal house, elsewhere also every five years.[2] Herod could have selected for this purpose one of his Syrian or Phœnician towns, but he preferred to build an amphitheatre near

---

[1] Antiq. xvii. 2, 5. [2] Suet. Oct. 18; Dio, 53, 1.

Jerusalem itself. Prize-fights, gladiatorial contests, combats of animals—in short, all the abominations of the Gentile—found a place at this festival of Cæsar. It was on account of no greater evils that the Maccabees had once drawn the sword against the Syrians; those times of the raving Antiochus seemed returned, of which they read in the first book of the Maccabees, "They built a place of exercise at Jerusalem according to the customs of the heathen."[1] In crowds the Greeks streamed up to the festival in order to carry off the rich prizes offered by the king in the various kinds of forbidden arts, and the two and four-horse chariot-races, from the Jews, who were unpractised in such abominations. The Rabbis regarded this building with abhorrence, for its Gentile style of architecture proclaimed contempt for the law; the people with grief beheld human life fall a sacrifice in the combats with wild beasts.

But not content with this, the king proceeded even to build a theatre in the holy city. The Jews, who had never heard of a play, looked upon this building with horror. Around it were portrayed, on a ground of gold and silver, the deeds of Octavianus; while the Greek mimics strutted about in rich costumes and sparkling jewels. As there were no Hebrew dramas, the contents of the plays were also abominable and blasphemous. Yet in true Rabbinical manner, the hatred of the pious was especially directed against certain ornaments arranged as trophies upon the pillars, behind which, in their suspicion, they assumed human figures were placed, these being directly forbidden by the Decalogue, and even exceeding in abominableness flat representations. In order to appease this suspicion, the king one day invited the most discontented members of the Sanhedrin into the theatre, and asked which were the decorations that were so offensive to them; and then he immediately commanded the coverings to be removed, so that the bare wooden posts presented an odd appearance. Nevertheless, there was but little laughter upon his side.[2] The Rabbis only preached the more continually

[1] 1 Maccabees i. 14.   [2] Antiq. xv. 8, 2.

that Jehovah would send all the punishments which stood written, as retribution for such abominations; and at last ten zealots conspired to strike down the tyrant in his theatre, contented if even an unsuccessful attempt should at least remind him of the people's zeal for the law. So thoroughly was their fanaticism excited, that a blind man even associated himself with them, in order that he might at least participate in the merit of having thrust this new Antiochus aside. But a conspiracy which is intended, as was this one, to be a testimony and a religious act for an example to all the people, is seldom kept very secret. When the conspirators, consequently, met in the theatre on the day appointed, they found, not the king, but his body-guards, who arrested them. They died like heroes, and the informer was torn by the people literally into pieces, which were thrown to the dogs. But the participators in this tumult also were discovered by means of torture, and they and their families destroyed.

After these events it was no longer possible for the king to conceal from himself that he was hated by those around him. He thought of plans for making his life more secure. Laws were enacted for his safety which had been quite unnecessary during the earlier period of his government under Antonius. A network of espionage was spread over the land. Every road in town and country had its appointed number of spies; and it was reported that the king did not himself disdain stealing about at night, disguised, in order to ascertain the feeling of the people. All gatherings and meetings in private houses were forbidden. Any one convicted of transgressing the royal commands was condemned without mercy; but numberless persons also vanished secretly, being conveyed to the fortress of Hyrcania, where either death or years'-long imprisonment awaited them.[1] To the body-guard of Gauls which Augustus had presented to him, Thracians and Germans were now added.[2] At the same time, Herod surrounded the country with forts, and especially sought to make an insurrection in Jerusalem impossible by enlarging the fortifi-

---

[1] Antiq. xv. 10, 4.   [2] Antiq. xvii. 8, 4.

cations of the king's palace, and the citadel Baris, called by him Antonia, in honour of Antonius, which was close to the temple, and menacing the city by a line of other towers. In the same manner he fortified Straton's Tower on the coast, Gaba in Galilèe and Hesbon in Peræa. Samaria, which had been rebuilt by Gabinius, he made a fortress of the first rank, extended its circumference by half a mile, and settled his veterans in the new works. Naturally this erection of the king was especially hateful to the Jews, who in the benefactor of Samaria were the less inclined to acknowledge *their* own sovereign. All these fortifications and castles, however, would not have sufficed, in the present state of popular excitement, to have prevented an outburst of public rage, had not the year 25 B.C. afforded an opportunity for exhibiting the advantageous side of the intimacy with foreign countries.

There was a failure in the crops, and, in consequence of the famine, diseases of every kind made their appearance. The misery was indescribable. Herod had reason to fear a people which despair rendered capable of anything. He therefore made provision against the want with all energy, and succeeded in making a contract with Petronius, procurator of Egypt, for a supply of corn. As, notwithstanding his usual avarice, he never allowed a question of money to interfere when important interests were at stake, so now he unhesitatingly sold with all possible speed his valuable furniture and emptied his treasury in order to purchase corn, and organized a system of relief as thorough as it was practical. He gave both corn and bread, and even provided what clothing was required for wholly impoverished villages. At the same time, he knew how to encourage work, and distributed seed-corn gratuitously. Finally, he was able to succour the province of Syria also. We possess, in the fifth psalm of the Psalms of Solomon, a prayer against famine belonging to this period, which presents us with the disposition of the community at such a visitation. "Let not Thy hand bear heavily upon us," does the Psalmist pray at an earlier visitation of this kind, "so that we may not fall into sin through want. Also when Thou rejectest us, we will not desist, but come unto Thee. When I am an hungered I cry unto Thee, O God, and Thou givest unto me. Thou feedest the birds and the fish, when Thou sendest rain in the spring time in the wilderness to cause food to grow on the pastures for every creature. . . : . A man is kind to his friend, and the day after, if he give unto him a second time without murmuring, so is it a matter of astonishment. But Thou, O God, givest out of Thy goodness much and abundantly; and whoso placeth his hope in Thee, O Lord, will never want Thy gifts. Over the whole world, O Lord, does Thy pitying goodness extend. Happy is he whom God provideth for with sufficient measure. Has a man too much, so does he fall into sin; sufficient is moderation with righteousness. In this does the blessing of the Lord consist, that a man is satisfied in righteousness." We see that the religious feeling of Israel still gave a full tone when deeply agitated, and the strings upon its harp were not all rent. On this occasion the God of Israel had sent help by the hand of the notorious Idumæan, who was able to accomplish more than perhaps a David or a Josiah could have done, and we can well understand that the people were grateful to him for this generosity. It is calculated that altogether he distributed eight hundred thousand Attic measures of corn, and even the pious discovered that this salvation of the country atoned for his previous sins. They therefore bore his Gentile customs more readily for some time, for the sake of the material advantages, although only under necessity and distress of conscience.

Besides, it must not be overlooked that Herod took a far more serviceable part in these Augustan improvements than by merely building theatres and inland fortresses. He strengthened his Arabian frontiers, in the Roman method, by a chain of castles and watch-towers, which were to give timely warning of the movements of the enemy.[1] The strong connecting points of this system were Phasaelis in the Ghor, the castles Thrax, Taurus,

---

[1] Bell. vii. 6, 2; Bell. i. 21, 2; Strabo, Geogr. 16, 2.

Dagon and Cypros above Jericho,[1] Masada upon the western, and Philadelphia, Hesbon, Machærus and Herodium on the eastern shore of the Dead Sea.[2]

As he there built bulwarks against the hostile Arabians, in order to preserve peace for the Romans, so too upon the coast he began at this period to found a magnificent place for commerce which was of benefit to three provinces.[3] Through the stipulations of the year 30 B.C., he had again obtained possession of Straton's Tower. This place was so far of great importance because there was no other harbour between Dor and Joppa, a distance of almost half the length of the coast, than that of Straton's Tower; but during the wars the town had fallen into ruin and its harbour become choked with sand. The want was especially felt in the trade between Syria and Alexandria, because, owing to the want of a station upon the coast, the commerce had to come to an end very early in the year. The king determined to form a harbour here which should not be inferior to the Piræus. He threw out a dam 200 feet broad into the sea, under the protection of which he was enabled to widen and deepen the old harbour. For more than twelve years was this colossal work in execution, being dug out, built up and secured on firm foundations; but the result corresponded to the labour. Here he built what was for the succeeding centuries the capital of Palestine.

---

11. Herod and Augustus.

The more the king had endeavoured, in these latter years, to serve those interests upon which the present potentate of the Roman empire laid value, the more necessary did he find it to

---

[1] Strabo, Geogr. 16, 2.

[2] Phasaelis, Bell. i. 21, 9; Antiq. xvi. 5, 2. Cypros, Bell. i. 21, 4. Masada, Bell. vii. 8, 3. Herodium, Bell. i. 1, 10. Thrax, Taurus, Philadelphia, Strabo, 16, 2. Machærus, Bell. vii. 6, 2. Hesbon, Antiq. xv. 8, 5.

[3] Antiq. xvi. 5, 1.

fill the chief places in his court with foreigners who could satisfy
the demands of the new times. There was a couple of clever
brothers especially, Nicolaus and Ptolemæus of Damascus, descended from a very respectable family there, which the king
now honoured with his confidence. The talent of Nicolaus pre-
eminently was adapted to lend a certain kind of splendour to a
court like Herod's in the eyes of the Roman world. Nicolaus
was a naturalist; he had published some geographical works,[1]
and corresponded with Augustus about a newly-discovered kind
of date.[2] He had farther made a paraphrase of the Metaphysics and some other books of Aristotle.[3] Even poetry had been
attempted by him.[4] Among other things, he had dramatically
treated the story of the chaste Susanna, a significant subject
for the circumstances, and one that had every expectation of
pleasing at the same time both the children of the world and the
pious. Without doubt the piece was also performed at the
theatre in Jerusalem.[5] His historical works, however, were more
important than his poetical. He wrote a history of the world
in a hundred and forty-four books, which seems to have concluded
with the life of Augustus.[6] Moreover, this really learned man
was an elegant sophist of the most practised description, a clever
logician, a skilled lawyer and polished courtier. Nearly all the
law-suits of his prince were conducted by him,[7] and he was
frequently in attendance on the imperial court on account of
business. In the year 16 B.C. he defended the Asiatic Jews
against the Hellenic cities before Agrippa, and it was at that
time that he made that collection of the Roman edicts on the
Jewish privileges which Josephus borrowed from him.[8] Similarly is it through him, too, that Josephus is so exactly informed

[1] Strabo, Geogr. xv. 1.   [2] Plin. Hist. Nat. xiii. 9, 4; Athenæus, xiv. 22.
[3] Nic. Dam. de Arist. reliq. in Roeper. Lectionar. Abulpharag, 35—43.
[4] Suidas, iii. 623.
[5] The piece, according to Dionys. Perieg. v. 976, bore the title Σωσάνις.
[6] Antiq. xii. 3, 2; Athen. vi. 249; compare Müller's Fragm. Hist. Græc. iii. 356.
[7] Bell. i. 29, 3, ii. 2, 1; Antiq. xvi. 2, 3; 9, 4; xvii. 9, 4; 10, 5, &c.
[8] Compare Niese, Hermes xi. 478.

about the most private secrets of Herod's seraglio, in that he, as the confidant of the king, had acquired a most intimate insight. At the extent of servility which he displayed in the biography of his master, even Josephus is shocked.[1] Although less celebrated, yet his brother Ptolemæus, chief chancellor and keeper of the seals of the king, was not less useful to him. The former brother's duty was the representation, the latter's the practical conduct of business. Like his brother, Ptolemæus belonged to his most confidential circle, and had been presented by Herod with the village Arus and other estates in Samaria.[2] He was an equitable man, and tried as much as possible to restrain the passions of the king, the advocate of which was Nicolaus. Other Greeks and half-Greeks also—like Sapinnius, Andromachus and Gemellus, who served him, some in the administration, others as ambassadors, and others as tutors and travelling companions of his sons—now stood high in the favour of the king, and retained it until the obscuration of his last days.[3] Certainly the evil kind of Hellenic sycophants, which usually infested courts then, were not wanting in Jerusalem, and were represented by the rhetorician Irenæus, who by his ready tongue had gained the character of being a skilled member of the administration,[4] and the still worse Eurycles of Lacedemon, ever unsettled, who made money by acting as spy and false witness. The scribes in mockery termed these parasites "the proselytes of the royal table."[5]

The munificence of the king and the intellectual importance of his companions were certainly among the reasons why Herod confirmed himself more and more in the favour of Augustus. The shrewd man upon the Tiber had yet other reasons, however, for especially distinguishing the Jewish king. Augustus was no warrior, and desired no war. But the Arabian desert and the Euphrates were the weakest frontiers of his empire. It was therefore of inestimable value to the emperor to know that there

---

[1] Antiq. xvi. 7, 1.   [2] Antiq. xvii. 9, 4, and 10, 9, xvi. 7, 2, 3; Bell. ii. 5, 1.
[3] Antiq. xvi. 8, 2.   [4] Antiq. xvii. 9, 4.
[5] Grätz, iii. 308; Jerusalem Kiddush, c. 4, p. 65 b.

was here a shrewd prince bound to the Roman interests and at
home in all its complicated relations, one who was in a position
to point out better ways for the Oriental politics of the empire,
which since the days of Pompeius had received only shameful
losses and fatal defeats. The emperor was convinced of this for
the first time in the year 24 B.C., when Gallus, his procurator
of Egypt, allowed himself to be involved in most Utopian
designs, for which Augustus could personally be made answerable.
Augustus had not only retained Egypt under his own administration, but also never sent any officials of senatorial rank
there, because the post was too influential. The more therefore
did the chief nobility in their malignity rejoice when the cousin
of the court poet Propertius, Ælius Gallus, who belonged to one
of the knightly families, seriously compromised the imperial
knowledge of men.

In his anxiety to advance the work of civilization and point
out peaceful laurels to the Roman people, Augustus commissioned his procurator to discover the shortest way between Upper
Egypt and Arabia Felix, in order that spices and precious stones,
the chief commercial products of Arabia, might be directly introduced into the capital. The cousin of Propertius, in order to
accomplish this task, trustingly confided in his chief official, the
so-called "brother" of the Nabatæan king Obodas. Now if any
one were interested in throwing obstacles in the way of this
project, it was the Nabatæans, through whose capital the caravan
road ran. Ever since they had been strengthened by the first
διάδοχοι,[1] they had caused difficulties to the Indian trade of the
Ptolemies, and plundered the Egyptian travellers to India, in
order to prevent any competition with the caravans.[2] The crafty
vizier Syllæus naturally did not allow this to be discovered, but
he determined to play the same trick upon the Romans that
Abgarus had played upon Crassus, and Artavasdes upon Antonius, without the honest Romans afterwards becoming one hair's

---

[1] The name given by historians to the successors of Alexander the Great.
[2] Diod. iii. 43.

breadth the wiser.[1] So he informed the credulous Gallus that the goods were in the first place to be seized at the sea-port of Leuce Come, whither it was necessary to transport the army. Accordingly, Gallus built a fleet, although the great commercial road from Rhinocorura, which passed through Petra, led to this place. When the triremes were built, it was found that they could not be used in the shallow and rocky Arabian bay. Merchantmen, therefore, had to be built. These were sent by Syllæus to a southern point for the army to be embarked. While man and beast perished as they marched along the coast through the stony desert of Troglodytica, half the vessels were destroyed on the rocks by the ebb and flow of the tide as they sailed round the coast. At last the army was transported across to Leuce Come on the Arabian coast; but owing to the want of necessary supplies, the whole force was already fit for the hospital. They had at once to betake themselves to winter quarters. In the spring, the vizier repeated the same game. He did not take the commercial road, but conducted the army to the Sabæans through deserts where the water had to be carried upon camels. Thus they proceeded for fifty days before coming in conflict with a tribe hostile to Syllæus. Then one Arab village after another was taken, and at last they were only a two days' journey distant from the land of spices, when Gallus saw it was absolutely necessary to return, as sickness was terribly thinning the ranks of his army. A kind of typhus had broken out, which carried off the men in a few hours.[2] Fortunately Herod, who must have seen through Syllæus' game, had sent a small squadron of five hundred cavalry to their assistance by the shortest way, without whose aid hardly a Roman would have returned to Egypt.[3]

They led the army, which had taken eighteen months for the march there, back to Alexandria in ten weeks.[4] That the emperor was spared a yet greater disgrace was due entirely to Herod. For without his aid, this scientific-mercantile expedition

---

[1] Strabo, xvi. 4 (p. 777). [2] Dio, liii. 29.
[3] Antiq. xv. 9, 3. [4] Strabo, xvi. 4.

—in which only seven men had died by the sword of the enemy, all the rest having perished through hunger, thirst and disease— could very possibly have severely shaken the position of the monarch. Augustus, however, was one of those sovereigns who learn from their mistakes. He determined for the future not to undertake any Oriental transaction without first consulting Herod. Already in the year 23 did the desired opportunity of distinguishing the meritorious vassal occur. Herod gave a new queen to his seraglio, and now determined to send the sons of Mariamne, the eldest of whom was about thirteen years old, to Rome.[1] The princes were to grow up among the influences of the capital, and from their youth become initiated into the relations of the Imperial court. The Jewish royal family took up their quarters with Asinius Pollio, during whose consulship Herod had first been raised to kingship. The mentor for superintending the education of the boys[2] was not badly selected. Pollio was a learned and well-read man, who, after a protracted military and diplomatic service, had now thrown himself into the fine arts, and wrote historical tragedies in the tragic trimetre. They cannot have been anything very extraordinary, for Horace, who was so fond of praising, can only say of them,

> Pollio regum
> Facta canit, pede ter percusso ;[3] . . . .

But in any case his Tusculan villa was one of the more respectable of the Roman houses; and the princes were well brought up under his indirect superintendence by the well-intentioned pedagogue Gemellus.[4] The finest spirits of Rome visited here, and it was not forgotten that in the year in which Pollio, as consul, had conducted Herod, the newly designated king of the Jews, to

---

[1] For the chronology, compare Antiq. xv. 10, 1, and Bell. i. 20, 4. According to these passages, Herod had received the highlands on the other side of the Jordan on his journey to Rome. The journey took place at the expiration of the first games of Actium, that is, in the year 23.

[2] Pliny, Hist. vii. 30, xxxv. 2, xxxvi. 5.

[3] Hor. Sat. i. 10, 42; Virgil, Eclog. viii. 9.   [4] Antiq. xvi. 8, 2.

the Capitol, the immortal Virgil dedicated his fourth eclogue to the consul on the occasion of the birth of a son, in which the Messianic expectation of the Jews is brought into connection with the consul's child in the cradle. With this Messiah of Virgil the Jewish princes were now to enter into friendly relations. In his audience with Augustus, the expectations of the king were exceeded. The emperor allowed Herod to introduce his sons, assured him that he recognized them as the heirs to Judæa, and interested himself in their education. Nicolaus of Damascus also was treated with distinction by the emperor.[1]

At the same time, however, there were greater plans proposed to Herod. The proconsul of Syria, Varro, had at that time been making vain attempts to restore order in the Lebanon district. The former domain of Lysanias was still in the hands of Zenodorus, dynast of Ulatha, to whom it had been leased by Cleopatra. But this petty princeling had not been at all in a position to maintain order among the hordes of robbers there, and so long as he personally received no injury, he was also indifferent to the complaints of his neighbours, who were molested by the Ituræans and Trachonites; nay, it was even said of him that he shared with these highway robbers in the proceeds of their plundering. The merchants of Damascus, therefore, addressed their complaints to Varro, the proconsul of Syria; but he would have been compelled to have stationed whole legions here in order to keep a guard upon the hundreds of caves and subterranean retreats. Such a condition of things might have long continued under Antonius, but with Augustus the disturbance of trade and breaking the public peace were the greatest of all crimes. Zenodorus consequently was promptly deposed, and the whole territory presented to Herod, who knew of old how to deal with these troglodytes. The king, after these favourable results of his journey, returned home, in order that he might without loss of time zealously pursue his contests with the caves, in which he had won his spurs some twenty years before. His first step

---

[1] Athen. xiv. p. 652 a.

was to obtain guides and spies who were acquainted with the entrances to the caves. Then he cut off one of the subterranean villages which had its outlets on the upper surface, and destroyed its inhabitants by the means already approved by him. When, notwithstanding, the caves were afterwards again inhabited, he planted military colonies in a series of strongholds, for which he formed, shortly before his death, a centre in the fortress of Bathyra,[1] so that under his successors these extensive territories could be regarded as tranquillized.[2]

Ituræa with Trachonitis alone would certainly have been of very doubtful value, since the administration of these territories cost more than their whole revenue was worth;[3] but united to the fruitful plain of Hauran and the splendid valleys of Cœle-Syria, it was an acquisition, not only politically but also pecuniarily, of great advantage. The slighted Zenodorus, it is true, in consequence of his forfeiture, incited the Arabians against Herod, who did not recognize their treaties with the previous lessee; he also betook himself to Augustus in order to arouse suspicions about Herod; but the king silenced the Arabians by presents, and Augustus unceremoniously dismissed Zenodorus. In the following year, 22 B.C., Herod was able to give an account of his successes in person to the minister who, having fallen out at this time with his master, was directing the administration of Syria from Lesbos. Agrippa received him in a friendly manner at Mitylene, and displayed the most respectful consideration towards him, deciding all complaints which were there brought before the mighty Roman in favour of the king. Augustus also shortly afterwards in person at Antioch rejected the intrigues of Zenodorus, and when the injured dynast shortly afterwards died, Herod received also Ulatha and Paneas in the year 20 B.C., in order to round off his frontiers.

Thus he had in fact become a great king, for he was now

---

[1] Under the proconsul C. S. Saturninus, 10 to 6 B.C.
[2] Cass. Dio, liv. 9; Antiq. xv. 10, 2, and xvi. 2, 1.   [3] Antiq. xvii. 2, 2.

master of the territory from Lebanon to Damascus and southwards to Mount Alsadamus, a territory which no Jewish king before had ever possessed. These new acquisitions embraced Batanæa, Auranitis, Trachonitis, Ituræa, the dominion of Ulatha with Paneas, the principality of Abilene and Chalcis, together with the possessions upon the western slopes of Lebanon. Moreover, Augustus, who had now become tired of his officials' blunders, commanded, during his present stay in Syria, that they should not undertake any important enterprize without the approbation of the king, so that Herod became, as it were, Agrippa's deputy for the eastern provinces. And thus he could now with truth be termed the most powerful sovereign of Asia on this side of the Euphrates. These, perhaps, were the happiest years of his troubled life. It seemed, in fact, as though the storms which had raged within him after Mariamne's death had subsided, and he had regained his former equilibrium. In the year 23 he had even married again, taking for his wife "the most beautiful woman in the world," as the Jews extravagantly termed her—the daughter of Simon ben Boëthus; and in order that the relationship should not be too humble, he deposed the high-priest Jesus, the son of Phabi, and promoted his father-in-law to this office. That this man belonged to an Egyptian Levitical family, and consequently was without any standing in the country, only made the king the more determined upon the change.[1] Thus the new nobility of the family of Boëthus thrust themselves in among the Sadducees, whom they soon even surpassed in arrogance and violence. In fanaticism for the letter of the law, the family of Boëthus equalled the Sadducees; they differed from them politically through their attachment to Herod. It was in virtue of his royal relationship that the first of the family of Boëthus held his priestly office; it was owing to a family dispute in the royal house that it was finally lost.

[1] Antiq. xv. 9, 3. Josephus varies in his statements on this point, terming the high-priest in one place the brother-in-law, and in another the father-in-law, of the king. Compare Antiq. xix. 6, 2; compare also Schürer, the ἀρχιερεῖς in N. Test. Stud. und Krit. 1872, p. 599.

Besides, it was impossible that the special Jewish interests could remain without being injuriously affected by the acquisition of so many Gentile territories. The king's first act was to found a temple of white marble to Augustus on the mountain of Pan, at the sources of the river Jordan; and very soon was it unnecessary to travel far up the country in order to learn that Jehovah had to endure many gods besides Himself in His own land. In Samaria, also, Herod built a temple to Cæsar, which he surrounded with a sacred court, a stadium and a half in size. Statues and busts of Herod, too, were not wanting.[1] On the other hand, in Jerusalem itself, a new palace, quite in the Gentile style, with wide halls, colonnades and baths, was commenced upon Mount Zion, one wing of which was called Cæsar's building, the other Agrippa's. The Castle Herodium also, which he placed upon the hill at the falls of the Wady Ain Ghuweir, where formerly he had fought so bravely with the Jews on his retreat before Antigonus, acquired the appearance of a Roman citadel in an Italian town, having great aqueducts and round, staring towers about it. In a similar manner was the building of Cæsarea proceeded with. When the great harbour-dam was finished, another narrower one was erected opposite it, provided with signal towers, the greatest of which was called Drusion, after Augustus' son. The outlet, which was to the south, the harbour being protected from the north wind by its situation, was adorned with massive columns. Widely extended quays, elegantly arranged bazaars, spacious basilicas and convenient lodgings for the sailors, were intended to contribute to aid the establishment of the great world of commerce. The whole of the quarter near the harbour was built of white stone in the showy style of that period, and above the town, visible far and wide to the sailors, arose a temple with colossal statues,—one of Augustus as Zeus Olympius, and another of the Roma Dea as the Argos-Juno. Theatre and amphitheatre were not wanting. The king built a

[1] De Vogüé and Waddington found the pedestal of a statue of Herod in the Hauran: Syrie Centrale. Archit. pl. 2, 3.

palace for himself, to the gorgeous halls of which the procurators afterwards transferred their prætorium. But what appeared to the Jews as especially beneficial was the subterranean system of drainage, by which, as the drains were washed out by the sea, the town was kept cleaner and healthier than any other in Syria. Notwithstanding, the completely Gentile character of Cæsarea created yet greater exasperation against the king, because it especially commended itself to the hated Samaritans.

Although the inland districts of Judæa remained undisturbed by any attempt to erect buildings of such purely Gentile character within them, yet there arose along all the military roads cenotaphs, mausoleums, Cæsareums and similar monuments; and as the king had a passion for giving the names of the members of the imperial family to all his creations, it was possible for a stranger to suppose that he was transported to Italy, so many Latin names of places came into use. Herod, moreover, was never short of money for proving his friendly interest to the neighbouring Gentile towns, by building them gymnasia, colonnades, theatres or aqueducts, and endowing a "Herod's prize" at every public game in the world. It seemed as though the throne of David existed only in order to enable heathendom once more to flourish. The Jews were the more sensitive upon this point because Herod did not favour a single Jewish town with even the least adornment, and quite openly confessed that only his Gentile subjects were dear to his heart, the Jews having become thoroughly distasteful to him.[1] With all the more mistrust, therefore, must it have been received by the scribes, when he suddenly proposed a most magnificent scheme with regard to their sanctuary at Jerusalem.

[1] Antiq. xix. 7, 3.

12. Jewish Politics.

It was in the fifteenth year of his reign that Herod summoned an assembly of the people, in order to announce to them his intention of rebuilding the temple of Zerubbabel, because it in its antique poverty stood no longer in suitable relation to the new, magnificent buildings which the king had lately erected in Jerusalem. That some sort of demand was made upon Herod to this end is certain; and according to a perhaps somewhat doubtful account in the Talmud, it was Rabbi Baba Ben Bouta who demanded of Herod that he should atone for his deeds of violence in the eyes of the people by a work of this nature.[1] It seems, however, that in this undertaking there was a political motive also present,—that of uniting his name inseparably with the central point of the theocracy. The speech which Josephus puts into the king's mouth on this occasion has been sometimes regarded, too, as a proof of Herod's intention of convincing the Jews, by this undertaking, that his government was that promised time of the restoration of the kingdom—nay, that he himself was the promised king of the Jews.[2] For one of the standing articles of the Messianic expectation was that the restorer of Israel would replace the poor temple of Zerubbabel by a more splendid one, as the prophet Haggai even had consoled the elders of the people. And the favourite book of Enoch placed before their view, as the end of the eighth week of years, a time "when they would acquire houses through righteousness, and a house would be built to the praise of the great king for ever and ever."[3] Herod had to assume a position with regard to this popular belief that it was the work of Messiah—relatively of the Messianic time —to replace the temple of Zerubbabel by a worthier one: and there appears indeed to have been a party which saw in him

---

[1] Baba-bathra, 36; Bamidbar-rabba, cap. 12: in Derenbourg's Histoire de la Palestine, d'après les Talmuds, 152.

[2] Antiq. xv. 11, 1, &c.   [3] Henoch 91, 13; compare 90, 28.

the fulfiller of the Messianic promises; for the Church fathers Epiphanius and Tertullian regard the Herodians of the Gospels as those who had accepted Herod as the Messiah.[1] According to Josephus, even Herod himself referred to the promise of the prophet Haggai concerning this point. "Who is left among you," had the prophet asked of the elders after the completion of the building of the temple, "that saw this house in her former glory? and how do ye see it now? Is not such an one as nothing in your eyes? Yet .... fear ye not. For thus saith Jehovah, Yet once it is a little while, and I will shake the heavens and the earth, and I will shake all nations, and the desirable things of all nations shall come: and I will fill this house with glory, saith Jehovah..... The latter glory of this house shall be greater than the former, saith Jehovah; and in this place will I give peace, saith Jehovah."[2]

This was the theme which Herod took as the foundation of his speech to the people and their elders. His assumption was, that the time of peace had now begun after great commotions, and that he, by his measures, had so firmly established the security of the country, that by the will of God he had been enabled to raise the Jewish people to a degree of happiness and prosperity, of splendour and respect, which had never before been attained; that now the time of enduring peace, of great riches and large revenues, had arrived; and it was now therefore a duty so to restore the temple, which wanted sixty cubits of the height of Solomon's temple, that it should even surpass the glory of the first house.[3]

A universal consternation was the result of these communications. The people were afraid that the king would pull down the temple, and not build it up again. Thus some opposition

---

[1] Compare also the Scholium to Persius, v. 180; Grotius, de verit. relig. Christ. edit. Cleric.: Amsterdam, 1709, p. 247, nota. 4; Tertullian, Præscr. 45: Herodiani, qui Christum Herodem esse dixerunt.

[2] Haggai ii. 3—9.

[3] Compare Gerlach. die Weissagungen des Alten Testaments, in d. Schriften des Josephus, p. 87; Gfrörer, Urchristenthum, i. 46, &c.

arose, and it was demanded that Herod should desist from his plan, as it was doubtful whether he would be able to complete a new building. In reply, the king promised that not a single stone should be removed before the whole of the materials for the new building had been prepared and hewn ready to hand, a promise against which no further opposition could be entertained. But now the question arose, Would not the sacred precincts be desecrated if workmen of every tribe, perhaps even Gentile overseers, were to work at the temple? According to Josephus, the king promised to have a thousand priests instructed in carpentry and masonry, in order that they might undertake the work in the sacred precincts. From this magnanimous offer, also, there was no escape. In fact, Herod procured a thousand priests and ten thousand workmen, and it seems that now the outer courts were built by ordinary workmen, those of the Israelites being built by Jews, while the sanctuary itself and the forecourt of the priests were built by priests alone.[1]

Meanwhile the king had the priests whom he had procured instructed in many hundred workshops in Palestine, and provided them with the necessary priestly garments, and thus by his energy in executing what had been deemed impossible he cut away the last ground of objection from the Rabbis. In eight years the forecourts were so far advanced that it was possible to begin the temple itself.

Singular as all these demands of the people upon Herod appear, yet his very compliance proves that he did not underestimate the fanaticism of his subjects about the temple, and was well aware that he was working in dangerous proximity to most terrible passions. The guarantees which the people demanded for the safe preservation of their sanctuary appear even moderate when we read how the writer of the book of Enoch had imagined the rebuilding of the temple. He makes Jehovah himself, at the Messianic renovation of the temple, proceed with far greater reverence for the old building than the

---

[1] Reminiscences of this are found in Baba-bathra, 3 b, in place before quoted.

Jews demanded from Herod. "I saw," the seer declares,[1] "how the Lord of the sheep surrounded that ancient house, and all the pillars were carried out, and all the beams and the decorations were at the same time covered over, and they were carried out and laid in a place in the south of the land. And I saw the Lord of the sheep until he brought a new house, greater and higher than the first, and set it in the place of the first which was covered over." Any pulling down of the old temple, in which the old materials should be carted away as rubbish, was even in the Messianic kingdom inconceivable to the author of the book of Enoch; how much more need was there, then, of Herod's paying regard to such susceptible piety! For the belief prevailed that the temple was altogether inviolable; and the author of the Christian Apocalypse was still of the opinion that the ark of the covenant and the pot of manna of Solomon's temple had not perished in the first destruction of Jerusalem, but had been carried off to heaven, whence they would be revealed on the day of judgment.[2]

Whilst the temple service, therefore, was proceeded with in its usual course, the great work was carried on assiduously, from year's end to year's end, by ten thousand workmen and a thousand waggoners. It was deemed necessary to surround the whole of the temple-mount with buttresses, in order to furnish a firm foundation for the greater buildings. Blocks of colossal size were provided for the purpose. "Master, see what manner of stones," did the disciples at a later day say to their teacher of Capernaum, when they went with him down the temple-mount towards the valley of the Kidron. Even at the present day such pieces of workmanship, twenty feet long by four feet high, remain an object of astonishment.[3] A farther difficulty was how to obtain the masses of marble employed in the external facing of the walls and the temple-house; for there are no marble quarries in Palestine, and the transport from Arabia was still

---

[1] Henoch 90, 29. [2] Rev. xi. 19, ii. 17; compare also 2 Maccabees ii. 4—8.
[3] Furrer, Wanderung, xxxiv.

more difficult than from the Greek islands.¹ When the building
had advanced as far as to the highest terrace, it took the king
still a year and a half to have the temple-house put together,
piece by piece, by the most clever of the priests who had become
stonemasons. The priesthood insisted so strongly upon the point
that only priests should be allowed to enter the inner court, that
even the king, who had often been present at the building of the
courts and terraces, was now forbidden entrance and oversight of
the work.² The Rabbis also pretended to have observed that
during the latter period, when the inner temple was being built,
rain fell only at night, so that the work should not be hindered.³ When the whole approached completion, the king
managed that the consecration fell upon the day of his accession to the throne, so that it henceforth was reckoned among
the Jewish festivals.⁴ The festival itself was celebrated on
Herod's day, in the year 14 B.C., with a pomp which far
surpassed that of every previous temple festival. The lowing of
300 oxen at the altar of burnt sacrifices announced to Jerusalem
the first sacrificial hour of the temple of Herod. Even the
Rabbis were compelled to acknowledge that he who had not
seen the temple of Herod had seen nothing beautiful.⁵ But it
seemed as though the king were determined to studiously prove
to the scribes that their praise or blame was to him a matter of
perfect indifference; for scarcely had he won their hearts through
the completion of this great theocratic work, when he all the
more deeply revolted their feelings by placing a large golden
eagle above the principal gate of the new temple,⁶ and by this
means grossly transgressed the commandments of the Decalogue.
Thus here too, finally, did the cloven hoof appear.

The Roman eagle probably had been placed on the temple-gate

---

[1] Antiq. xii. 4, 11; Diodorus Siculus, ii. 52.   [2] Antiq. xv. 11, 5.

[3] Antiq. xv. 11, 7. Talmud: compare parallel passages in Derenbourg, Histoire de la Palestine d'après les Talmuds, 153.

[4] Antiq. xv. 11, 7; Persius, Sat. v. 180.   [5] Succa, 5, b; Baba-bathra, 4 a.

[6] Antiq. xvii. 6, 2.

at a time when Herod was expecting a visitor from Rome, perhaps Agrippa, who had sacrificed in the old temple. But already, during the whole time the temple was rebuilding, the relations with the people appear to have been again in a state of extreme tension. For although the laws for public security had never been more ruthlessly maintained, yet the undertakings of the king were publicly characterized with indignation and exasperation as an attempt to at once "undermine religion and morality." Then Herod suddenly took the people by surprise by remitting more than 33 per cent. of the taxes, without however, being able to entirely remove their ill-humour. Indeed, this actually increased when he published a law by which convicted thieves were to be sold abroad as slaves. The precepts of Leviticus, as well as natural feeling, were opposed to such a severe punishment. The stricter school of the Rabbis, which insisted, as Shammai had done, upon the very letter of the law, referred to Exodus xxii. 1—4, where restitution—and, in case where the thief has no means, then his being sold until the sabbatical year —is permitted. The milder school, on the other hand, following Hillel's method of interpretation, even proved that there was a fundamental contradiction between the law and this decree; for, said they, when a man has been sold to the Gentiles he cannot keep the law, and thus loses the blessing of Abraham; he therefore goes to Gehenna, and will be eternally damned on account of a theft.[1] The discontent was great, but Herod's position was then so assured that he did not need to concern himself about it. When, in the year 19 or 18 B.C., he went to Rome in order to bring his sons home, he was again loaded by Augustus with favours. In the year 15, Agrippa, who was now Augustus' son-in-law, came a second time to the East,[2] and with full powers. Herod hastened to meet him, and accompanied him to Syria, where Agrippa had business.[3] He could not lose the opportunity

---

[1] Antiq. xvi. 1, 1.
[2] Antiq. xvi. 2, 1; Dio, liv. 19; compare Müller, Fragm. Hist. Græc. iii. 350, n. 2.
[3] Eusebius, in Ol. 191; Strabo, 16, 2.

of also personally showing a minister so enthusiastic about the construction of aqueducts and roads, that they did not remain behind the demands of the times in Palestine. In the year 15, therefore, Agrippa came to Judæa in compliance with the urgent requests of the Jewish king. They first inspected the quays and harbour arrangements in course of construction at Cæsarea; next the barracks and temple to Cæsar at Sebaste; and then made excursions from Jerusalem to the fortresses of Alexandrium, Herodium and Hyrcania. The people of Jerusalem went to meet their exalted guest in festive processions. According to Philo's description, it appears to have been the time of the feast of Tabernacles. The mighty Roman conducted himself on this occasion with great prudence. "Agrippa," does Philo relate to Caligula, "thought fit to go up from the sea-coast to the metropolis, which was inland. And when he had beheld the temple, and the adornments of the priests, and the piety and holiness of the people of the country, he marvelled, looking upon the whole matter as one of great solemnity and entitled to great respect, and thinking that he had beheld what was too magnificent to be described. And he could talk of nothing else to his companions but the magnificence of the temple and everything connected with it. Therefore every day that he remained in the city, by reason of his friendship for Herod, he went to that sacred place, being delighted with the spectacle of the building and of the sacrifices, and all the ceremonies connected with the worship of God, and the regularity which was observed, and the dignity and honour paid to the high-priest, and his grandeur when arrayed in his sacred vestments and when about to begin the sacrifices."[1] Then Agrippa, without offending their customs, gave a splendid feast to the people, sacrificed a hecatomb in the temple, and showed it honour by his gifts. So much had he charmed the Jews by his affability, that in all the places through which he passed on his return, the people accompanied him, and strewed

---

[1] Philo, Leg. ad Caium; Frankfurter Ausgabe, 1033; Bohn's Translation, by C. D. Yonge, Vol. iv. p. 164.

his path with branches and flowers, and parted with him on his ship at Cæsarea with loud cries of hosanna.[1]

In the spring of the year 14, Herod paid his return visit at Sinope,[2] where he found Julia also, whom Augustus, anxious about her fidelity to her husband, had sent after him to the camp. Both gave Herod a proof of their friendship; for Agrippa, at Herod's intercession, remitted the exorbitant fine which he had laid upon the town of Troas because the community, by neglecting the regulations for safety, had endangered Julia's life in the passage across the Scamander.[3] The journey there had cost Herod large sums of money, for all the Greek cities through which he passed besought the support of the rich Jewish king; upon his return, which he made from Sinope by land to Ephesus in the train of the princely pair, the Jews of the Diaspora flocked to him, in order to obtain his intercession for them with Agrippa. We possess in Josephus the Roman edicts and communal decrees — collected, probably, on the occasion of this process — of the cities of Ephesus, Sardis, Halicarnassus, Pergamus, Miletus, Laodicea, Cos, Delos and others, by which the relations of the Jews to the communal duties and rights at the time of Julius Cæsar had been defined;[4] but where the decisive will of a Roman official did not watch over their execution, the natural disinclination of the Hellenes to the Jews always manifested itself. The chief complaints of the Jews to Agrippa were at this time also, that they were purposely called before the tribunals on their holy days, that their collections for the temple were frequently sequestered, that their exception from military service was not respected, that they were subjected to personal services incompatible with their law, and had to purchase immunity from those very things to which Cæsar, out of regard to their law, had promised they should not be liable. It was at Lesbos where Agrippa, at Herod's

---

[1] Antiq. xvi. 2, 1. Philo, in passage last quoted.
[2] Antiq. xvi. 2, 2, and Cass. Dio, 54, 24.
[3] Antiq. xvi. 2, 2; Nicol. Dam. de vita sua, 3; Müller, Fragm. Hist. Gr. iii. 350.
[4] Antiq. xiv. 10.

request, appointed a day for hearing their case, when the king's friend Nicolaus of Damascus pleaded the cause of the Jews. That the positive law stood upon their side, their very opponents could not deny; but the latter returned now, too, to their ancient Hellenic canon, "That if the Jews wished to share in the same rights, they ought also to worship our gods."[1] Many complaints were raised on this occasion of how the Jews drained the communities, and were a cancer to many a commonwealth. Nevertheless, Agrippa gave judgment in their favour in every essential point, and Herod began his journey home with the blessings of the Diaspora of Asia Minor. In Jerusalem, the people—to whom the prince on his return home communicated the results of his journey in a public assembly—accepted his services to the Diaspora with great approval; and the king, being in a gracious humour, heightened their joy by remitting a fourth part of the taxes due for the current year.

13. New Family Disputes.

Before Agrippa's arrival in Judæa, Herod had brought his sons back from Rome. The elder, Alexander, was about eighteen, and the younger, Aristobulus, somewhere about seventeen. During their residence in Rome, they had grown up to fine figures which did not belie the nobility of their mother. In Italy and on their return in Judæa, the princes were greeted by the people with marked sympathy. They had in their intercourse with the leading Roman families acquired an open, straightforward manner, which was in advantageous contrast with that of their cringing Idumæan relations on Mount Zion. Certainly, the depravity of the capital had also found a place in their education, and they habitually indulged in vices which were punishable by death in Israel.[2] Augustus had given Herod

---

[1] Antiq. xii. 3, 2.   [2] Bell. i. 24, 7.

full permission to nominate one of them as heir of his united kingdom, which would have crossed many plans formed in Jerusalem during their absence. But the princes on their side, too, felt a repugnance to their Idumæan relatives. Images of their beautiful mother, they had often been reminded of her in Rome, and had pondered much on her fate. Their inexperienced youth cherished the idea of restoring the honour of the mother who had perished on the scaffold, by a revision of the trial and bringing her calumniators to punishment. Herod observed the division between the two sides of his family, and sought to remove it, as the practice was in Rome, by intermarriage. He caused Aristobulus, the younger son, to marry Berenice, daughter of Salome, who, of good disposition from the first, grew up afterwards into a worthy matron, but was at this time undeveloped, and entirely under the influence of her mother's intrigues.[1] For Alexander, the heir to his throne, on the other hand, the father sought out a king's daughter as wife. He found a court which was worthy of him. Archelaus, a descendant of the sacerdotal princes of Comana, had been declared king of Cappadocia by Antonius. The temple at Comana had the same repute as the temple of Aphrodite at Corinth.[2] One of the courtezans, named Glaphyra, had so captivated the father of Archelaus, that he had raised her to be his queen.[3] As such, she had contracted an attachment with Antonius, and this was supposed to be the reason why her son received the kingdom of Cappadocia in the year 36 B.C.[4] In order that this ignoble origin of the dynasty should not be allowed to be forgotten, Archelaus had also given his daughter the name of Glaphyra, and she it was whom Herod now sought as wife for his son. To this Greek princess, Mount Zion, with the numerous wives of the king, received into his harem rather on account of their beauty than their breeding, appeared very barbarous. The Idumæan relatives of her husband, in particular, did she find

---

[1] Antiq. xviii. 6, 1. [2] Strabo, xii. 3.
[3] Dio, xlix. 32. [4] Martial, xi. 20; App. Bell. c. v. 7.

completely beneath her, and boasted not a little that she herself was descended on her father's side from Hercules, and on her mother's from the Persian royal family.[1] She bred her children up in Gentile manners, and on every occasion let her contempt for the barbarism of the Jews be known.[2] Thus the disputes of the various wives were soon once more in full swing. Aristobulus did not see why he should have had to marry the daughter of Salome, when Alexander had married a king's daughter. The more exasperated did Salome become with Glaphyra; for the latter, besides, had never learned to bridle her Hellenic tongue, and her husband threatened that when he was master he would make his brothers village clerks, and set his father's wives to spin, and clothe them in hair-cloth instead of the royal garments of Mariamne which Herod had bestowed upon them.[3] Salome, in return, swore that he and his brother should be sent to the grave of their haughty mother, together with their three little brothers, who bewailed the Asmonean princess with them. Owing to the imprudence of the princes and the Cappadocian princess, the family scandals of the court were soon the one subject of conversation in the town.

Unfortunately, Herod's last remaining brother, Pheroras, declared himself likewise upon Salome's side. He had been engaged to be married to a daughter of Herod, and had received from the latter the title of tetrarch and the whole revenue of Peræa, but had then fallen so completely into the trammels of one of his female slaves, that Herod broke off the engagement. While the king showed a great attachment to him, Idumæan faithlessness constituted the real nature of this youngest son of Antipater. He was believed to have already entered into a conspiracy with the sheikh Costobar against Herod. Then the relations of the servant-girl whom he made his wife exercised great influence over him, which was the more disastrous because she had inherited from the lower orders, from which she derived her origin, an unconditional reverence for the sanctity of the Pharisees.

[1] Bell. i. 24, 2.   [2] Antiq. xviii. 5, 4.   [3] Bell. i. 24, 3.

Among other things, it was from the revenues of Peræa, which Herod had bestowed upon his brother, that the fines were paid which had been inflicted upon the Pharisees on account of their refusal to take the oaths. As Pheroras could not live without entering into conspiracy, and might well feel enraged at the pert jokes which Glaphyra made at the expense of his plebeian relatives, he allied himself with Salome for the destruction of the two princes. When Herod returned to Jerusalem, after his visit to Agrippa in the year 17 to 16 B.C., he found his whole household at enmity. The elder members proclaimed themselves to be the party of the king, the younger sullenly withdrew. The easier was it for the brother and sister to persuade their royal brother that designs had been made upon his life. They alarmed him especially by the news that the Cappadocian king had promised the young princes that he would desire Augustus to institute an inquiry into the trial of Mariamne.

Herod was deeply affected by this information, which had already reached him from another quarter, and in which he could only see a design upon his crown. To his misfortune, the idea now entered his head of recalling to the court Antipater, the son of his first marriage with Doris, who had hitherto grown up in the obscurity of a country town, in order to show the lads that there was a still older Herodian who could inherit the crown as well as they.

This step became the greatest curse of his life. Antipater had grown up hating the old royal house and despising his father. He had scarcely been allowed to visit Jerusalem upon the festivals, in order that the aristocratic relations might not be reminded of his plebeian existence.[1] In this banishment his heart had grown hard as iron in hatred of the Asmonean to whom his mother, and of her sons to whom he had been compelled to give place. His malignant disposition could have but one object, that of supplanting the young intruders. All the Idumæan relations at once took his side in his contest with the sons of

[1] Bell. i. 22, 1.

Mariamne, and the chancellor Ptolemæus, who considered it his duty to act as mediator and reconciler, soon found his position endangered by him. Antipater played his game cautiously enough. A word of complaint against the young princes never passed his lips, while a troop of informers in his interest worked upon the king. Herod's evil genius had ever been suspicion, the offspring of his evil conscience. He now watched every step of the princes with injurious mistrust; angry expressions about his "nobly born" sons, allusions to their legitimacy, betrayed what was passing in his mind,[1] and insulting neglect engrafted a hatred in their hearts which was not there at first. The sons of Mariamne, again, were indignant at seeing the child of a plebeian mother elevated above themselves: especially so as Herod, in order to thoroughly humiliate them, took Doris back again as wife, so that every hope for the crown which had been promised them seemed to have vanished. Pheroras and Salome, moreover, inflamed the emnity between them by poisonous insinuations, suggesting to Alexander in particular that Herod had designs upon his attractive wife, the beautiful Glaphyra.[2]

When Agrippa, in the year 13, returned from Asia to Rome, after his ten years' administration,[3] Herod, on his departure, sent Antipater to Rome with him, thereby seeming to put his succession to the throne beyond question. But even from this distance the practised intriguer knew how to keep his father's suspicion alive, and his tale-bearing at last brought the old king to such a state of mind that he took ship with his two sons for Italy, and at Aquileia besought the Cæsar in person to punish the patricidal young men. Now for the first time did the two princes learn the full extent of their father's suspicions, and, horror-struck, burst into tears with protestations of innocence. That they were tried here was, however, fortunate for them. In the bright halls of Augustus the ghosts of the Jewish court faded away, and Alexander's straightforward manner obtained a better arena here than

---

[1] Bell. i. 26, 2.   [2] Antiq. xvi. 7, 4.
[3] 741 A.U.C.: Fischer, Zeittafel, 407.

in the gloomy Jerusalem, where he was sold to the groundless falsehoods of the Oriental courtiers. Augustus, moreover, unravelled the complications in an intelligent and benevolent manner, and the king appeared to forget all his suspicions at his exhortation. No one, however, more loudly proclaimed his joy at this happy reconciliation than Antipater, with whom the father and brothers now returned to Jerusalem. To the people there, Herod announced that he should divide his possessions among the three sons proportionately to their relative ages.

But, naturally, the war of parties did not end here. "Antipater possessed quite a peculiar skill in contriving that the brothers should be accused by others, while he personally defended them."[1] One of his chief instruments for this purpose was the hatred existing between the young wives, Glaphyra and Berenice; for since the latter did not believe that she was sufficiently defended by her husband, Aristobulus' most private expressions were often betrayed by her, during her fits of weeping, to her mother, who busily reported them again. Fortunately, Herod discovered that Pheroras was attempting to make his son Alexander jealous about his relations with Glaphyra, so that the old king began to doubt his brother's and sister's veracity, and for some time rejected all their insinuations. Antipater alone had played his part so skilfully, that no suspicion attached to him, and he waited quietly until Herod had another gloomy fit upon him, and then suggested that the immediate followers of the princes should be interrogated, by means of the rack, about certain pretended plans of murder. The tortured slaves of course confessed whatever Antipater desired, and accused Alexander of conspiracy. The latter, thus hunted down and full of disgust at such a mode of life, drew up a very foolish document, in which he declared that he was guilty, but that all the immediate relatives and friends of the king were accomplices. Neither Salome, whom he accused of forcing herself upon him at night, nor Pheroras, Ptolemæus, Sapinnius, nor any other

[1] Antiq. xvi. 7, 2.

courtier was forgotten; the only exception made by the poor young man was in favour of his trusty friend Antipater. Naturally, everything now pointed to his death. Just as the stroke was about to fall, the king of Cappadocia, Alexander's father-in-law, made his appearance. The man who was all his life a comedian, and finally saved his life, under Tiberius, by feigning to be mad,[1] here also had planned a clever part. With the words, "Where is my accursed son-in-law? where is the patricide? where is my fine daughter?" he one day entered the house of the Jewish king, and by apparently accepting Herod's fixed ideas, he first won his confidence and then managed to gradually transfer his rage to Pheroras. When he now, however, proposed to withdraw his daughter from the wretched court, under pretext of a divorce, Herod was thoroughly prepared to pardon Alexander, in order that he might avoid such a humiliation. Indeed, after his fits were over, he even became so compliant as to engage to go to Rome, so that he might in person recall his last letters to Augustus. While in Rome, however, confessing *pater peccavi*, the amours of the old Salome brought matters to such a pass in Arabia as almost to deprive him of Augustus' favour.

In Trachonitis, during the last few years, affairs had again become unsettled. The unfruitful, rocky soil yielded but poor results to the miserable husbandry in which Herod was determined that the inhabitants should become practised. They only waited to be freed from his dominion to recommence the old gay robber-life. Whilst Herod was in Rome with his sons,[2] the rabble of Trachonitis, on the report that the tyrant had died upon the way, attempted to regain their freedom, but had been already subdued by the garrisons of the king when the latter returned home from Rome. Forty of the chief banditti, however, made their way to the Arabians, where Syllæus granted them the mountain fortress of Raipta on the Jewish frontier, so that they might levy contributions on the farther provinces of Herod. This enmity on the part of the

[1] Dio, 57, 17.   [2] Antiq. xvi. 4, 6, and 9, 1.

vizier was occasioned by a double rejection which he had experienced from Herod. The enterprizing Nabatæan desired, after long and mutual feuds, to enter into an alliance with Herod, in order to prepare Hyrcanus' fate for his own master, the indolent Obodas II., and make himself king. Under the pretext of business, he had visited Jerusalem, and there begun a ludicrous amour with Salome, who, although a mother and grandmother, yet had no scruple in engaging herself secretly to the far younger and, on account of his bad habits, even disreputable Arabian. But when the vizier now formally begged for the hand of the venerable sister of the king, Herod made many difficulties. He hesitated about supporting the designs of Syllæus against Obodas, who was such a peaceable neighbour. Upon the demand, which in Herod's mouth could only be understood as chicanery, that Syllæus, for the purpose of obtaining the object of his desires, should first embrace Judaism, the courtship was broken off. Enraged, the Arabian rode homewards, where he soon found an opportunity of avenging himself upon Herod by receiving the fugitive Trachonites. Exasperated that he could not check their plundering, Herod put the families of the robbers which had remained behind to death; but now the war, under pretext of revenge, was waged by them with greater boldness than ever. When their number amounted to a thousand, and their marauding expeditions resembled regular campaigns, Herod demanded from the court at Petra the delivery of the banditti, and also payment of a sum of money which was due. Syllæus refused the first demand, and referred the second to the governor-in-chief of Syria. This man, C. Sentius Saturninus, who governed Syria from the year 10 to 6 B.C.,[1]—a strict Roman administrator, the terror of tax-gatherers and farmers of revenue,—was inclined to regard all irregularities in these respects very seriously,[2] and commanded that Obodas should pay the money within thirty days, and that each of the two governments must deliver up the

[1] Sanclem, De vulg. æræ emendatione, Rom. 1793, fol. 338—346.
[2] Dio, 54, 10, 51.

subjects of the other when a criminal charge was made against them. Instead of obeying this decision, Syllæus had the audacity to go to Rome, where his treachery to Gallus had hitherto, from political grounds, been ignored, but by no means forgotten.

Herod now lost all patience; he requested and obtained from Saturninus permission to put his demands into execution himself. With a military force he crossed the frontier, took Raipta, and repulsed the Arabians who were hurrying to its defence. Conscious of his rights, he then rendered an account of his proceedings to Saturninus, and next proceeded to make the tranquillity of Trachonitis and Batanæa more secure by establishing fresh garrisons of Idumæans there. When Herod thus ventured to break the peace of the Roman empire, upon which Augustus laid such stress, he certainly did so in the conviction that sentence could not be given in favour of the vizier of the Nabatæans, who had so treacherously deceived Rome fourteen years ago, and against him, the constant friend of Rome. But this time the king had deceived himself as to the strength of the emperor's principles. On Syllæus presenting himself at court, complaining that Herod had broken the public peace, slain 2500 Arabians, plundered Raipta, and levied contributions upon the sick and helpless Obodas,—and as the ambassadors of Herod, moreover, on being interrogated, acknowledged their master's expedition, Augustus angrily rejected all excuses, and wrote to Herod that hitherto he had regarded him as a friend, but that henceforth he would treat him as a subject. Now the wily Nabatæan felt that he was in his element. At a hint from him, the Arabians put an end to the fulfilment of peace dictated by Herod and Saturninus; the pasture-lands of the king which had been taken on lease, they declared to be their own property; and, in open alliance with the Trachonites, made assaults upon the military colonies and Idumæan garrisons of Herod in Trachonitis. As Herod dared not again violently disturb the peace of the empire, this being the special hobby of the emperor, he acted only on the defensive, and sent an embassy to Augustus; but

Cæsar, injured in his most sacred principles, refused to receive it. The higher, consequently, were the stakes for which Syllæus now played his daring game.

The sick Obodas II. had died while his vizier was intriguing at Rome, and his son Æneas succeeded him in the government as Aretas VI. As he, however, perhaps upon the instigation of Syllæus, did not in any way report his accession to the throne to the emperor, the latter was now enraged with Aretas also, and Syllæus believed that he should be able to obtain the dominion for himself from Augustus. In fact, Augustus did not receive a deputation which was sent later on from the Nabatæan king, and now neither Aretas nor Herod were able to do anything to check the robber bands which were daily becoming more daring. In his ill-humour about breaking the imperial peace, the emperor had brought it to pass that the Arabian-Jewish frontier had fallen into the most absolute anarchy. The king, in his extreme necessity, determined to send Nicolaus of Damascus, whom the emperor esteemed as a learned man, to Rome, so that at least one voice might be able to reach Augustus himself. Nicolaus first of all put himself in communication with the Arabian opponents of Syllæus, and came before the emperor as the advocate of all whom the vizier had wronged by his deeds of murder, treachery, adultery and other crimes. In the course of these proceedings, an opportunity was found of correcting the emperor's impression about the breach of peace which it had been pretended Herod had committed. All the treachery and falsehood of the vizier was now brought so clearly to light, that Augustus sent him to Arabia to unravel the business yet remaining there, and then to be brought back to Rome for punishment. As, instead of doing what he had been commanded, he made an attempt, by means of the royal body-guard, to send Herod out of the world, he was, upon his return to Rome, punished by being put to death.[1] To the king, on the other hand, Augustus wrote a most appeasing letter, and entered

[1] Antiq. xvi. 10, 9; Strabo, 16, 4.

into consultation with those who understood the state of affairs, as to whether it would not be better to confer the crown of Arabia upon Herod, instead of upon the young and doubtful Aretas. The decision seemed about to turn in favour of Herod, when a fresh embassy arrived, bringing letters from the latter which deprived the emperor of any desire to entrust another kingdom to a man who raged like an executioner and torturer among the members of his own family.

The stupor, however, under which the king had allowed the injuries of the Trachonites and Arabians to take place at this time, was due to yet another cause than fear of Augustus. The state of affairs in his seraglio had by this time passed beyond the control of the aged despot, and had brought him to absolute mental derangement. Since the last disclosures of the falsehood of Pheroras and the intrigues of Salome, who was at that time beseeching the interference of the empress Livia in her love-affair with Syllæus,[1] he never trusted any one again. Those who came to him frequently were suspected by him, but still more those who came seldom. A friendly attitude aroused his distrust, an earnest one his suspicion; to keep silence was dangerous, but to speak was also to incur peril.[2] Thus in self-defence was it necessary in this miserable court always to lead the king's suspicions on to another person. Those who did not calumniate others as much as they themselves were calumniated, hopelessly lost their equilibrium. Under these circumstances it is no wonder that finally a stranger, the Lacedemonian adventurer Eurycles, just because he appeared perfectly impartial, threw the casting weight into the scale. He had calculated that Antipater out of hatred, Herod out of gratitude, and Archelaus as a fee, would give him a large sum of money if he were to bring affairs to an issue. Everything co-operated to make this object easy of accomplishment: Glaphyra's levity, who took the Greek into her confidence because he had been her father's guest, as well as Alexander's contemptuous openness. Moreover, it was

---

[1] Bell. i. 28, 6.   [2] Bell. i. 26, 4; Antiq. xvi. 8, 2.

not difficult to deceive one deranged. Thus the knot was quickly tied. A pretended assassination, preparations for flight, forged letters to the commander of the fortress of Alexandrium, were communicated to the king, who immediately threw his sons into chains and had their servants examined on the rack. Who confessed, was immediately stoned. The princes were at first spared, their father not venturing to put them to death, as he dared not give the angry Augustus another cause of complaint against himself; at the same time it was well known that everything which occurred in the palace was reported by the love-sick Salome to Syllæus, while she herself besought Herod night and day to execute her son-in-law and Alexander. The new examinations caused only more terrible scenes still; among which, the confronting of the fettered Alexander with the indiscreet Glaphyra proved so painful, that even the aged chancellor Ptolemæus quite forgot that he had an official duty to perform. At last the king despatched messengers to the capital, with the commission to demand the punishment of the princes from the emperor as soon as Nicolaus should have brought him to another opinion concerning Syllæus. The execution of this commission cost Herod the crown of Arabia. When the emperor had read the new communications, he declared that here was no longer the man to whom he could entrust new kingdoms, and upon whose advice Roman triumvirs had once laid weight, but a deranged old man, who did not even know how to keep his own house in order. Nevertheless, he gave Herod permission to deal with his sons according to his royal and paternal authority. Augustus was just learning from his own household the misery which degenerate children cause.[1] He doubted not but that in Jerusalem also the father might be in the right. A tribunal was accordingly summoned at Berytus, composed half of Romans and half of Jews, before which the king appeared in person as the accuser of his sons. Proconsul Saturninus brought his three sons with him hither in order to awaken Herod's paternal feelings. But

[1] Agrippa's death in 12 B.C. occasioned stronger suspicions against Julia: Dio, 55, 10.

the king behaved like a madman, presenting his accusations in a most passionate manner, and making up for want of proof, in the most irrational fits of rage, by the constant assertion that his royal prerogative and the Jewish law made the verdict of this tribunal unnecessary to him. The Romans were disgusted at this insight into the palace intrigues of an Oriental seraglio, and no one understood why a father, who had so many lawyers at his command, should have undertaken in person the hateful part of accuser. Meanwhile the verdict was given in accordance with his wish. The proconsul Saturninus and his three sons alone gave their vote against the punishment of death. Herod deliberated some time before carrying out the sentence. An honest soldier, who excited his rage by his representations, and then his barber, who desired to earn some money by the information of a new conspiracy, soon put him again in the mood in which he was accustomed to come to a resolution. On account of the pretended conspiracy, three hundred soldiers and their officers, as well as the informer, were put to death at Cæsarea. The princes, however, were taken to Samaria, and there, where Herod had married their mother Mariamne, were strangled in the year 8 B.C.

He caused them to be buried in the sepulchre of the Maccabees at Alexandrium, in order to show that he regarded them, even in death, more as Maccabees than as his sons.

14. The End.

If the unhappy man, however, now expected that by this stroke he would at last obtain rest, he knew his own people but badly. The hatred which Antipater had cherished for the brothers was not diminished for their children, in whom he saw that new rivals were growing up. Fresh disputes arose about their education and betrothment; yet Antipater found it desirable under present circumstances, and as he had attained his chief object, to be sent to Rome as ambassador to conduct the suit there with the Arabians. Even the experienced Saturninus he had known how to deceive, so that he obtained from him a recommendation to be sent thither. In Herod's neighbourhood everything now remained quiet, and the last three years of his life were extremely eventless and dreary. Glaphyra returned home, at the command of the king, to her father in Cappadocia, whence a very exceptional fate brought her back at a later period as queen to Jerusalem. Berenice went with her children to Rome. The others, after the complete victory of their relatives, maintained a mutual friendship; but so morbid had the mistrust of the king become, that he regarded this sociableness as a conspiracy against himself, so that before him they had to feign that they were at enmity and hostile, and only at night, in well-guarded rooms, enjoyed any intercourse. The husband-seeking Salome had been compelled by her brother—with the assent of the empress Livia, who had been already previously importuned by Salome with her schemes of marriage—to contract a, to her unwelcome, marriage with his courtier Alexas. Antipater, on the other hand, though in Rome, pursued his old course of behaviour. His suit against the Arabians gave him opportunities of coming into contact with many eminent Romans. Inferior men he won by bribery. Even in the train of the empress Livia had he bought the services of a Greek slave-girl, who proved useful for his treachery. His younger brothers, Archelaus and Philip, who lived in Rome, he incited against their father, and then denounced them, again, to him. He attempted to arouse his uncle Pheroras to form plots against Herod, and generally strove, with the restlessness of an evil conscience, to compass the end of the aged king, in order that the entire tissue of his falsehoods might not be dragged into the light of day before his father's death.

He was not alone, however, in wishing for the king's death. The Pharisees also had entertained thoughts as to the succession to the throne, and hoped to carry Pheroras, who was favourable to them, his wife, mother-in-law and sister-in-law being extremely

Pharisaic, and courting support among the popular party. The three ladies soon observed that Salome had discovered traces of this scheme; they consequently separated and lived apparently in great enmity; but their wily sister-in-law was not thereby deceived. She knew who, at the time, had paid the fines for the Pharisees, and suspicously watched all her brother Pheroras' relations with the pious. The latter observed far less secrecy with regard to their plans, and published the prophecy, "that it was ordained by God that Herod and his descendants should lose the kingdom, which would then fall to the wife of Pheroras and her husband." The kingdom which Pheroras was to inherit was not meanwhile entirely of this world. It was far more the belief of the Pharisees that the days of the Messiah were at hand. Their prophecies found believers especially among the slaves and courtiers, who, in harmony with their mistress, expected great things from the coming Messianic times. The eunuch Bagoas was referred by the pious friends of Pheroras, among other things, to the prophecies of Isaiah: "Let not the eunuch say, Behold, I am a dry tree! For thus saith Jehovah unto the eunuchs that keep my sabbaths, and choose the things that please me and take hold of my covenant: Even unto them will I give in mine house and within my walls a memorial and a name better than sons and daughters; I will give them an everlasting name that shall not be cut off."[1] In still more material terms had Enoch promised to the righteous that he should live in the Messianic kingdom long enough to beget a thousand children.[2] With these promises the eunuch was allured. He was assured that the power to marry and beget children of his own would be restored to him; nay, that it was ordained that he should raise up the son for the childless Pheroras who was to establish the kingdom, so that he would be called "the father and benefactor of the Messiah." The catamite Carus, also, who was held to be the most beautiful youth in the country, was drawn by the Rabbis into

---

[1] Isaiah lvi. 3—5; compare Haverkamp on Jos. Antiq. xvii. 2, 4.
[2] Henoch x. 17.

their toils, quite regardless of the part he should play in the accomplishment of this prophecy. Thus we find that the aged tyrant was in fact surrounded by the rumours of the coming Messiah, which we find interwoven in his history in the narrative of the wise men from the East.[1] The eunuch, from the representations made to him, was the most excited of all, and began to behave in the palace in a foolish manner. By this means an inquiry was occasioned, and the king, who hated the Messianic prophecy, as he did everything connected with the national hopes of the people, had the Pharisees who were most concerned in the affair, Bagoas, as well as the page Carus, put to death. The superstitious wife of Pheroras, as source of all the disturbance, was called to account, and Herod demanded of her husband that he should put her away. The pious woman, however, had such influence over her otherwise faithless husband, that he preferred to leave the court, and withdraw with her to his tetrarchy. But the king "slew all of his household who had consented to what the Pharisees had said."[2] What had been further said by the Pharisees, has probably been recounted by Nicolaus of Damascus, whom Josephus here makes use of; but Josephus passes lightly over this Messianic movement also, and thus farther particulars escape us. Nevertheless is it a remarkable fact, that at the very time at which, so far as we know, Jesus was born, on Mount Zion and at the court of the Tetrarch of Peræa the Messiah was actually expected, and that information of it gave occasion for a sanguinary persecution.

But another "slaughter of children" than that of the page Carus took place, too, in this last period of the king. A sickness which first prostrated Herod and then Pheroras seemed to bring these aged brothers once more together. Then Pheroras suddenly died. The whisper arose that all had not happened aright. An inquiry brought the most unexpected discoveries to light. "Then did the ghosts of Alexander and Aristobulus go round all the palace, and became the inquisitors and discoverers of what could

---

[1] Matthew ii. 1.   [2] Antiq. xvii. 2, 4.

not otherwise have been found out, and brought such as were freest from suspicion to be examined," says Josephus.[1] The poison by which Pheroras was supposed to have been killed was certainly found, but it was intended for Herod by his favourite son Antipater, who had sent it to Pheroras. And now Herod learned the real nature of the men to whom he had sacrificed his wife and children. An exceptional revenge, therefore, should now fall upon him who had thus cheated the king out of his last possession. In assumed friendliness, Herod recalled Antipater from Rome, as though he wished to give him his last blessing. It seemed remarkable to all that, after the action had continued seven months, and had already led to the casting off of Doris, Antipater was without any information as to its latest direction. No one had warned him, because no one was his friend. "Perhaps," says Josephus, "the ghosts of his murdered brethren stopped the mouths of those that intended to have told him."[2]

It was only when he found at Cæsarea that there was not a single person in the harbour to welcome him, that he perceived that affairs were serious. But after he had come so far, he could not return. Sullenly he rode on to the capital and entered the king's palace. Only when his suite was there separated from him, did he perceive that he was lost. Collecting all his energy, he endeavoured to embrace his father joyously, but the latter thrust him back, and turned to Quinctilius Varus, proconsul of Syria, and afterwards the notorious hero of the Teutoburgian forests, who was present, and begged him to try this murderer of father and brothers. The investigation did not prove difficult, for every one pressed forward to give witness against the hated man. Nicolaus of Damascus, as chief counsel for the prosecution, clearly summed up the condemnatory evidence. That Antipater had sent the vessel containing poison for the purpose of being employed against his father, was sufficiently proved. Then Varus ordered a criminal who had been condemned to death to come and drink off the contents of the goblet. As the man imme-

[1] Bell. i. 30, 7.   [2] Bell. i. 31, 2.

diately grew pale and sank down, Varus turned to depart. Antipater, however, was led away in chains.

These terrible scenes had destroyed the yet remaining energy of the aged king. He only kept up until he had sent an account to Augustus. Then he fell into a mortal sickness. The news that the tyrant was dying spread like wildfire in Jerusalem. Now was the scribes' opportunity for action. Among the Rabbis at Jerusalem were Judas ben Sariphai and Matthias ben Margaloth, the two most determined opponents of the Romans. A great number of youths crowded to them in order to hear their exposition of the law, so that there was daily collected around them quite an army of young men.[1] When they received the news of the king's condition, they declared to their disciples that the king's sufferings were the long-predicted punishment of Jehovah for his violations of the law. What was especially condemned by the people was Herod's breaking into the tombs of the kings, where his body-guard had sought for gold in the year 9 B.C.; but, it was reported, they had been driven back by a supernatural fire which burst forth from David's sepulchre. "After this desecration of the graves, Herod's house became more unfortunate from day to day."[2] Rabbis Judas and Matthias now demonstrated to their disciples that this desecration, for which Jehovah was punishing the king, dared no longer be endured; that an end of it must be made at once, and the untheocratic erections of the tyrant destroyed together. They determined to make a beginning with the great golden eagle which the king had set up over the chief gate of the temple. In the middle of the day, the people thronged into the sanctuary. Several disciples let themselves down from the temple roof by ropes, so that they could reach the eagle, and threw it down into the forecourt, where the people, rejoicing, broke it into pieces. Mobs immediately swarmed into other places also, in order to demolish the images upon the remaining buildings. The commander of the city garrison meanwhile easily dispersed the unarmed crowds, and took pri-

[1] Bell. i. 33, 2. [2] Antiq. xvi. 7, 2.

soners forty young Pharisees who offered resistance, together with their instructors, who themselves demanded their own arrest. On the king asking who had incited them to destroy the eagle, they replied with emotion, "The Law." Herod at once deposed the high-priest as a participator in the affair. The Rabbis, with their disciples, were imprisoned and tried at Jericho on the charge of temple desecration. The two teachers and those who had climbed up and thrust the eagle down were burned alive; the forty disciples of the Rabbis were beheaded. In the same night the moon was eclipsed.

From this hour the king, who yet had been personally present in the theatre at Jericho during the trial, began visibly to fail. A fever-heat raged within him, his feet swelled, ulcers in his bowels caused him terrible sufferings. "All those who claimed to have a knowledge of divine things unanimously declared that Jehovah had inflicted this punishment upon the king for his manifold wickednesses."[1] The physicians had him brought to the hot sulphur baths of Callirhoë on the other side of the Jordan. Here he was placed, first in hot water, and then in hot oil. But as this treatment brought the seventy-year-old man almost to the point of death, he had himself carried to Jericho in order to end his days there. The court were afraid that he might die before Antipater was executed, and therefore they communicated to the king that the prisoner was rejoicing that he should survive him. "Then despatch him," the king roared, louder than, from his weakness, could have been expected. According to a later story, Augustus, who had advised with regard to Antipater also that he should be spared, mockingly said, when informed that Herod had now put the third son to death, that upon the whole it was better to be the Jewish king's swine than his son.[2]

As the ulcers increased, the sickness of the king became so loathsome that only a few persons could endure to remain at his side. At last he tried to put an end to his anguish by his own hand. Demanding that an apple should be given him, and

---

[1] Antiq. xvi. 6, 5.   [2] Macrobius, Saturn. ii. 4; compare Strabo, xvi. 2.

a knife that he might pare it, he suddenly attempted to thrust the knife into his heart; but the commander of his body-guard, his faithful cousin Achiab, seized his arm and prevented the accomplishment of his purpose. He had to drain the cup to the lees; and whilst he writhed in the agonies of death, the cries of the crowd, rejoicing in the deliverance of Israel from the bloodthirsty monster, sounded in the chamber of pain. Raging, he once more collected his powers, and ordered that the city elders throughout all Judæa should be summoned to Jericho. When they were assembled, he commanded that they should be kept in custody in the Hippodrome, and that the moment he was dead they should be put to death, so that the Jews should lose all inclination for rejoicing.[1] Thus he died as he had lived. His successors had no desire to execute his testament. Alexis and Salome set the prisoners at liberty before the body-guard had received news of the king's death. He had survived Antipater only five days. He was when he died, at Easter of the year 4 B.C., in his 70th year, and, receiving the government in the year 40 B.C., had reigned thirty-seven years.

The latter period of the king's life had been so exciting and terrible that it quite extinguished for the next generation all memory of the former part. The features of the tyrant when distorted by madness were more deeply imprinted in men's minds than the picture of the clever, energetic and courageous prince, which nevertheless he had once been. He lived in popular imagination only as the man of blood.

In the lapidary style of ancient Israelitish historical writing, has the "Prophecies of Moses" especially pronounced its judgment upon the government of Herod, the eight and thirty years' misery of which is compared to the eight and thirty years of wandering in the desert, ordained by God as a punishment because the Maccabees had made God's state into their own kingdom. Therefore also it was that Herod had most violently

---

[1] Antiq. xvii. 6, 5. A reminiscence of this is found in Megillat Ta'anit, § 25; see Grätz, iii. 426.

raged against the Maccabees. "An insolent king succeeds them," does the seer prophesy,[1] "who is not of the race of the priests, a rash and godless man, who will judge them as they deserve. He destroys their eminent ones with the sword, and buries their bodies in unknown solitary places, so that none know where they rest. He kills the elders and does not spare the youth. .... And he will hold judgment upon them, as the Egyptians did upon them for thirty, yea forty years. And he will punish them and beget sons who, as his successors, will bring yet more dreadful times upon them."

The gospel narrative also, which places the blood-thirsty figure of Herod at the cradle of Jesus, rightly conjecturing that the time which bore the Saviour of mankind in its bosom was in not its least important part the work of Herod, has collected together all the worst features of his character.[2] It has depicted him as he was in his later days, fearful, suspicious and ferocious, as the Herod who dreads the usurper of his throne even in the child, and kills a hundred innocent in order to reach *one* whom he hates. His alarm about the baby of Bethlehem recalls vividly the long hunt which he instituted for the sons of Babas, the haste with which he proceeded against Bagoas, the believer in the Messiah, the hypocrisy with which he conducted the rebuilding of the temple in order that he might prove at least *one* Messianic passage false. The crafty manner in which, in the legend, he invites the magi to return to him, resembles the feigned tenderness which enticed even the cunning Antipater into the net. The murder of all the children of Bethlehem, however, has always been compared to the sentence of death passed upon all the elders at Jericho, which had for its purpose also that a crying should be heard, much weeping and wailing from Jerusalem to Ramah. As in the gospel narrative the mothers of Bethlehem raise their lamentations over the blood-thirsty tyrant, so also in the history of Josephus is the commencement of his public life characterized by the lamentations

---

[1] Mose Prophetic. viii.; in Volkmar's edition, p. 30.   [2] Matthew ii.

of the mothers who demand back from Hyrcanus their children which the young Herod has killed; and its termination by the lamentations of the daughters of Jerusalem who weep over their sons' blood that the aged king has shed on account of the destruction of the golden eagle.[1] It is in these features alone that the character of the terrible king has been preserved in the memory of the people, and history has in great measure followed in these footprints. In the confusion which his death occasioned, and in face of the moral bankruptcy which his creation was hardly now in a position to conceal, it is certainly quite possible to overlook the material successes which nevertheless he obtained by his energy and the unquestionable geniality of his foreign policy. He was, whatever else one may think of him, still the only king of Israel who enabled the land to obtain those natural frontiers which had hovered before the eyes of Moses and Joshua. He made, moreover, much out of this land. The Arabian frontier was, under Herod, stronger and better respected than it was even at the time when Judæa had become a Roman province. Galilee he delivered from the control of robber-bands and Bedouins. The territory east of the Jordan was permanently tranquillized by settlements of Parthian Jews and Idumæan military colonies. Altogether, the capability of the country for defence, which was so conclusively proved in the Jewish war, was his work. Numerous fortresses, magazines and arsenals derived their origin from him. The majority of the Jewish fortresses were either newly built by him, or else rebuilt in order to meet the requirements made by the improved Roman weapons of assault, acquaintance with which the Jews had made in the war with Pompeius. Jerusalem was made by him into one of the greatest strongholds of Asia. A line was drawn against the Arabians by Scythopolis,[2] Pella,[3] Hesbon,[4] Herodium,[5] Machærus[6] and Philadelphia;[7] and a second

---

[1] Antiq. xiv. 9, 4, xvii. 9, 1; Matthew ii. 16.   [2] Strabo, xvi. 2.
[3] Bell. i. 6, 5; 7, 7; ii. 18, 1; Pliny, Hist. v. 16; Antiq. xiv. 4, 4.
[4] Antiq. xv. 8, 5.   [5] Bell. i. 21, 10.   [6] Bell. vii. 6, 2.
[7] Strabo, xvi. 2.

line behind that by Phasælis,[1] Alexandrium, Dagon,[2] Cypros,[3] Therex,[4] Taurus, the castle of Herodium[5] and Masada.[6] Even if this double line were broken through Jerusalem, Samaria and Hyrcanium could still hold out for a long period. Trachonitis was protected by Bathyra,[7] Carmel by Gaba,[8] and the road to Cæsarea by Antipatris.[9]

It is remarkable that Herod did so little for the defence of Galilee,—a sign that his mistrust was especially directed towards Judæa, and that it was not his aim to protect his country against Rome, but against the Arabians and Parthians. The growth of commerce upon the coast was not less due to him. Moreover, he had shaken an inexhaustible cornucopia filled with gifts over the Gentile world, building gymnasia in Tripolis, Damascus, Ptolemais and Nicopolis, theatres in Damascus and Sidon, an aqueduct in Laodicea, baths in Ascalon, temples in Tyre and Rhodes, colonnades in Tyre and Antioch. The towns of Byblos and Berytus owed to him their city walls; Athens, Sparta, Nicopolis, Pergamum and Cos received ostentatious gifts or prizes for their games; and had it not been for his permanent regal endowment, the Olympian games would probably have come to an end.[10] The Jews abroad reaped the benefit of their king's generosity, quite apart from the fact that through his influence with Augustus he enforced a strict observance everywhere of the privileges granted them by Cæsar, and made the oppression of his people's relatives by the proconsuls of the empire a very disagreeable thing.

Nevertheless, there are a hundred witnesses to testify that the Jewish people had no regard whatever for these services rendered by his government, while for its shadowy side they had the most intense susceptibility.[11] "The generation which lived under Herod

---

[1] Antiq. xvi. 5, 2; Bell. i. 21, 9. [2] Antiq. xiii. 8, 1. [3] Bell. i. 21, 4.
[4] Strabo, xvi. 2. [5] Strabo, xvi. 2. [6] Bell. vii. 8, 3.
[7] Antiq. xvii. 2, 2. [8] Bell. iii. 3, 1; Antiq. xv. 8, 5.
[9] Bell. i. 21, 9; Antiq. xvi. 5, 2; Acts xxiii. 31.
[10] Bell. i. 21, 11, 12. [11] Antiq. xv. 9, 1.

endured more tribulation than all their forefathers together, since the return from Babylon," cried the deputy of the people emphatically before Augustus. Herod knew this feeling regarding him well. He had, when any failure in the crops occurred, to make almost superhuman efforts to render assistance, because otherwise feelings of hatred would have been directed towards himself.[1] He had to keep down the country by a system of castles and strongholds, and spread a network of espionage over every village.[2] During the whole of his reign the fortresses were filled with prisoners.[3] When he left the country, he had to imprison his Asmonean relatives, or else put them at once to death; and, on the other hand, in order to protect his own blood relations from the rage of the people, he had to shut them up in fortresses. For his festivals and contests in the amphitheatre, he had to seek not only performers, but also spectators, from beyond the frontiers, and at every wild-beast fight and show in the circus be prepared for a riot.[4] Thus, although he prevented every greater insurrection by his prudential measures, and even appeared to the Romans to be an unsurpassable sovereign, yet he was himself perfectly conscious that he stood upon the edge of a volcano, which sooner or later would overwhelm him and his work. With his alarm about the Maccabees, which became in his case actual madness and fear of ghosts, was associated a dread of his own people, yoked to a hatred of mankind, that met him like a tormenting secret, keeping silence like the Essene Menahem. In this feeling he did not deceive himself. He was scarcely buried when the insurrection was knocking at the doors of the palace.

15. THE INHERITANCE.

Herod in the days of his last illness had destroyed an earlier will, made a new one, and then again cancelled that. His last

---

[1] Antiq. xv. 9, 1.
[2] Antiq. xv. 10, 4.
[3] Antiq. xvii. 8, 4.
[4] Antiq. xv. 8, 1; 10, 4; xvi. 1, 1.

will was now opened. Only as a compromise between the various palace intrigues can we understand why in this will he shattered into pieces the creation of his life,—the last-won territory beyond the Jordan being bequeathed to Philip, son of Cleopatra of Jerusalem, who had been received into his harem on account of her beauty; Galilee, with Peræa, being bequeathed to Antipas as a tetrarchy, and Judæa, with the title of king, to Archelaus, the two latter being sons of Malthace; whilst at first Herod had intended to leave the entire realm to the son of the second Mariamne, Herod Boethus.[1]

Salome, too, was not forgotten. She received Jamnia and Ashdod on the coast, and Phasaëlis, the city of palms, in the valley of the Jordan, in order that she might have a residence for each season of the year. As the result of her friendship with Livia, Augustus left her the palace also in Ascalon, and presented her, after the banishment of her nephew Archelaus, with the new town of Archelaïs, which the latter had built in a valley of palms lying to the north of her possessions near Phasaëlis. Thus endowed, the sister of Herod lived some fifteen years longer, corresponding industriously with the empress Livia, to whom finally she bequeathed her palm-groves and towns upon the sea.[2]

Immediately after the opening of the will, Archelaus received the homage of the troops and betook himself to Jerusalem. Here he harangued the people in the temple, who quietly listened to him, but then demanded that he should grant a relaxation of the customs and taxes and release the prisoners. Archelaus granted both requests, and then withdrew to the palace. But as evening drew on, tumultuous crowds collected, who raised an alarming lamentation over Rabbis Matthias and Judas and the young Pharisees put to death by Herod, and with uproar demanded the deposition of the new high-priest and the expulsion of the Gentiles.[3] The troops which were sent to prevent

---

[1] Bell. i. 30, 7.   [2] Bell. ii. 6, 3; compare Antiq. xviii. 2, 2.
[3] Nicolaus Dam. in Müller, Fragm. iii. 353.

the crowds increasing, without making use of their arms, were driven back. As it was close upon the Passover, and the first visitors were already beginning to arrive, Archelaus was compelled to forcibly interfere if order were to be restored before the assemblage of the masses of the people. A great fight in the streets was the result. Three thousand corpses covered the scene of the contest. The visitors to the festival were shut out of the city, and had to return home without celebrating the Passover. What would be the result no one knew.

No sooner was a momentary peace obtained than Archelaus entrusted the commandership-in-chief of the troops to the trusty old Achiab, and appointed his step-brother Philip vice-regent of the kingdom and superintendent of his household. He himself went to Cæsarea and there embarked, in order to obtain in Rome the emperor's confirmation of his father's will. With him travelled Doris, Salome, Ptolemæus and Nicolaus. Others sought to reach Rome by other routes; but even from Archelaus' own suite, Salome and Ptolemæus went over to his brother Antipas, who had gained the services of the eloquent Irenæus, and on the strength of an earlier will laid claim to the kingship.[1] To keep the Jewish kingdom together was the ambition of not one of them. Those who were not personally candidates for the throne sought that the country should be united to the neighbouring Roman province, in order to keep some later inheritance in view. Whilst the worthy family of the late king were thus quarrelling about their claims in the ante-rooms of the Roman nobility, and affording them the disgraceful spectacle of relations wrangling over their inheritance, proconsul Q. Varus permitted the popular party likewise to send an embassy to utter their protest against Archelaus, and to pray that the theocracy might be restored. This news was received by the Jews of Rome with shouts of joy, and eight thousand members of the community accompanied the fifty deputies of the people when Augustus granted them an audience in the Temple of Apollo. These deputies recounted the

---

[1] Bell. ii. 2, 1, 2; Antiq. xvii. 9, 4.

long register of Herod's infamous deeds to Augustus, and begged that the theocracy might be again restored, under the supervision of the Syrian proconsul, and that Archelaus—who was represented by Nicolaus of Damascus—might be dispensed with. They did not gain their point. The emperor's feelings of regard for his friendly ally of so many years' standing, Salome's friendship with Livia, Berenice's favour with Antonia, perhaps, too, the disinclination to allow the high-priesthood of the ever-extending Jewish people to become so powerful, stood in the way. The Herods might be despicable, but they could be made of use. The more ineffaceable were the lines with which the self-humiliation of the royal house and the tension of those weeks so full of expectation were engraved in the remembrance of the Jewish people. Jesus (Luke xix. 12), in his parable of the Ten Pounds, needs only to allude to the journey of Archelaus, and every one knows whom he means by the prince whose people cried before the foreign throne, "We will not have this man to reign over us." So vivid were these memories in even the third decade afterwards.

But whilst the Herods were thus making themselves the subject of ridicule in Rome, the one honourable member of the family, Philip, son of Cleopatra of Jerusalem, who had remained behind as vice-regent, sought in vain to keep the Jews in check. Varus had to march upon Jerusalem with one of his legions to restore peace. He had returned subsequently to Antioch, whilst Philip followed his relations to Rome, as the emperor himself sent a procurator to govern Judæa, until the succession to the throne had been definitely settled. This man, Sabinus, thought that he ought to make the best use of his time, and drove the Jews into a fresh revolt by his extortions of every kind. At the feast of Pentecost, the Romans were hunted out of the temple by the festival-keepers, who had come up with evil intent, this time chiefly from Peræa, Galilee and Idumæa. The soldiers, however, continued the contest from the fortress of Antonia, setting fire to the halls, which were roofed with cedar wood, and thus drove the Jews out of the sanctuary.

The temple treasury was taken by Sabinus under his own administration, and was immediately relieved of 400 talents. Hereupon the favourite rallying-cry, Corban! Corban! was raised. When the Gentiles had thus violated the Jews' most sacred possession, the revolt immediately spread throughout the whole land. Even the Herodian troops deserted in great part to the side of the rebels. In Idumæa, Achiab found himself actually attacked by the veterans of Herod. But the most important of all was, that the old banditti chiefs who were scattered in the mountains now called their former pursuits to mind, and summoned their terrible confederates to fresh work after their long holidays. The banditti of Peræa placed a slave, whose name was Simon, at their head as king of Israel.[1] He established himself in the defiles between Jericho and Jerusalem, and thoroughly plundered Herod's palace at Jericho. Judas, the son of the Hezekiah whom Herod had executed, summoned the wild shepherds from the Galilean mountains, and with their aid stormed Sepphoris, six miles north of Nazareth, the armoury of which was broken open; and thus provided with arms, the troops poured forth over the immediate home of Jesus, in order to prepare for war everywhere against the Romans. Other bands rendered the valley of the Jordan unsafe, and Athronges, one of the robber shepherds of the Steppes, found, in his untamed strength and muscular greatness, and the support of his equally gigantic brothers, the means of assuming a sort of Messianic character, and pressed forward to Jerusalem, carrying with him the golden crown and purple robe. At Emmaus, almost under the eyes of the Roman garrison, he surrounded a cohort, which only escaped the treacherous arrows of his rabble with heavy losses.

Meanwhile, Varus had received news of the condition of the country from Sabinus, who was shut up in the fortress of Antonia, and summoned all the neighbouring allies against the insurgent Judæa. With delight did the Nabatæan king send numerous auxiliaries; the town of Berytus, too, provided 1500 Syrian mer-

---

[1] Tacitus, Hist. v. 9.

cenaries, and Philip pushed forward with the remnants of Herod's army to the two legions which Varus was leading. All the deadly enemies of the Jews were collected. Columns of smoke from Sepphoris, and long trains of Sepphorites sold for slaves, proclaimed at once to the Galileans how Varus intended to conduct the war. The possessions of Ptolemæus were laid waste by the Arabs. One village after another was set on fire. Jerusalem also was soon purged of rebels, but it cost much heavier sacrifices to follow up the rebellion in the country into all its ramifications, and the flames often broke out again from the ground behind the cohorts where they thought they had left the most profound peace. The more inhumanly did the Bedouins of Aretas rage against the hated Jews; and Varus, too, here learned that savage barbarity by which he ten years afterwards drove the Germans at the Weser into revolt. These few weeks had inflicted deep wounds upon the land. The flower of the Jewish youth lay slain upon the fields of battle; in Galilee and Judæa the smoke of the burning towns and villages rose to heaven, and the corpses of two thousand brave patriots rotting upon as many crosses were far and wide a warning against similar attempts. Samaria alone was spared, as it had taken no part in the revolt, the one exception here being the possessions of Ptolemæus, which the Arabians plundered out of hatred of the minister of Herod. As a reward, one third of its taxes were remitted to the Samaritans, and this much more added on to the Jews, who thus found new ground for hatred towards the foolish people of Sichem.

Sixth Division.

THE HISTORICAL RELATIONS OF THE LIFE OF JESUS.

THE HISTORICAL RELATIONS OF THE LIFE OF JESUS.

1. THE LORDS OF THE LAND.

THE will of Herod had been confirmed by the emperor Augustus, in the autumn of 4 B.C., in all its essential features.

PHILIP received Batanæa, Auranitis, Trachonitis and a part of the dominion of Zenodorus.[1] The chief heirs were the sons of the Samaritan woman. The younger, ANTIPAS, obtained Galilee and Peræa; the elder, ARCHELAUS, Idumæa, Judæa and Samaria, a well rounded-off territory with the towns of Cæsarea, Samaria, Joppa and Jerusalem. Hippos and Gadara, however, were once more incorporated in the Decapolis, and Gaza in the Syrian city alliance. The title of king, which Herod had intended that the eldest son of his Samaritan wife should wear, alone was refused by Augustus. Archelaus was to be called ethnarch until he had proved himself worthy of the rank of king. It was without doubt the result of the urgent complaints which the Pharisees and sacerdotal nobility had made in Rome, that Archelaus was thus put upon his good behaviour. Another consequence of this deputation was, that Augustus placed a maximum limit upon the taxes which might be raised by each prince. Philip was thus limited to 100, Antipas to 200, and Archelaus to 400 talents, and the manner in which these taxes might be raised was at the same time prescribed.[2]

---

[1] Bell. ii. 6, 3; Antiq. xvii. 11, 4. For Ituræa, compare Antiq. xviii. 6, 11, with Tacitus, Annals, xii. 23; Dio, 59, 12.

[2] Antiq. xvii. 11, 4.

PHILIP, son of Cleopatra of Jerusalem,[1] in age the middle one of the three brothers, having been educated in Rome with the sons of Malthace, and always enjoying the firm confidence of these otherwise capricious and distrustful despots, stood in especial regard not only with his own family, but also with the Roman officials. In the eyes of the Jewish people he was preferable to his brothers because his mother had been no Samaritan, but a daughter of Zion. The territory which he had received was in extent the greatest, as regards the work of governing it the most difficult, and in revenue the smallest. He had, in the inhabitants of the caves and the robbers of the Trachonites, to look after a troublesome people, and yet might not lay more than 100 talents as taxes upon his district. Under such circumstances, journeys to Rome and politics on a large scale were manifestly forbidden; instead, Philip, during his reign of thirty-seven years, was to his subjects a mild sovereign, and to the surrounding dynasts a peaceable neighbour. In contrast with the petty despots around, he had the reputation of the good king Alcinous, who took his *sella curulis* with him on every excursion, being ever ready to set up his prætorium in market-place or field, and allowing the stolen sheep and cattle to be recovered by means of his body-guards from the caves of the Trachonites. A few friends formed his court, which he seldom changed. He provided a splendid capital for his kingdom by rebuilding the ancient Paneas at the sources of the Jordan—where the old Herod had built a temple to Augustus—in the style of the times as Cæsarea Philippi, and in order to provide it with inhabitants declared it to be an asylum.[2] Jesus, too, do we find here at the sources of the Jordan, on the green spurs of Hermon, in the days when he was leading a fugitive's life. "And Jesus went out, and his disciples, into the villages of Cæsarea Philippi; and by the way he asked his disciples, saying unto them, Whom do men say that I am?"[3]

Below, on the north-east shore of the lake, Philip enlarged the

---

[1] Bell. i. 28, 4; Antiq. xvii. 1, 3. [2] According to the coins, Eckhel, iii. 491.
[3] Mark viii. 27.

village of Bethsaida into a town, which, in honour of the notorious daughter of the emperor, he called Julias. Between the court of Antipas and Herodias, which settled, towards the end of Philip's life, at Tiberias, and his own, a friendly intercourse prevailed. For he led the daughter of Herodias, Salome, home as his bride, probably in order that the neighbouring territories should once more become united, in one way or another, into one country again. His magnificent grave, too, did he erect at Julias.

For science, too, this man of peace seems to have had some understanding. He proved that the lake Phiala and the so-called source of the Jordan of Panium were connected together. "He threw chaff," Josephus tells us, "into Phiala, and it was found at Panium."[1] The correctness of this observation has been called in question by later geographers, it is true. His delight in building is to-day witnessed by the ancient ruins at Banias. Moreover, his coins prove that he regarded himself as a Gentile sovereign over Gentiles; for they bear the images of Augustus and Tiberius with laurel, and even four pillars which are to represent the temple of Augustus at Paneas. But his desertion of the Mosaic law was not prejudicial to his virtues as ruler. Death summoned him, in the year 34, from a well-ordered sphere of action. That he had not squandered his subjects' money in Rome, had dispensed equitable justice, and discharged the duties of government with zeal, was counted doubly high in a son of Herod.[2]

HEROD ANTIPAS, too, was, according to the standard of these times, not altogether a bad ruler. Educated in Rome, he was anxious to keep up his relations with the capital.[3] But the smooth and devoted Jew found less favour with Augustus than with Tiberius, who succeeded to the empire in 14 A.D. This emperor kept up an epistolary correspondence with him, much to the dislike of the Syrian proconsuls. Vitellius, especially,

---

[1] Bell. Jud. iii. 10, 7.   [2] Antiq. xvii. 2, 2; xviii. 4, 6.
[3] Antiq. xvii. 1, 3; xviii. 5, 1; 7, 1, 2.

could not endure the wily sneak, as he made him very emphatically feel after the emperor's death.[1] Pilate also hated him,[2] probably from the same reason. He had provided for the safety of his territories beyond the Jordan, in his prudent manner, by marrying the daughter of the Arab king Aretas, perhaps at Augustus' command, who was fond, as Suetonius informs us,[3] of forming family connections between allied princes, in order that peace might be more easily preserved. Of all the sons of Herod, he had inherited most of his father's love of magnificence. He indulged in expenses which were altogether out of proportion to the income of his tetrarchy. When, for example, the Parthian king Artabanus was discussing terms of peace with Vitellius in the year 35 A.D. on the Euphrates,[4] Antipas had a large tent erected on the bridge in the midst of the stream, and there entertained the Parthian and Roman authorities.[5] This was in accordance with the taste of the time, which loved to reverse the order of nature; turning the sea into dry land for the purposes of a banquet, and enjoying spring in winter, the north in the south, regardless of the cost. At such carousals, in his intoxication he was able to taunt his relatives with the bread he found them, or to promise some female dancer an execution; whilst at other times he was not wanting in caution and understanding. In addition to the ostentatiousness, he had inherited also the old Herod's love of building. In order to flatter the empress Livia, he built the town of Livias,[6] in the south of Peræa, on the site of the ancient Beth Haran; for the tetrarchs held it as no mean honour to themselves that the empress-mother was their neighbour as landed proprietor since the year 12 or 13 A.D.; for by the testamentary depositions of her estates by the dying Salome, the town of Jamnia and its neighbourhood, together with Phasaëlis and Archelaïs, in the valley of the Jordan, had been bequeathed to her.[7] Livia also now enjoyed the character of being a friend

---

[1] Antiq. xviii. 4, 5.   [2] Luke xxiii. 12.   [3] Suet. Aug. 48.
[4] Tacitus, Annals, vi. 37, corresponding with Antiq. xviii. 4, 5.
[5] Antiq. xviii. 4, 5.   [6] Antiq. xviii. 2, 1.   [7] Antiq. xviii. 2, 2.

to the Jews, as she had presented golden goblets and cups
and other costly presents to the temple.¹ Then Antipas made
Machærus, the fortress of the southern frontier of his states, once
more inhabitable, and rebuilt Sepphoris, which had been destroyed
in the last war by Varus, in a more magnificent manner.² But
soon Sepphoris, which was hidden in the mountains, did not at
all satisfy him, and he determined to build a new residence on
the Sea of Gennesareth, near the warm springs of Emmaus.³ It
was to be kept in the most modern Roman style, and as during
the time of Augustus every third town was called Cæsarea or
Sebaste, so it was to be called Tiberias. The situation was one of
the most beautiful on the sea, being on a narrow strip of level
ground which was extended towards the south, washed on its
eastern edge by the waves.⁴ When the foundations were being
dug, traces of an ancient cemetery were discovered, and the Rabbis
demanded that the building should cease, as the place was
unclean. Antipas paid no heed to this request; but when the
first streets were finished, he found that he had to bring together
a concourse of foreigners to inhabit it, and finally compel his
subjects to settle there, since no believing Jew cared to live in
an unclean place. He allotted ground and sites even to slaves
and beggars, built houses for them and gave them privileges,
only to see his imperial town inhabited. Even at a later period
every one was accounted unclean for seven days who took up
his abode here, and had to observe for himself and others all the
usual regulations regarding purity, so that strict Jews preferred
avoiding the place altogether.⁵ In the Synoptic Gospels the
name of Tiberias is not mentioned,⁶ and Jesus seems never
to have gone there, which however can also be explained from
the fact that the building of the town was only first begun when

---

[1] Philo ad Caium. Frankfurt Ausgabe, 1036; Bohn's translation, iv. 169; Pliny, Hist. Nat. xiii. 9, 4.

[2] Antiq. xviii. 2, 1.   [3] Antiq. xviii. 6, 2.

[4] Antiq. xviii. 2, 3; Bell. iii. 10; Pliny, v. 15. Furrer, Wanderungen in Palestine, 314.

[5] Antiq. xviii. 2, 3.   [6] John vi. 1, xxi. 1, speaks of the Sea of Tiberias, however.

Pontius Pilate was procurator in Judæa.[1] But in spite of the opposition, Antipas now transferred his residence from Sepphoris here, and to the great grief of his people adorned his newly-built palace according to the unlawful Gentile style of architecture. The façade, in particular, which was adorned with the figures of animals, gave offence to the Rabbis. The interior was decorated with exceptional magnificence, and for long afterwards was mention made of the gilded roof, the valuable candelabra and furniture of solid metal which here met the eye. When the people, at the outbreak of the war, stormed the palace, lamps of Corinthian brass, magnificent tables and complete stores of uncoined silver, were carried off, in such a princely manner had the tetrarch furnished his residence.[2] Shortly afterwards he built a race-course spacious enough to hold the largest assembly of the people,[3] and other Roman pleasure-grounds, all of which were like a thorn in the eye to the Rabbis.[4] Even at the present day, on the shore at Tiberias, there are to be found fragments of buildings, granite pillars, blocks of marble, porphyry and syenite. The ruins of an amphitheatre also call to mind this godless tetrarch.[5] The constitution of his Versailles was chosen by the little federal prince quite after an Hellenic pattern. The town had a council of six hundred,[6] with ten elders,[7] an archon,[8] an exarchos,[9] an agoranomos,[10] and so on.

But yet the Jews were not quite forgotten. He built them a synagogue, "a large edifice, and capable of receiving a great number of people,"[11] in the roomy basilica of which the Galilean assemblies of the people were usually held during the period of the revolution. Hither, too, were the archives and seat of government transferred, and a castle erected for the garrison, in the

---

[1] After the appointment of Pilate, 26 A.D., Josephus mentions the commencement of the building, and accordingly Eusebius puts it in the Chronicon in the year 27.

[2] Vita, 12, 13.   [3] Bell. ii. 21, 6.   [4] Vita, 12, 13.

[5] Furrer, Wanderungen in Pal. 316.   [6] Bell. ii. 21, 9; Vita, 12, 34, 55, 61, 68.

[7] Vita, 13.   [8] Vita, 27, 53; Bell. ii. 21, 3.

[9] Bell. ii. 21, 6.   [10] Antiq. xviii. 6, 2.

[11] Vita, 54.

armoury of which were weapons provided for seventy thousand men.¹ For the next fifty years Tiberias was the undisputed capital of Galilee, and, with the exception of Cæsarea on the sea-coast, the most beautiful town in the land of the Jews.²

Although Antipas, as a rule, governed with moderation and judgment, yet the Jews no more recognized him as prince of their people than they had the old Herod. Son of an Idumæan father and Samaritan mother, he, too, was to them only a stranger in Israel's gates, and his followers were called briefly "the Herodians"³ by the people, as though the tetrarch were merely the leader of a party. But the worst period of his life began first when the wife of his brother Herod Boethus,⁴ who lived in Rome, unsettled his mind. From this most peace-loving of the Herods—(for, curiously enough, after their unhappy childhood amidst the passions and perpetual unrest of their father and his relatives, all of them had the same longing for rest and apathy)⁵—from whom his brothers had snatched the crown that had been bequeathed to him in an earlier will, Antipas now too carried off his wife HERODIAS, daughter of Berenice and granddaughter of Salome. All the passionate, restless, ambitious and cruel temperament of her grandmother Salome and her grandfather Costobar had been transmitted to this daughter of the executed Aristobulus. She was in Galilee what the pendulum is to the clock, and finally brought ruin upon herself and Antipas.

The son who most resembled Herod was ARCHELAUS. This at least was the opinion of the people. "When Joseph heard that Archelaus did reign in Judæa in the room of his father Herod, he was afraid to go thither," says the evangelist.⁶ His own relations in union with the inhabitants of Jerusalem had desired

---

¹ Vita, 9; Bell. ii. 9, 1; Antiq. xviii. 7, 2. ² Vita, 9. ³ Mark xii. 13.

⁴ We call him Herod Boethus from his mother, the daughter of Boethus, in order to distinguish him from his two brothers, Herod Antipas and Herod Philip, son of Cleopatra.

⁵ Antipas, too, in Antiq. xviii. 7, 2, is called ἀγαπῶν τὴν ἡσυχίαν.

⁶ Matthew ii. 22.

to prevent his obtaining the throne. His stay in Rome had been to him an unending series of humiliations. With self-degradation had he had to purchase the confirmation of his father's will, and literally beg for the crown upon his knees. He returned home with the determination to repay his opponents for these mortifications. Philip alone, the good and faithful servant whom he had placed as administrator of his inheritance, had not deserted him; all the others had more or less intrigued against him, his present subjects the most determinedly. From the first, his violent reign was regarded as a government of revenge. Thus Jesus describes the commencement of Archelaus' reign in his parable of the Ten Pounds. "A nobleman," as he is there termed, "went into a far country to receive for himself a kingdom and to return. Then he called ten of his servants, and delivered to them ten pounds, saying to them, Trade until I return. But his citizens hated him, and sent an embassy after him to say, We will not have this man to reign over us. Nevertheless, he received the kingdom, and when he had returned commanded his servants to be called before him, in order that they might give an account of their stewardship. Of the faithful ones, one is set over ten cities and another over five; but a third, who had delayed, knowing that his lord is an austere man taking up what he laid not down, and reaping where he had not sown, he casts forth from the court. And then he cries, But those mine enemies which would not that I should reign over them, bring hither and slay them before me."[1]

It was with this season of requital that the government of Archelaus had begun.[2] His next step was to deprive the Boethusian Joazar of his office as high-priest, accusing him of having taken part with the rebels; then he decreed all manner of stringent penalties on Jews and Samaritans, which were so oppressive that the two hostile peoples even forgot their mutual hatred for the time in order to take common action against the tyrant. But what especially aroused the hatred of the Scribes

[1] Luke xix. 11—27.   [2] Bell. ii. 7, 3.

and Pharisees was his marriage, in violation of the law, with his brother's widow Glaphyra, whom he had married, although she had borne children to his brother Alexander.[1] The frivolous Cappadocian had, after the death of her first husband, married Juba, king of Mauritania, who won a great reputation as an historian. Soon, however, she separated from her learned husband,[2] and returned home to her father. Here she met Archelaus, who fell violently in love with her, put away his wife, and took the spirited Glaphyra back to Jerusalem. In the melancholy royal palace, it seems that the remembrances of her first marriage overpowered her. She died after her first husband had appeared to her in a dream. It seems, almost, as though her case had formed the basis of the Sadducees' marriage parable. Glaphyra, it is true, had not had seven husbands, like the wife in the narrative of the Sadducees, but still she had had three when the first appeared to her in the dream, and demanded her soul in order that she should belong to him in that other world, and not to the two others. The problem of the Sadducees had been solved, consequently, by the ghost.

Nine years long did the contest of the Pharisees with Archelaus continue, in the course of which the ethnarch was twice more obliged to change the high-priest. His relations, too, hostile to him from the first, may very probably have kept stirring up the strife. In the beginning of 6 A.D. the discord reached its height; the nobility of Judæa and Samaria had sent an embassy to Rome to complain there of the ethnarch. Archelaus at the same time dreamed that he saw ten ears of corn which were eaten up by some oxen. Superstitious as his deceased wife, he sent for an Essene, whose name was Simon, to the palace to explain the dream. "The oxen denote a change, because in ploughing they turn over the land, and the ten ears denote the ten years of thy reign," replied the Essene. The ethnarch's dreams were no

---

[1] Antiq. xvii. 13, 1.

[2] Josephus thought that death had put an end to her marriage, but Juba was still living in the year 18; see Schuerer, Neutest. Ztg. 248..

longer difficult to interpret. Only five days afterwards an imperial message summoned Archelaus from his court banquets to Rome. Augustus deprived him of all his possessions, and sent him to Vienna Allobrogum on the Rhone, where he could meditate upon the change in affairs spoken of by the Essene.[1]

His reign left scarcely a trace behind. The newly-erected palace and aqueduct in Jericho, and the beautiful walks of Archelaïs which now fell to Salome, alone remained to call the ethnarch to mind, who otherwise was distinguished for nothing except cruelty and extortion.

A deeper impression, according to Rabbinical tradition, was produced when about this time the celebrated Rabbi Hillel died. All Israel mourned at his grave. "Alas for the meek, alas for the pious, alas for the disciple of Ezra!"[2] He remained in the memory of the people as a pattern of patience, of devoted, peaceful, enduring faith. The stories related of his peaceableness show that his good-nature had become proverbial, so that the fertile imagination of the people made many extraordinary examples of it. Thus it is related that Shammai demanded absolute truth in the marriage-song about the bride, in order that it might produce an effect upon the newly-married; Hillel, however, declared that the standpoint of the bridegroom must be taken, and even though the bride were ugly, yet the song must be, "Oh thou lovely, charming bride!"[3] In the same manner he sought to help the husband who did not feel happy in his marriage, by simplifying divorce. According to Deuteronomy xxiv. 1—4, a man was only allowed to put away his wife when he found some "shameful thing" in her; Shammai understood by this a morally shameful fault; but Hillel taught that a man might put away his wife even for having burned his food in cooking.[4]

---

[1] Bell. ii. 7, 3; Antiq. xvii. 13, 2.

[2] Sota, 9, 6. Chronology. According to b. Sanh. 15 a, Hillel became president of the Sanhedrin 100 years before the destruction of Jerusalem, that is, in 30 B.C., and occupied the office forty years, until his death, which would be in 10 A.D. He lived to be 120 years old. Beresh Rabba, § 100.

[3] b. Ketuboth, 16 b to 17 a. [4] Gittin, 9, 10.

This love of peace led him sometimes into downright untruthfulness, so that once, in order to avoid a contest with the followers of Shammai, he declared that an ox, which was being slaughtered in the fore-court of the temple as a sacrifice, was a cow, waving the tail of the animal to and fro in order to hide its sex.[1]

More authentic than such anecdotes are the proverbs, some of which are very beautiful, that the Pirqe Aboth refer to Hillel the old, so far as such characteristic sayings bear witness of themselves. "More flesh, more worms; more treasures, more care; more maid-servants, more lewdness; more men-servants, more theft; more women, more witchcrafts (Nah. iii. 4); more Thorah, more life; more wisdom, more scholars. He who has gotten to himself words of Thorah, has gotten to himself the life of the world to come. He who increases not, decreases; and he who will not learn, deserves slaughter; and he who serves himself with the tiara, perishes."[2] As the sum and substance of the law, he enjoined on a Gentile, much as Jesus did after him, "That which is unpleasing to thee, do not to thy neighbour: that is the whole law, and all the rest is but its exposition."[3] "Be of the disciples of Aaron, loving peace and pursuing peace, loving mankind, and bringing them nigh to the Thorah."[4] "A name made great is a name destroyed. Trust not in thyself until the day of thy death .... and say not, When I have leisure I will study; perchance thou mayst not have leisure. If I am not for myself, who is for me? and being for my own self, what am I? If not now, when?"[5] Although much real wisdom is contained in these precepts, yet they gain in weight from the importance which the man possessed for several decades. By his canons of interpretation he had awakened a fresh zeal for the exposition of the Scriptures. Antiquated regulations he had put aside by these means without breaking the law. With the delight in the law he had also kept Israel's faith in herself alive. "Am I, Israel, here, then is everything here; am I absent, who is to be

---

[1] b. Beza, 20 a.   [2] Pirqe Aboth, ii. 7; i. 14; iv. 5.   [3] Grätz, iii. 226.
[4] Pirqe Aboth, i. 13.   [5] Pirqe Aboth, i. 14; ii. 5.

found?"[1] had he said at a time when many were discouraged. On the other hand, he had treated Gentiles also with mildness, patience and respect. In case he really was president of the Sanhedrin exactly forty years, which is a somewhat suspiciously round number, he personally experienced the defeat of his own party by the stricter and passionately patriotic school. It was from the exciting and strained relations of the times that the extreme tendencies now again came uppermost.

2. The Incorporation of Judæa into the Province of Syria.

When the Jewish deputies had previously repeatedly requested that the kingship might be abolished and the high-priest be made directly subject to the proconsul of Syria, they were thinking, doubtless, of the favourable condition of the Phœnician cities, the archons of which carried on public business according to local custom, and practically had to come into contact with the proconsuls only on military or taxation affairs. It was forgotten that the land of the Jews was much too large for such a relation, the population too difficult to manage, and its position one of extreme military importance, and that such dependencies of greater provinces were usually governed by a procurator *vice præsidis*.[2]

The news that Judæa was to receive a procurator was perhaps the first disappointment the Jews experienced when rejoicing at the removal of Archelaus, for they had not desired that one should govern them. Moreover, the then governor of Syria, P. Sulpicius Quirinius, who was administrator of this province from 6 to 11 A. D., showed that he was not at all inclined to undertake the

---

[1] Grätz, Geschichte der Juden, iii. 174.

[2] Such procurators were stationed in both provinces of Mauritania, Rætia, Vindelicia, Noricum, Thracia, in the Cottian Alps, Corsica, &c. Tacitus, Hist. i. 11; ii. 16; Höck. Röm. Geschichte, i. 2, p. 202. The title was procurator et præses, or procurator vel præses; procurator et prolegatus; procurator cum jure gladii.

incorporation of Judæa with the forbearance towards the Jewish peculiarities that was so imperatively necessary. Quirinius was a *homo novus* of mean descent. He came from Lanuvium,[1] and had received the consulship from Augustus on account of his zeal in military service as well as the affairs of state. In the last years of Herod he had—presumably as proprætor of Galatia—earned the honour of a triumph for wars in the Taurus. The Homanades, a tribe of predatory mountaineers—who possessed, in the steep mountain ravines of the Taurus, where the frontiers of Lycaonia, Pamphylia and Cilicia meet, forty-four castles which were deemed impregnable[2]—had killed Amyntas, king of Galatia. Quirinius did not venture to follow them up into their ravines and caves, but starved them out, and then carried away all the men capable of bearing arms, sending some into exile, and others he distributed among the legions. Afterwards he conducted the affairs of the young Caius Cæsar, grandson of Augustus, in Armenia to the satisfaction of the emperor, and was rewarded with the province of Syria. He was deemed a malignant, avaricious character, who, twenty years after he had been divorced from his wife, commenced an action against her for mixing poison, in order to gratify his malice.[3]

The procurator whom he had assigned to Judæa was Coponius, an otherwise unknown Roman knight. Both appeared in Jerusalem and took possession of Archelaus' property in the name of the emperor. The royal palace now became the prætorium, where, henceforth, the procurator took up his abode during the festivals. To the Herods the ancient Maccabean castle on the Xystus was ceded.[4]

After the strong illusions which had been formed, during the violent contest with Archelaus, of the blessings of a direct subjection of Judæa to the Syrian proconsul, the disappointment was the greater when Quirinius now proclaimed that the first business incumbent upon him was to take a census of the people and

---

[1] Tacitus, Annals, iii. 48; Dio, 54, 28.　　[2] Pliny, v. 53.
[3] Tacitus, Ann. iii. 22; Sueton. Tiberius, 49.　　[4] Antiq. xx. 8, 11.

assess their property, in order to measure by these means the country's capacity for taxation.

New assessments have never been popular with the common people. The more exact control over the income, the stricter levying of the excise, the imposition of new burdens, the intermixture of estates, the necessity of fresh declarations as to means, which are the results, constitute the real ground of such antipathy. As regards the census of the people, the objection in Judæa was based, moreover, upon religious grounds'; for since the fatal census of king David, such enumerations, if not forbidden, were yet surrounded by peculiar formalities. Was it desired to obtain an estimate of the number of the population in Judæa, the Passover lambs at Easter were counted, their number multiplied by ten—since, on an average, ten to twelve persons partook of a lamb—an allowance being made for the lepers and unclean; and in this way was it believed that the number of families and heads of the district could be ascertained.[1] In formal census of the people, half a shekel per head had to be paid, as an atonement for the guilt incurred thereby, to the temple. At the same time the men over twenty alone ought to be included in this enumeration, and the sons of the tribe of Levi were to be quite free because they were not liable either for military service or taxation. As these regulations were difficult to carry out, the milder school allowed that every one should give a coin, and that finally the coins should be counted, and thus the necessity of any other atonement avoided. The more strictly inclined, on the other hand, rejected every kind of census. According to their theory there was no blessing whatever in what was numbered, but men especially fell under the power of evil as soon as they had a number. "When the anger of Jehovah was kindled against Israel,"[2] they declared, "he moved David against them, saying Go, number Israel and Judah; and when he had done so, there

---

[1] Bell. vi. 9, 3. According to the Targum on 1 Samuel xv. 4, Samuel even had counted the people by means of the Passover lambs.

[2] 2 Samuel xxiv. 1—15.

died of the people seventy thousand men." Or else they referred to the word of the prophet, "Yet the number of the children of Israel shall be as the sand of the sea, which cannot be measured nor numbered."[1] Thus the Roman administration, on its very first action in the newly-acquired province, encountered an opposition, of the deeper motives of which it had manifestly no presentiment.

To Quirinius, a census of the people was the simplest thing in the world. So little had he calculated upon any opposition, that he came to Jerusalem accompanied by only a few followers. It is very probable that he regarded the sale of the property of Archelaus, and the confiscation of his estates in favour of the imperial treasury, as the most difficult task. For the census of the people, on the other hand, there were the prescribed methods according to long-accustomed rules. In the first place, the counting of the communities, that is, the so-called *capitatio*, had to be made, either according to houses or according to families (according to *regio* or *tribus*). Upon the basis of the *capitatio*, the poll-tax was then imposed, according to which every father of a family had to pay a sum yet to be fixed for each person in his *familia*, as was the case also in the older parts of the province.[2] The capital-tax in Syria, at the time of the first triumvirate, amounted to one per cent. of the personal property. Since the time of Antonius it had probably been increased. The trade-tax also was to be regulated upon the basis of these schedules. It was more difficult, on the other hand, to settle the *tributum agri*, since comprehensive surveys were necessary in order to make the land-tax equitable in the several districts. For this purpose, separate divisions of the fields (*juga*) were made, so that their capital value was about a thousand ducats [guineas] (*solidi*).[3] Within these divisions, regard was paid to the fertility of the several plots of land, and there was a distinction between the

---

[1] Hosea i. 10. The opinions of the Rabbis, see Taanith, fol. 8.

[2] App. Syr. 49.

[3] Cassiod. ii. 38. [The solidus, or aureus, of the Roman emperors was at that time worth 119·6 grains pure gold = £1. 1s. 1d.]

arvi primi, arvi secundi, prati, silvæ glandiferæ and *silvæ vulgaris pascuæ*.[1]

Without doubt, both sides were struck with consternation when proconsul and members of the Sanhedrin first learned the rules which were recognized by the others for the work to be undertaken. Apart from all Rabbinical amplifications, the directions given in Exodus xxx. 11—16 were undoubtedly the proper rule for Israel: "Jehovah spake unto Moses, saying, When thou takest the sum of the children of Israel by those of them that are mustered, then shall they give every man a ransom for his soul unto Jehovah, that there be no plague among them when thou musterest them. This they shall give, every one that passeth over to them that are mustered, half a shekel after the shekel of the sanctuary: twenty gerahs to the shekel: an half-shekel shall be the offering to Jehovah. Every one that passeth over to them that are mustered, from twenty years old and above, shall give an offering unto Jehovah. The rich shall not give more, and the poor shall not give less than half a shekel, when they give an offering unto Jehovah to make an atonement for your souls." Moreover, there was the farther direction that *one* tribe was not to be counted at all: "Only thou shalt not number the tribe of Levi, neither take the sum of them among the children of Israel."[2] And just as little were they accustomed to count women and children, because they did not come into consideration in the military purpose for which the enumeration was made.[3] The Romans might well have been astonished when the Jewish councillors proposed these principles of statistics to them.

But it was still worse with regard to the land-tax. From ancient times it had been the doctrine in Israel that every Jewish man held his soil and ground only as a fief from Jehovah, and paid his tithes for it to the lord of the land, who handed them over

---

[1] Compare Huschke, Census und Steuerverfassung der röm. Kaiserzeit; Berlin, 1847, pp. 106—121.

[2] Numbers i. 49.   [3] Exodus xxxviii. 26.

to the Levites.¹ The Pharisees therefore maintained "that it was not permitted to pay any taxes to the Romans, inasmuch as by so doing another suzerain would be recognized in addition to Jehovah."²

That this pretension was possible, makes it probable that Herod and Archelaus had up to this time avoided any open competition with the temple tithes; and perhaps the civil imposts known hitherto to the Jews as highway-rates, house-tax, excise, market-tax, poll-tax,³ salt-tax, crown-tax⁴ and tolls⁵ pressed so heavily upon them, because the states' necessities had, in order not to violate religious custom, to be raised in a perfectly irrational manner. Certainly Herod appears to have derived a revenue from the field produce,⁶ but probably in so doing he avoided the form of a tithe, just as Cæsar forbade the application of the Roman forms of taxation in Judæa, in consequence of the representations of Antipater.⁷ Under any circumstances, the Roman land-tax, which claimed a tenth of corn and two-tenths of wine and fruit, was regarded as an encroachment upon the rights of Jehovah.⁸ At the head of the opposition appeared the Pharisee Zadok; among the people, a native of Gaulanitis, Judas of Gamala, generally called Judas the Galilean, incited to a revolt. Perhaps it is the same Galilean Judas, son of the Hezekiah executed by Herod, who had immediately after Herod's death stormed Sepphoris, obtained possession of the armoury and begun the war with Varus, that now was again opposing the Romans. The learned Jews, too, would not at all listen to this proposal for the new census; but Quirinius was not the man to trouble himself about Galilean robbers or the theology of the Sanhedrin. He had the reputation of generally recognizing no

---

¹ Leviticus xxvii. 30—33; Numbers xviii. 21—24.
² Nehemiah xiii. 5; Jubilees 13 (p. 6).
³ Ezra iv. 13, 20, vii. 24; Antiq. xvii. 8, 4, xviii. 4, 3, xix. 6, 3.
⁴ 1 Macc. x. 20.   ⁵ Antiq. xii. 3, 3, xiii. 8, 3 xiv. 18, 6.
⁶ Antiq. xv. 9, 1.   ⁷ Antiq. xiv. 10, 1—6.
⁸ Bell. ii. 8, 1; Matt. xxii. 17, ἔξεστι δοῦναι κῆνσον καίσαρι, ἢ οὔ.

motives other than avarice and ambition; and as he had reduced the Homanades by starvation and barbaric conscriptions to quietude, so he intended here, too, to establish order. Then the Rabbis began to draw back.

The high-priest Joazar, an Herodian of the house of Boethus, was the first to be convinced that the opposition of the people rested upon prejudice, and, according to the traditions of his family, was the first to go over to the Gentiles. He was fortunate enough to again appease the mob and remove their exaggerated fears. In Jerusalem, the census of the people and the survey proceeded, consequently, even without any opposition.

But now a division took place in the party of the Pharisees itself. The most extreme members were tired of the Rabbinical opposition of significant speeches, concealed references and pointed disputations about words in the synagogue. They separated themselves from the Pharisees, and founded, as Josephus expresses it, "a new school." The new doctrine of this school was the doctrine of the dagger, for which reason the adherents of this "philosophy" were afterwards termed briefly the *Sicarii*. Before their adoption of these last means, they had been called ZEALOTS, in memory of the legacy of the dying Mattathias: "Be ye zealous for the law, and give your lives for the covenant of your fathers."[1] To the exhortations of their former associates to honour the decrees of government, they retorted: "Whoso receives upon him the yoke of Thorah, they remove from him the yoke of royalty and the yoke of worldly care; and whoso breaks from him the yoke of Thorah, they lay upon him the yoke of royalty and the yoke of worldly care."[2] Thus the prophecies that the census of the people would cause death as at the time of David did not remain unfulfilled. But the threshing-floor of Araunah was this time Gamala on the lake of Gennesareth. It was in the very country where the census was not to take place that the revolt commenced, and the destroying angel which went through the land was Judas the Galilean.

[1] 1 Maccabees ii. 50; 2 Maccabees iv. 2.   [2] Pirqe Aboth, iii. 8.

Judas the Galilean belonged to those idealistic characters which do not the less inspire youth because they are fools; for it is not a knowledge of the world, but honest conviction, that carries men away. He was one of the historic holy simpletons who aim at what is impossible and run their heads against walls; effecting nothing outwardly, and yet exercising the greatest influence because they leave an irresistible example behind them. In comparison with the terribly effective legacy which the hero of Gamala bequeathed to the future, the sanguinary revolt which he raised seemed so unimportant that Josephus leaves it altogether out of sight, passing into womanish complaints about the unspeakable misery which was attached to the name of the Gaulanite. The watchword which Judas gave especially to the Pharisaic youth ran simply, "No Lord but Jehovah; no tax but that to the temple; no friend but the zealot." It is idolatry to reverence Cæsar, idolatry to pay the denarius to the Gentile state, a breach of the purity of clean goods to pay toll or tithe to the unclean, and he who demands it is an enemy of God, enemy of Israel, doubly punishable when he is a Jew. War against Rome and civil war, consequently, always went hand in hand with these zealots. Whenever the curved scimitar of the Galilean clashes on the short sword of the Romans, the country-houses of the Sadducees begin to smoke, and red flames devour the granary of the satisfied friend of the Romans. It was with such terrors that the Galilean at once took the field. The dominion of God, as he interpreted it, could only be established by the sword, for his God was a jealous God, who suffered no other Lord beside Him. Had Judas succeeded in establishing his kingdom of God, it would have resembled neither the theocracy of the Sadducees nor the dominion of God according to the Pharisees, but would have been more like the Maccabean state, the prophet of which would have quickly attacked the unbelievers of the neighbouring countries also. But the brave Galilean was defeated. That there was furious fighting is proved by the fanatical reverence with which the national party clung to the memory of the man of Gamala. Otherwise our sources of information say nothing. It is from the Acts of the Apostles alone that we learn that Judas himself perished. "Judas of Galilee," said Gamaliel in the Sanhedrin, "rose up in the days of the census, and caused much people to follow him and rebel: he also perished; and all who obeyed him were dispersed."[1] In any case, the revolt in which Judas shed his blood was quickly suppressed, and Israel, in spite of all opposition, was numbered from Beersheba to Bethshean. Nevertheless, the procurators never again desired to attempt a census of the people; and under Nero the proconsul Cestius Gallus had the enumeration actually taken by means of the Passover lambs, such a thorough lesson had this revolt occasioned by the census taught the Roman administration.[2] But far more important than this intimidation of Rome on this single point was the moral effect upon the youth of Judæa, especially as there arose in the sons and grandsons of Judas a new family of Maccabees that reverenced the bequest of the fallen hero. James, Simon, Menahem, Eleazar—these were the sons of the Galilean, of whom not one died upon a sick bed, but all met their end in fighting against Rome, on the lofty cross, on the bloody battlefield, or by their own hand. When there was nothing more left to the Jews in Judæa beyond a tower at Masada, a grandson of the Galilean who was the commander, said with pride to his companions, "We were the first to revolt against the Gentiles, we are the last who fight against them;"[3] and when every prospect of deliverance had vanished, Eleazar slew the nine hundred persons who had come to him for protection, and set the fortress in flames, in order that hungry Rome might gain nothing at his hands save ashes and corpses. And these Galilean principles seized upon those around with terribly contagious power. It was the ideas of the Galilean which Paul, in his Epistle to the Romans, had to contend against even in the followers of Jesus; these it was which gathered a faction together at Thebes in Egypt, and that a weaver, Jonathan, carried to Cyrene. This

---

[1] Acts v. 37. [2] Bell. vi. 9, 3. [3] Bell. vii. 8, 6.

radical fanaticism spread like an epidemic, and Josephus was not wrong when he declared that this Galilean, who had not been able to hold out for two months, had disturbed Rome for seventy years, turned Palestine into a desert, destroyed the temple, and scattered Israel over the face of the earth. This, too, was a part of Galilean idealism, that Galilee was capable of producing such prophets, and, even after their ignominious end, of *thus* believing in them. For the present, it is true, the clumsy executioner, Quirinius, remained master of the field.

At the end of the year, success had been so far gained that the poll-tax, land-tax and tolls could be newly assessed in accordance with Roman principles, not with a view, however, of abolishing the older taxes, such as the house-taxes and market-taxes, the latter of which especially were much hated by the people.[1] Nevertheless, the calculations gave a result below the Roman expectations. Whilst Herod had been believed to have been the richest king of the East, the estimates did not show a twelfth part of the taxes of Egypt.[2] In the usual course of business, the census lists were next sent to the emperor, who determined the amount of the taxes by the so-called *indictio*, which were then advertised in order that they might be farmed to the *publicani*. The *ager publicus*, that is, the public estates which had been confiscated for the imperial treasury, the harbour dues, the fisheries, mines, &c., were usually dealt with in the same manner.

But the opposition of the people to these Gentile taxes was only broken and in no way internally overcome. The Rabbis clung to their precept that the land was desecrated by tribute paid to the Gentile emperor; and a later saying even declares that, since purity had been removed from out of Israel, fruits had lost their savour and smell, and that since the tithes were not duly paid—which was soon afterwards the case, as the Romans did not trouble themselves about the temple-tax—the produce of the fields had decreased.[3] Thus the question of the

---

[1] Antiq. xvii. 8, 4, xviii. 4, 3, xix. 6, 3.   [2] Bell. ii. 16, 4.
[3] Mishna, Sotah, ix. 12, 13.

Pharisees about the tribute-money was not whether a man was bound to pay his taxes, but whether it was "*lawful*" (i.e. permitted by the law), on account of the purity of the land, to pay tribute to the emperor.[1]

Under these circumstances, the most vehement opposition was directed against those inhabitants who, after the revenues of the country had been farmed out to one of the Roman finance companies, placed themselves at its disposal in order to collect the tolls. The people knew how to torment these officials of the Roman customs with the petty cruelty which ordinary people develope with irreconcilable persistency, whenever they believe this persistency to be due to their moral indignation. In consequence of the theocratic scruples about the duty of paying taxes, the tax-gatherers were declared to be unclean and half Gentile. As among the Greeks the words "tax-gatherers and sycophants,"[2] so among the Jews the words "tax-gatherers and sinners,"[3] "tax-gatherers and Gentiles,"[4] "tax-gatherers and harlots,"[5] "tax-gatherers, murderers and robbers,"[6] and similar insulting combinations, were not only ready on the tongue and familiar, but were accepted as theocratically identical in meaning.[7] Thrust out from all social intercourse, the tax-gatherers became more and more the pariahs of the Jewish world. With holy horror did the Pharisee sweep past the lost son of Israel who had sold himself to the Gentile for the vilest purpose, and avoid the places which his sinful breath contaminated. Their testimony was not accepted by Jewish tribunals. It was forbidden to sit at table with them or eat of their bread. But their money-chests especially were the summary of all uncleanness and the chief object of pious horror, since their contents consisted of none but unlawful receipts, and every single coin betokened a breach of some theocratic regulation. To exchange their money or receive alms from them might easily put a whole house in the condition of being

---

[1] Matt. x. xii. 17, ἔξεστι; Luke xx. 22.   [2] Stobæus, Serm. ii. 34.
[3] Matt. ix. 10, xi. 19.   [4] Matt. xviii. 17.   [5] Matt. xxi. 31.
[6] Mishna, Nedar, 3, 4.   [7] Matt. xxi. 31.

unclean, and necessitate many purifications.[1] From these relations of the tax-officials to the rest of the population, it can be readily understood that only the refuse of Judaism undertook the office. Everywhere thrust out from respectable intercourse, they often did really abandon themselves to vice, and made their houses the refuge of all who had fallen out with the theocracy. Often a merry life was passed there, surrounded by the wine-cup, bottle and harlot,[2] and the one object of care was remorselessly to fill the money-chests that were so offensive to the Jews by all means in their power. These mutual relations urged them also on their side to wage war against this irrational and fanatical people. Shameless overcharge of the taxes, and ruthless harshness in exacting them, were henceforth quite an every-day occurrence.[3]

3. The Procuratorial Administration.

The procurator, who henceforth was to be administrator of Judæa, under the supervision of the Syrian legate, was in right of office commander-in-chief of the troops of Judæa and Samaria. He had charge of the administration of finance and exercised justice, so far as the latter had not been entrusted to the Sanhedrin. The penal judicature was reserved to him; and in case a Jewish subject were condemned to death by the Sanhedrin on account of some religious transgression, of which the decision lay with it, the procurator had to confirm the sentence. Hence the cry, Crucify him! at the judgment-seat of Pilate.

Nevertheless, in this division the priesthood had been the gainers, even though all their hopes had not been fulfilled. The Gentile procurator could not meddle so much in the affairs of the theocracy as the Herods had done. Thus we see the leading families of the Sadducees now coming forward with an

---

[1] Mishna, Baba Kama, 10, 1.   [2] Matt. xi. 19, xxi. 31.
[3] Luke iii. 13, xii. 58, xix. 8.

importance far other than that exercised by them in the days of
Herod. It is one family of priests, pre-eminently, that up to the
time of the last war stands at the head of the theocracy. Before
Quirinius left Jerusalem, he elevated Annas, the son of Seth, to
the high-priesthood, thus sacrificing Joazar, who had become
hated on account of the part he had taken in the census of the
people. Annas and his house were henceforth the soul of the
Sadducean government which succeeded that of the Herods.
On this occasion, too, the Pharisees were those who were over-
reached; and that it was not they, but the Sadducees, who obtained
the upper hand, can very probably have been among the reasons
which urged them subsequently into an alliance with Herod
Agrippa I., a thing contrary to all their previous traditions.

For their small share in the government the Pharisees found
compensation in their growing influence among the population,
whose hatred towards the Gentiles was gratified in the strict
fulfilment of their teacher's precepts against uncleanness. They
knew a hundred means by which they could annoy the Gentiles,
in consequence of which the Romans came to the opinion that
the Mosaic law had no other purpose than that of planting hatred
between Israel and every other people. Gentile coins with the
head of the emperor and inscription were at the most available
for taxes to the Gentile state. The titles of honour upon them
were names of blasphemy; and that no one can buy or sell without making himself unclean,[1] is reckoned among those machina-
tions of Satan which he contrives. Thus there were pious people
who never touched a piece of money, and excluded themselves
from all trade or commerce, because they would not carry the
image of the emperor or the gods in their pockets, and preferred
not entering a town at all to passing under a gateway adorned
with images.[2] If a Jew only visited a bath that was adorned
with Gentile statues, he was called to account.[3] So that he should
not incur the guilt of participating in the worship of idols, he
was forbidden to transact any more business with Gentiles three

---

[1] Revelation xiii. 17.   [2] Hippolyt. Ref. 9, 26.   [3] Aboda Sara, iii. 4.

days before the Gentile festivals, or to visit the Gentile city on a festival day; and he dared not purchase any Gentile wine because it might be wine offered to idols. To provide his army with proper oil was one of the most important cares of the Pharisee Josephus. "It is forbidden to employ for any purpose whatever wood that has been taken from the idol's grove. An oven that has been heated with it is unclean; bread baked with it is not to be eaten. If it be made into a weaver's shuttle, the cloth woven is not to be used."[1] "All Gentile houses are to be avoided, for merely entering them makes a man unclean."[2] "No sort of food prepared by a Gentile may be partaken of by a Jew; he is not allowed to sit at the Gentile's table.[3] The Gentile may be invited by the Jew to his table, indeed; but if it happen that the Gentile remain a minute alone, then everything which stands upon the table becomes unclean, and may no longer be partaken of."[4] These were the weapons with which the Rabbis fought the Romans.

When we remember how, in the Gospel narrative, the Pharisees watch Jesus, or call to mind the centurion of Capernaum or the widow of Tyre, we have a vivid picture of these relations. But the tribute money in particular was the favourite theme of the Pharisees at the time of Jesus.

As the lax Oriental countries could not in general endure the tension of a regular taxation, and least of all the Roman system of raising revenue, there was a state of war, consequently, from one year's end to another. Even the milder school of Hillel declared every means by which the plundering of the tax-gatherers could be escaped to be permissible.[5] And yet the Pharisees did not do nearly enough in such matters according to the stricter-minded. "We complain of you Pharisees," does a controversy in the Talmud declare, "that you place the emperor's name beside the name of Moses in bills of divorce." To which

---

[1] Aboda Sara, ii. 3, iii. 9. In Schuerer, Neutest Zeitgeschichte, 386.
[2] John xviii. 28.
[3] Acts xi. 3; Galatians ii. 12.
[4] Aboda Sara, v. 5.
[5] Nedarim, 27 b, 28.

the sons of Hillel reply, not without a show of reason, that in the very Scriptures the name of Jehovah is mentioned beside that of Pharaoh, which finally satisfied them in this matter.[1]

The ZEALOTS, however, would know nothing whatever of waging war with such petty means; they wanted iron and blood. "It was our youth," does Josephus complain, "that, by their fanaticism for that unprecedented doctrine, brought the state to destruction;"[2] and this doctrine was, "that Jehovah alone was to be honoured as the Lord of the land, that death was not to be dreaded, and the slaughter of their neighbours was not to be heeded if it concerned the freedom of their country."[3] The family of the fallen Gaulonite remained at the head of this movement. Two of his sons were afterwards crucified by Tiberius Alexander for insurrection;[4] and whilst a third one, Menahem, was the first to begin the war against Florus by taking Masada,[5] his grandson, Eleazar, was the last contender for freedom, burying himself with the last of the Zealots under the ruins of this fortress.[6] It is at the same time worth observing that, after 7 A.D., in no part of Palestine was public security cared for worse than in that directly under the Roman administration. If the traveller even from Jerusalem to Jericho falls among robbers,[7] how must it have been in the lonely and deserted ravines beyond Hebron?

The condition of affairs, moreover—although Augustus endeavoured to make allowance[8] for the peculiarities of the Jews, little as he loved them—was not at all favourable for giving the people that feeling of security in their religious life, without which there was no peace in Judæa. The Samaritans, well aware that now their opportunity had come, boldly lifted up their heads. Since the banishment of the ethnarch, their dependency

---

[1] Grätz, iii. 209.   [2] Antiq. xviii. 1, 1.   [3] Antiq. xviii. 1, 6.
[4] Antiq. xx. 5, 2.   [5] Bell. ii. 17, 8.
[6] Bell. vii. 8, 1; compare ii. 17, 9.
[7] Luke x. 30; Bell. iv. 8, 2; Antiq. xx. 5; 1, 2, 3, 4; 6, 1.
[8] Compare Philo, Leg. ad. Caium. Frankfurter Ausgabe, 1014, 1035, 1036; Bohn's translation, by C. D. Yonge, iv. 167—169; on other hand, see Suet. Oct. 93, 96.

on Jerusalem had ceased. Their council of elders rejoiced in a power that they had long wanted.¹ But the foolish people of Sichem used their freedom in a way devoid of dignity. Under Coponius, the sanctuary at Jerusalem was desecrated in the night before the Passover by the Samaritans. For as the gates of the temple, according to custom, were thrown open immediately after midnight, several Samaritans had stolen secretly into the temple during the night, and strewed human bones in the courts, so that in the morning the crowds coming to the festival had to be sent away from the temple gates by the high-priest Annas, in order that they should not themselves be defiled. The people withdrew to their houses enraged, and the temple was consecrated anew; but of punishing the Samaritans we hear nothing. That the temple ought to be watched, seems to have been the decision of the procurator.² The two successors of Coponius, M. AMBIVIUS and ANNIUS RUFUS, were less important characters, and not able to check the prevalent misery.³ Of the first, all we are told is that under him Salome died; and of the second, that it was during his administration that Augustus died. Their successor sent by Tiberius, VALERIUS GRATUS, who governed Judæa for full eleven years (15—26 A.D.), meddled so much in the affairs of the Sadducean temple-nobility, that he had to install and depose five high-priests during his administration. This fact alone shows what was the real state of the "rest" and "peace" that it is believed were spread over Judæa until the time of Pilate. First of all, the wily Annas was removed; a year afterwards, his successor Ismael, to whom the enviable privilege fell of having to prepare the ashes of a red cow. Then Annas's son Eleazar was installed, whose place again was taken within the course of a year (18 A.D.) by a Simon ben Kamhith. Simon is celebrated in Rabbinical annals on account of an accident which befel him on the night preceding the feast of Atonement. In order to shorten the length of the night-watch, he had entered into conversation with an Arabian sheikh, when the

¹ Antiq. xviii. 4, 2. ² Antiq. xviii. 2, 2. ³ Tacit. Annals, ii. 42.

vehement-speaking Gentile sprinkled his garment with a drop of saliva, and so made him unclean. His brother had now to attend to the sacred offices in his place.[1] The last high-priest of this batch was Caiaphas, the judge of Jesus. The highest office of the theocracy, however, lost so much respect by this perpetual change, that the deposed high-priest Annas remained, in spite of his successors, the theocratic authority of the country.

In addition to these grievances, the burden of taxation was so unendurably increased under Valerius Gratus, that serious commotions had to be feared in Judæa, as in Syria. A deputation in Rome, in the year 17, besought for some alleviation from this taxation. Tiberius declared in the senate, "that the wisdom of Germanicus alone could check the commotions in the East." But the effect of sending Germanicus was lost in the dispute with Cneius Piso, the wilful legate of Syria, and, instead of any alleviation, the province nearly experienced a civil war.[2] The prince, who could be little moved from his purpose, expected to attain this alleviation without any exceptional measures, by determining to put an end to this rapid change of officials. "Every office," he philosophized, "leads as a matter of course to avarice; and if any one obtain an office, not as a permanence, but only for a brief period, without knowing when it may be taken from him again, the more will he make a point of plundering the wealthy. Were one to remain longer in possession of office, he would become tired of extortion as soon as he had amassed enough, and would then prove more moderate." "A wounded man," he used to add as an example, "lay by the roadside, and swarms of flies settled on his wounds. A traveller who came that way took pity on his sufferings, and thinking that the man was too weak to drive away the flies himself, came up and was about to drive them away for him. But the wounded man besought him not to do so, and, when the traveller inquired why he did not wish to be freed from such a plague, replied, You will only increase my sufferings if you drive them away; for

[1] In Derenbourg, 197. [2] Annals, ii. 42, 43, 71.

these flies are now almost satiated, and are already abating; but should a fresh hungry swarm come and find me in my exhausted state, they would be my destruction."[1] A frightful picture of the condition of the tortured provinces! But the misanthropic indolence of the melancholy emperor knew nothing of the duties of the good Samaritan in binding up such wounds; he consoled himself by thinking that the flies would soon become satiated. For Judæa it was certainly a doubtful advantage to possess a Valerius Gratus and Pontius Pilate for any real length of time. Moreover, the emperor himself hated the Jews, and the malignity which he made them feel in the capital was naturally imitated in the provinces. He counted it as an improvement in morals that, in the year 19, he, at the solicitation of Sejanus, banished the Jews from Rome.[2] In immediate connection with the decrees of the senate against the debauchery of Roman wives, Tacitus relates, "there was farther intervention on account of the expulsion of the Egyptian and Judæan sects."[3] This curious juxtaposition is explained by the circumstance that certain priests of Isis had cheated a superstitious aristocratic lady of her honour, and certain Jewish Rabbis had cheated another of gold she had destined for the temple.[4] The decree of the Fathers ran as follows: "That four thousand freedmen infected by this superstition, who were yet of vigorous age, should be transported to the island of Sardinia to reduce the hordes of robbers there; should the unhealthy climate destroy them, it was of small consequence; the others were to quit Italy unless they had before a certain day appointed renounced the unholy usages."[5] According to Suetonius, Tiberius even compelled the followers of this cultus themselves to burn their garments and vessels used in their worship;[6] whilst Josephus, on the other hand, recounts that the Jews distributed among the troops preferred becoming martyrs to their religion to breaking their law.[7]

---

[1] Antiq. xviii. 6, 5.
[2] Philo, Leg. ad Caium, Frankfurter Ausgabe, 1015; Bohn's translation, iv. 135.
[3] Tacit. Ann. ii. 85. [4] Antiq. xviii. 3, 4, 5. [5] Tacit. Ann. ii. 85.
[6] Sueton. Tiber. 36. [7] Antiq. xviii. 3, 4.

In Judæa, these manifestations of hatred were attributed to the influence of Sejanus.[1] The more significant must it have appeared that in the days of his greatest influence a change of persons took place; for in the year 26, PONTIUS PILATE took the place of Valerius Gratus. The servant was in fact worthy of his master. Mercenary, avaricious, cruel and even bloodthirsty, conscienceless, and yet at the decisive moment wanting in decision, his name soon became one of the most odious Roman ones in Judæa.[2] He introduced himself also in a most unfavourable manner to the inhabitants of Jerusalem. It had until now been the custom for the garrison of Antonia to leave the emblems of their *signa* behind at Cæsarea, as the Jews would not suffer the eagles and busts of the emperor in the holy city, because divine honours were paid them. Pilate, however, now commanded, probably when the first change of garrison was made,[3] that the troops that were freshly arriving should bring their standards, just as they were, with them into Jerusalem by night; and one morning the people of Judæa—whose chief commandment was, Thou shalt not make unto thee any graven image, or any likeness—beheld the Roman *signa*, with the silver busts of Tiberius, planted in view of the temple. A universal commotion arose in the city, and everywhere scribes and people consulted how the sacrilege was to be repressed. Soon the country people, too, poured in in crowds; but the sober-minded now again retained the upper hand in opposition to the zealots, and it was decided to go to Cæsarea, and beseech Pilate to remove the abomination. The procurator harshly rejected the demand of the crowd as an insult to the emperor, but the multitudes did not give way. Five days and five nights they besieged the palace of Herod, in which Pilate dwelt, always giving utterance to the same complaint and petition. Pilate desired to put an end to the matter, and commanded the Jews to present themselves, on the seventh day,

---

[1] Philo, Leg. ad Caium, 1015, 1033; Bohn, iv. 135, 164.
[2] Antiq. xviii. 3, 1; Bell. ii. 9, 3. Philo, Leg. ad Caium, 1034; Bohn, iv. 165.
[3] Antiq. xviii. 3, 1.

in the circus. During the night he had surrounded the place with his troops, and as the Jews again raised their mutinous clamour on his refusing their request anew, he suddenly commanded the soldiers to come forth with their weapons drawn. But he was mistaken with regard to the fanatically excited crowd. The Jews bared their necks, threw themselves down as though preparing for execution, and declared that they would sooner surrender their lives than their law. From such a massacre the procurator drew back alarmed, for he was afraid of the emperor's anger. Nothing remained for him but to order the *signa* to be removed.[1]

By this retreat, however, faith in his immovability was from the very beginning destroyed. The Jews had discovered a means of bending his will in that pertinacious clamour which we know so well from the history of the Passion. Still less tenable, however, became his position, when he afterwards made a very perverse attempt to repair the fault. Although the Rabbis had pleaded that their law did not allow the erection of images, yet there was nothing to prevent votive tablets being fixed on the citadel, as they were usually dedicated by other officials, also, to the emperor. He therefore suspended golden shields of this kind, inscribed only with the name of Tiberius and his own, on the palace on Mount Zion, where he himself dwelt. But a fresh storm was the result. At the next festival the Jews, with the four sons of Herod at their head—that is, probably, one of the sons of Cleopatra, Antipas, Herod Boëthus and Phasael— declared that they would still less tolerate such symbols, in that they were to be regarded as altars. "Cease," they cried, when he insolently began to snub them, "inciting to revolt and to war. The emperor is not honoured by dishonouring the law. It is the will of Tiberius that our law should be respected; or else show us some edict or new letter which decrees otherwise, in order that we may send an embassy to Tiberius."[2] Pilate

---

[1] Antiq. xviii. 3, 1; Bell. ii. 9, 2.

[2] Philo, Leg. ad Caium, Frankfurter Ausgabe, 1033—1035; Bohn, iv. 165, 166. For the four sons of Herod, see Antiq. xviii. 5, 1, and xvii. 1, 3.

trembled certainly at the thought of a complaint before Tiberius; for he was afraid, as Philo says, that an embassy to Rome would disclose all his delinquencies,—"the venal character of his judgments, his rapine, the ruin of whole families, all the meannesses of which he was the source, the execution of a multitude of persons who had been subjected to no judicial procedure whatever, and his excessive cruelty of every kind." Nevertheless, he could not go back, and had to allow it to come before the emperor for decision. As Antipas possessed the ear of the latter, and gladly took part in the opposition of the people to Pilate, the final decision was given against him. The decree of Tiberius was a complete exposure of the procurator, for he commanded Pilate to remove the shields from the Antonia and hang them up in the temple of Augustus at Cæsarea. The Jews even took comfort in the belief that the emperor had been very enraged at the follies of his procurator. From this time forth, consequently, Pilate heard on every occasion the mutinous cry of the multitude.

Soon afterwards he came into conflict with the people, even when he undertook a work that was of the most undoubted importance for Jerusalem, and for which he had certainly previously obtained the assent of the Sanhedrin. The conduit which provided Jerusalem and the temple with running water had become defective in course of time, and Pilate now undertook to build a noble aqueduct five, or according to one account even ten, leagues long, which was to conduct the neighbouring fountains up to the temple and join them to the gently flowing waters of the fountain of Siloam.[1] As the work was also to benefit the temple, Pilate unhesitatingly thought that he could make use of the temple treasury (corban) in order to supply means; but scarcely had news of this reached the multitude, when at the next feast there was again a wild commotion raised at the pretended temple robbery, and thousands thronged to the palace in order to repeat the tactics of Cæsarea. But this time the procurator was prepared. He had distributed numerous

[1] Antiq. xviii. 3, 2; Bell. ii. 9, 4; Eusebius, Ecc. Hist. ii. 6; Jerome on Isaiah viii. 6.

soldiers from his troops, dressed in Jewish garments, among the crowd, and when the Jews again raised their pertinacious clamour, the soldiers began at different points to beat the shouters with clubs, who, terrified, ran away, while some, severely wounded, remained on the spot. Perhaps it was on this occasion, when the works in the course of years were advanced as far as the fount of Siloam, that that tower at the pool of Siloam fell and killed eighteen men, which was interpreted by the Rabbis as a sign of divine wrath.[1]

As we learn from the Gospel narrative about the tower of Siloam, so do we also about another misfortune which occurred during the latter years of Pilate. Certain Galileans, who had in some way defied him, were slain by him in the temple over their sacrifices, so that their blood flowed into the same pool as that of their sacrifices.[2] The people's favourite, Barabbas, also, had committed his murders in a revolt against Pilate.[3] Upon the whole, if the name of Pontius Pilate has for us another repute than that of Marcus Ambivius and Valerius Gratus, it is because history has brought him into connection with the life of Jesus, which connection introduces us again more intimately to the internal movements of this period.

4. THE JORDAN BAPTISM.

After the termination of Herod's reign, the religious factor in the life of the Israelitish people was again unmistakably working with redoubled energy. Rumours of the approaching Messianic age had been whispered around the death-bed of the savage king.[4] The revolt of Matthias, Judas and the Pharisaic youth, had only anticipated those theocratic plans which it was intended should be put into execution after the tyrant's decease.

---

[1] Luke xiii. 1—5.
[2] Luke xiii. 1, &c.
[3] Mark xv. 7; Luke xxiii. 17.
[4] Antiq. xvii. 2, 4.

The rising of the robber kings, Simon and Athronges, also had been coloured in each case, more or less, by religious feeling. The deputation of the fifty to Augustus to obtain a restoration of the theocratic constitution, had set even the Jewish community in Rome in a perfect commotion. At last, however, this enthusiastic movement found in Judas the Gaulonite and his associate Zadok, leaders who knew how to defend their religious doctrines from the Scriptures, and prove them according to the rules of the schools, bequeathing an ideal of patriotism to the coming generation which ever fascinated the young anew, and was cherished by the old as the pride of their time. Henceforth patriotic excitement began to bear religious fruit also.

As had always been the case in Israel, so now too had political pressure awakened the slumbering expectations as to Israel's future. But hopes which formerly were confined to the soil of Judæa, excited a small nation, dominated over a generation or two, and then again fell asleep, this time set the world in motion. For these hopes now coincided with a widely-spread and energetic feeling—one that at that epoch thoroughly penetrated all nations alike—the feeling that the present state of the world was absolutely untenable. Tacitus' gloomy tales of the state of affairs at this period are known, as well as the numberless signs of misfortune which Rome anxiously endeavoured to interpret.[1] The ill-treated eastern portion of the Roman empire, especially, participated most strongly in this feeling, and the religious phenomena which occurred beyond the Jewish frontiers also, are signs worthy of attention, because they show that the age appeared to the neighbouring nations, too, to be pregnant with some mighty portents, although they did not, like the prophets of Judæa, hear the voice from above urging them themselves to perfect it.

Thus it is a singular coincidence that in the same year in which the Man appeared who preached and effected the regeneration of humanity, the Egyptian priests announced that the bird

[1] Tacitus, Annals, vi. 28—51. The years 34 and 35, Hist. i. 3.

called the Phœnix had been seen. "During the consulship of Paulus Fabius and Lucius Vitellius," the annals say,[1] "after a long course of centuries the bird Phœnix appeared in Egypt, and afforded abundant opportunity to the most learned of the natives and Greeks for inquiry concerning this miraculous phenomenon." Originally the mythological symbol of the sun, it now stood, in the belief of that time, as representing the cycle in which things move. It appeared at regularly recurring periods, and its appearance always betokened the end of the old age, for it came in order to destroy itself in the flames and rise anew from its ashes. Thus it had appeared at the time of Sesostris, of Amasis and of Ptolemæus, third king of the Macedonian dynasty. That it came again now seemed remarkable, since its periods previously had consisted of 1461 and 500 years, and not even 250 years had elapsed since the time of Ptolemæus.[2] Meanwhile, what was announced by the Egyptian priests was confirmed on the other side by the sacred colleges of the capital. Whilst the pious Egyptians were shaking off the anxieties of Tiberius' reign in the joyful belief that the ancient heathen bird was bearing the expired æon to its grave, the Roman colleges of priests had calculated that the world's year had come to an end, and that the age of Saturn was returning. At the death of Julius Cæsar, according to the opinion of the augurs, the ninth month of the world, and with it the reign of Diana, had reached its termination. Consequently the last month, that of Apollo, had begun. As the secular months were of unequal length, those who believed in such calculations confidently expected the end of all things.[3] The internal relationship of these expectations with the Jewish faith with regard to the future, was not unknown to the Romans,

---

[1] Tacitus, Ann. vi. 28. Pliny, Nat. Hist. ii. 2, places the appearance of the Phœnix more probably in the year 36.

[2] Tacit. Ann. vi. 28.

[3] Virgil, Eclog. iv.; see Ladewig on this passage; compare especially the lines 50—53:

    Adspice convexo nutantem pondere mundum,
      Terrasque tractusque maris cœlumque profundum,
    Adspice, venturo lætantur ut omnia sæclo!

and Virgil has painted the Saturnian age with pictures from Isaiah as the Sibyl whom he knew presented them to him.[1] The story also of the death of great Pan, which, according to Plutarch,[2] occurred in the days of Tiberius, has always been regarded as a deeply poetical expression of this presentiment of the ancient world that it was approaching its end. Near to Corfu a ship had been mysteriously becalmed at the time, when the Egyptian helmsman Thamnus heard a voice from the islands of the Echinades calling him by name, and charging him that when he passed the place called Palodes he should announce that the great Pan was dead. The Egyptian did as he was bid; but scarcely had he shouted his message across to the shore where directed, than a great sighing, mingled with cries of amazement, were heard around, so that the passengers were filled with astonishment, and when the news became known in Rome, the Quirites and the emperor Tiberius were not a little disturbed. For the great Pan was truly dead, and the other gods also began to sicken. Gloomy apprehension of approaching judgments, and anxious expectations of a coming universal catastrophe, are manifest in the declarations of the gods and oracles of this period. The bright days of the Augustan age were long past. Over Rome lay the fumes of the blood shed in the last years of Tiberius. Murder and suicide were the order of the day, and even women were not safe from the dagger.[3] Moreover, the common people were oppressed by actual want. Tiberius, in the year 33 A.C., had decreed Draconian statutes against usury, in consequence of which many loans were recalled, and bankruptcy followed bankruptcy. "At first," Tacitus relates, "there was dunning and petitioning, then the prætor's tribunal was besieged, and that which had been sought for as a remedy—sale and purchase—produced the opposite result, for the capitalists reserved all their money for purchasing estates. The number on sale depreciated the value; the more a man was indebted, the more

---

[1] Compare Part ii., Die Zeit der Apostel, i. p. 112.
[2] Plut. De def. orac. 17.   [3] Tacitus, Ann. vi. 9.

rigorously he was dealt with; the prosperity of many was engulphed; the destruction of one's property endangered at once rank and reputation."[1] It seems that the provinces also were strongly affected by this terrible crisis. Even sons of Herod were seen going about the country unable to meet their bills;[2] and the part which debtors, creditors and debtors' prisons played in the utterances of Jesus belonging to the year 34, has been already referred to. Altogether the eastern part of the empire was thoroughly depressed, less by violent disturbances than by an oppression, heavy as lead, which paralyzed everything, and by the bad prospects for the future. On the frontiers of Peræa, the Arabians were moving. On the Euphrates, the emperor had drawn the danger of a Parthian war upon himself by his malicious intrigues. Thus Israel was in the direct line of danger. Were the clouds on the Euphrates, or the storm behind the mountains of Gaulanitis, to be discharged, in both cases Galilee had to expect an inundation of enemies remembered with terror ever since the days of the first Herod. Even in Jesus' utterances there is a listening for the sound of arms in the distance. "What king, going forth to make war against another king, sitteth not down first and consulteth whether he is able with ten thousand to meet him that cometh against him with twenty thousand?" Jesus asks the Galileans.[3] In fact, the tetrarch of Galilee, who was staying in Tiberias until the end of the year 34,[4] was at that time preparing to travel, so that, in company with the Syrian proconsul, he might negociate at the Euphrates concerning peace.[5] Vitellius had received instructions from the emperor "to enter into friendly relations with the Parthian king Artabanus. The emperor was afraid of him because he had shown himself as an enemy, had already occupied Armenia, and was able to do yet

---

[1] Tacitus, Ann. vi. 17. [2] Antiq. xviii. 6, 3.
[3] Luke xiv. 31. [4] Matthew xiv. 1, 9.
[5] Antiq. xviii. 4, 4, 5. In the years 35 and 36. Jesus can very well have been living at the time when the quarrels began; indeed, during the first negociations. In Judæa they were much engaged with the affair, as the detailed account of Josephus proves.

greater harm.¹ The intermeddling of Antipas in these quarrels could hardly have been seen with joy in Galilee. In Judæa it was yet worse. Pilate could not even maintain public security, and the very road from Jericho to Jerusalem was known to Jesus as being proverbially a den of thieves. Bribery, violence, robbery, abuse, menaces, long series of iniquitous sentences of death—these are the only things mentioned as constituting in return the blessings of the procuratorial government.² Nevertheless, its authority had been already shaken. Since Sejanus' downfall, Pilate also had no longer been the same, for he too was not safe from Tiberius' anger. The more obstinately did the populace, sword in hand, stand opposed to his obstinacy. Even at the Passover of the year 35, a Barabbas was lying in the prison of the new castle on Mount Zion for participating in a tumult that had again been raging of late in the streets of Jerusalem, and cost human life.³

This, then, was the district in which political excitement first changed, according to Jewish method, into a religious movement.

The wilderness of Judah, the home of penitential Essenes, became, in the thirty-fourth year of our era, the scene of a great religious revival which is connected with the mightiest spiritual revolutions. About twelve miles east of Jerusalem the mountains begin to descend towards the Jordan and Dead Sea, forming a barren rocky region, abounding in caves, that was comprehended under the general name of the Wilderness of Judah. Here, between the gates of Jericho and Jerusalem, appeared in Pilate's time a prophet of the people, whose preaching, according to the concurrent testimony of Josephus and the Gospels, produced the most mighty effect upon the masses. In his external appearance he resembled those Essene ascetics who had settled in the habitable caves of the mountains of Judah, and there collected schools of zealous young men for strict exercises around themselves. Josephus himself passed

---

¹ Antiq. xviii. 4, 4.   ² Philo, Leg., Frankfr. Ausg. 1033.
³ Luke xxiii. 19.   ⁴ Matt. iii. 5.

three years with such an anchorite, who lived in the wilderness, wore clothes made of bark, ate wild herbs, and bathed day and night in cold water in order to keep himself pure.[1] Thus, too, did John, called the Baptist, appear before the people in his raiment of camel-hair and leathern girdle, not unlike a poor shepherd of the mountains of Judah, or an Essene in his winter garment. It was possible to regard him either as a prophet, like Amos, whom Jehovah had taken from his herds of cattle, or else as an Essene who, in the midst of his solitary exercises, had remembered his people. His occupation and his vocation were known to no one. He lived upon the wild honey of the bees which swarmed in the clefts of the rocks,[2] or upon the locusts which the south wind scattered among the valleys. His appearance caused great attention, chiefly from its peculiarity. Even after the whole movement was over, Jesus asked the people, "What went ye out into the wilderness to see? A man clothed in soft raiment?" The recollection of the raiment of John had well-nigh survived that of his preaching. This demeanour, estranged from human habits, creates an impression as though John had for no short time back associated with the spirits of the wilderness, and was intimate with "the house of thirst, where the dragons and demons howl." His very speeches borrow their images thence. The brood of vipers which lay coiled under the rock, the stones that were scattered in millions and out of which God's creative breath could raise up children enough, the barren olive, without fruit because its roots perished in the rocks, are images which show that his imagination had long been familiar with the figures of the wilderness.[3]

That his preaching was the announcement that the day of judgment of Jehovah was approaching with thunder and lightning, cannot be doubted, although Josephus here also has removed the Messianic element from his account. This message, however, was so far from being new in Israel, that it would not

---

[1] Vita, Jos. 2.   [2] Bell. iv. 8, 3.
[3] Keim, Jesus of Nazara, T. T. F. L. Vol. ii. p. 237.

explain the great sensation which this preacher of the wilderness, according to all the witnesses, caused. The same tidings could be read in the Book of Enoch and heard in the schools of the Pharisees and Essenes; but in John there was this in addition that was new: *he proceeded to action.* What Jesus did afterwards, that had he undertaken first; he aimed not at promising the Messianic kingdom, but at founding it. He was not satisfied with the mere waiting of the multitude, who trusted that for the seed of Abraham the kingdom was sure; nor with the purely negative work of the Pharisees, whose whole care was that the people should not fall away; nor, again, with the anxiety about purity of the Essenes, who abandoned the national character of the great promise in favour of a petty union. Since the kingdom promised to all Israel was at their very doors, as was everywhere believed, and as all signs presaged, *he*, with great, heroic, prophetic resolution, will begin it.

Thus in him did the belief of the age for the first time become practical. John's great thought was, that the kingdom of heaven was not only a gift from above, but a work of human labour; not a thing of dreams which hangs in the sky among the stars, but a kingdom that has to be founded and must be begun. Therefore did an ear-witness of John's preaching, Jesus, call him the greatest among those that are born of women; for, said he, before him the kingdom of heaven was prophecy, "but since the days of John the Baptist the kingdom of heaven is taken by violence, and the violent seize upon it." This violent seizure of the kingdom of heaven is what the Baptist wished to enjoin upon the people.[1]

This thought was not entirely strange to the age waiting upon the deeds of Jehovah. The Zealots had already found that in this perpetual waiting for the consolation of Israel no advance

---

[1] Matthew xi. 12, as the testimony of one immediately concerned, is to be preferred in estimating the preaching of John. Here we have the account of an ear-witness, whilst the fragmentary accounts of his preaching have been taken by those who have reported them from tradition.

was made, but that there was need for *action*. They declared
that the Pharisees were ever only dreaming of the kingdom, but
cast off all work.[1] This was also the opinion of the Baptist; but,
apart from the grander features which John's performance bore
throughout, the method of his procedure was an untried one. A
Samaritan prophet shortly afterwards adopted a purely external
course for the same purpose. He desired to discover the vessels of the tabernacle in Mount Gerizim, which it was supposed
would come to light for the day of the Messiah. In Samaritan
relic-worship, he expected that the possession of the insignia of
the kingdom would give him the kingdom itself. The Galileans
were more inclined to demand the kingdom from the Romans
with weapons in their hands, in the expectation that Jehovah
would not disown His people in arms. John, on the other hand,
desired to found the kingdom by means of a moral regeneration
of the nation. This means that the man of the wilderness of
Judah had been to the school, not of the Rabbis, but of the
prophets, as all the traditional words of John show—prophetic
passages being everywhere re-echoed in them. Above all, had he
thoroughly feasted upon Isaiah. The favourite images of the
great prophet, of God's planting, of the winnowing-fan and the
threshing-floor, are his also.[2] But not these ideas alone—even
his very appearance had he learned from Isaiah. The prophetic
word of the voice in the wilderness, of the time of grace which
would be manifested in the wilderness, had assigned him beforehand the desert as the scene of his activity. The question, also,
what it was necessary to do for the kingdom of God, he did not
seek to answer, as did the Rabbis, out of the book of Leviticus,
nor as did the Zealots, out of the book of Maccabees, nor as did
the Essenes, out of the Apocalyptic books; he again inquired
of Isaiah. "Wash you, make you clean; put away the evil of
your doings from before mine eyes; cease to do evil; learn to do

---

[1] Antiq. xviii. 1, 1.

[2] Isaiah v. 7, vi. 13, xxi. 10, xxviii. 27. Compare Keim's Jesus of Nazara, Vol. ii. pp. 216, 217.

well; seek right, reclaim the violent, judge the fatherless, plead for the widow"—these words, taken from the first chapter of the great prophet, were the theme not only of his preaching, but also of his activity,[1] and his utterances to the people, according to Luke, were only variations of these words. The kingdom of God was to be established, in the first place, through repentance for the sins of the people which lay between Jehovah and Israel, and then through "work worthy of repentance."[2] Pharisees and Essenes had held up their performance of the law to Jehovah. John would appeal to the repentance of the people, and not to any observance of the law. He had read less in the law, but all the more diligently in the prophets.

REPENTANCE, therefore, was the first thing that John demanded, and it, too, was demanded by him in the words of Isaiah: "The axe is laid unto the root of the trees; every tree which bringeth not forth good fruit is hewn down and cast into the fire."[3] A mighty preaching of repentance was what he—as formerly the son of Amos—aimed at beginning, in order that the people should put away their sins. In his mouth the promises of the kingdom of God sounded, not as sweet music, but as the terrors of the day of judgment. Were these promises usually to his contemporaries an $\epsilon\dot{\upsilon}\phi\eta\mu\acute{\iota}\alpha$[4] of the future, in which Israel would be full of joy, and the promises fulfilled which had been given to the seed of Abraham,—John, on the other hand, had read in the prophets of the terrors with which that time should begin: "O generation of vipers," he declared upbraidingly to the people, "who hath warned you to flee from the wrath to come? Bring forth, therefore, fruits meet for repentance. And think not to say within yourselves, We have Abraham to our father: for I say unto you, that God is able of these stones to raise up children unto Abraham." To individuals, also, did he point out their sins before the avenging God of Malachi, who is like a refiner's fire and like fuller's soap, and shall purify the sons of Levi as silver, that they may offer unto God an offering in

---
[1] Luke iii. 10. [2] Matt. iii. 8. [3] Matt. iii. 10. [4] Antiq. x. 11, 7.

righteousness, and is a swift witness against the sorcerers and against the adulterers, and against false swearers, and against those that oppress the hireling in his wages, the widow and the fatherless.[1] This was no joyful message, but one that deeply moved the conscience, for the prophet beheld the sword of Jehovah directed not against the Gentile in order to win freedom, a crown and tribute for Israel—its edge was towards Israel itself. "I will fan them with a fan in the gates of the lands; I will bereave them of children; I will destroy my people, since they return not from their ways," had the Baptist read in the prophets.[2] "His fan is in his hand," he cried, "and he will thoroughly purge his floor, and gather his wheat into the garner; but he will burn up the chaff with unquenchable fire." The very words, on account of which the people, according to Josephus,[3] hated the prophets, with the exception of the sweet-speaking Daniel, had penetrated most deeply into his heart. Of all the Messianic passages which we find written in Sibyls, Apocalypses and Jubilees, not one has struck this tone, which fell like rolling thunder on the people's ear.

Nevertheless, this reference to the falling axe, to the heated oven, to the purging fan which knows no consideration, did not at all betoken that the Messianic kingdom was to come upon them merely as an external, unavoidable judgment. Not resignation, but energy, would the preacher awaken. The people were to act so as to be able to show sound fruit on the tree to the threatening axe, golden corn to the blazing fire, and thus escape the coming wrath; but before all, would the Baptist urge Israel itself to establish the kingdom, in order that it might not happen that the punishment indeed should come, but the blessing be wanting. They should not trust to the hope that the kingdom could not fail Abraham's children; they should found it by repentance, conversion and fruits worthy of righteousness. Strongly as John emphasized the share of Jehovah in the coming kingdom,

---

[1] Malachi iii. 2—5; compare Luke iii. 13, 14.
[2] Jeremiah xv. 7.   [3] Antiq. x. 11, 7.

yet more emphatically did he insist, according to the testimony of Jesus, upon what the people themselves ought to *do to convert prophecy into fulfilment.* Consequently, he had assigned himself also an active part in the commencement of the Messianic period. "Behold," had he read in Malachi, "I will send my messenger, and he shall prepare the way before me: and the Lord, whom ye seek, shall suddenly come to his temple, and the messenger of the covenant whom ye delight in: behold, he shall come, saith Jehovah of hosts."[1] This prophetic word was the programme of his activity.

In fact, he proceeded in constituting the Messianic community with the bold courage of a man who is sure of the future. No contradiction disturbed him. "He is a fool," said the people of Jerusalem; but John was not the man to ask after the opinion of the multitude. "What went ye out to see? a reed shaken with the wind?" Jesus ironically asked, when he came to speak of the disposition with which the people encountered the Baptist. As little as the shaggy mantle which hung around his shoulders had to do with the soft raiment in kings' houses, so little could it be expected that he should bow before the opinion of the multitude. Reeds enough grew on the Jordan—he was a strong oak. Without caring either for doubt or opposition, he proceeded to prepare for the Messianic kingdom as he found that preparation described in the prophets. Thus he descended with his followers from the wilderness of Judah to the Jordan near Jericho, consecrating the covenant of the new life by a baptism in Jordan, as Isaiah's call, "Wash you, make you clean," seemed to demand. Israel's purgation and cleansing from all impurity was, according to the prophets, the first business of the Messianic kingdom. In that day, Zechariah had prophesied, "there shall be a fountain opened to the house of David and to the inhabitants of Jerusalem for sin and for impurity."[2] John resolved to point out this fountain to his people. If he thereby had in mind the signification of the proselyte's baptism, by which those

[1] Malachi iii. 1.   [2] Zechariah xiii. 1.

Gentiles who were entering into the congregation of Israel were declared purged from their Gentile impurity, then this would be the strongest possible condemnation of the condition of Israel; for he could not more strongly express the necessity for a new Israel than by demanding the Gentiles' baptism from those who wished to participate in the kingdom of God. They must first purge themselves of the people's sins before they could enter into the kingdom of heaven by the breach made by John. For what the Baptist had in view was nothing less than the foundation of a Messianic community. That this implied the formation of a *community*, of a proper *baptismal covenant*, Josephus expressly tells us.[1] The penitent were *to be united through baptism*[2] in the exercise of virtue, mutual righteousness and piety towards God. Immersion, consequently, was not to be merely a symbol of conversion, as in the baptism of proselytes, but an act of communion of the converted, combined with the mystic working of grace. Moreover, it was not to be employed for purification after separate sins, nor as the Levitical washings after every defilement; but only after complete conversion, when the soul had been already sanctified by an upright life, was it to be added as an act of covenant by which one united oneself to the community of the new life. The baptism of John, therefore, could be compared with nothing more exactly than with the community of meals and bathing among the Essenes, except that the latter were to prove the continuance of the covenant of brotherhood; whilst for John it was this very repetition of washing which was meaningless after the whole man had been once immersed. Just as the Baptist no longer dealt with separate sins, but with the sinfulness of the whole man, so, instead of the many washings, there was the plunge once for all in Jordan. According to Josephus, John asserted " that washing would be acceptable to God if they made use of it, not for the

---

[1] Antiq. xviii. 5, 2: βαπτισμῷ συνιέναι. Compare Keim, Jesus of Nazara, Vol. ii. p. 242; Strauss, Leben Jesu, p. 189.

[2] Antiq. xviii. 5, 2.

remission of some sins only, but for the purification of the body; supposing still that the soul was thoroughly purified beforehand by righteousness."

Consequently, there are three points to be distinguished in the procedure of the Baptist to found the Messianic kingdom.

That he had called the people into the WILDERNESS, had been the first step in the path of actual procedure; for it was in the wilderness, according to the prophets, that the time of mercy was to begin. The very summons of the people to this scene was a significant act, for it reminded every one immediately of the words of Isaiah: " In the wilderness prepare ye the way of Jehovah; make straight in the desert a highway for our God!" The significance which this point had for the Messianic expectations is also shown by the fact that Theudas attempted to lead the people across the Jordan into the wilderness in just the same manner, in order there to repeat the time of the wandering, and, as a prophet like unto Moses, to await the new revelation of Jehovah. Josephus tells of others also who exhorted the multitude to follow them into the wilderness, " where they, by God's assistance, would work manifest signs and wonders." Even during the Jewish war had the writer of our Gospel according to Matthew, still reason for warning them: " If they say unto you, Behold, he is in the wilderness, go not forth."[1]

Thus it is certain that John was not acting without design when he entered upon the scene of the Messianic theophany referred to by the prophets; where he knew how to effect its first preliminary condition—the requisite repentance of the people— by the thunders of his preaching. A repentant Israel encamped in the steppes of the wilderness of Judah. Then he accomplished the second step of purification and sanctification of the people at the Jordan by BAPTISM, which, in this form and designed as an action of the whole people, could only signify the inauguration of the Messianic kingdom. And now he did the last thing which could be done by human methods, and

[1] Antiq. xx. 5, 1, 8, 6; Matt. xxiv. 26.

founded a COMMUNITY of a new life worthy of the promises of God. From this moment, according to the words of Jesus, the kingdom of heaven had been taken by violence. As a mighty wrestler had he seized upon it. The first Messianic community was founded.

It was a Messianic community without Messiah, and the question presents itself whether John altogether expected one. The prophetic passages which, as the strong pillars of his preaching, survived the destruction of the rest, have been taken to prove that he did not, because they are such only as speak of the action of Jehovah on the great day of judgment, and not of Jehovah's champion, the Messiah.[1] In the Old Testament, the one who has the fan in his hand and purges his floor is certainly none other than Jehovah himself; but when the Baptist speaks of one whose shoes he is not worthy to bear, he cannot have meant Jehovah, but the Messiah alone. Of course, just as the first Christian community assigned the Baptist a position towards Jesus of which his own school knew nothing, so here, too, in referring to the speeches of the Baptist, a word of its own interpretation that has no historical foundation may just as possibly have crept in. The anticipated foundation of a Messianic community is in any case not easier, but more difficult, to explain, if it is assumed that John entertained the expectation of an immediately appearing personal Messiah *from the beginning*. But however he may have conceived the form of the Messianic kingdom, in any case he so vigorously hurled the terrors of the approaching judgment of the world at the masses, that soon half Israel streamed out in order to ensure their souls by acceptance in this new baptismal covenant. Unwillingly did the prophet—Matthew informs us—behold the Rabbis and priests participating. Although the Scribes had at first declared that "he was a fool," yet now the one drew the other into the religious movement. Even Josephus, the Jerusalem man of the world, twenty years afterwards, found that the memory of the

---

[1] Compare W. Lang, Zeitstimmen, 1865, p. 207.

exaltation of those days was held in high respect in his own, that is, the high-priestly circles.

It must certainly have been a popular movement of the greatest extent that Josephus considered yet worthy of mention after the great tragedies of the last years, at the time of composing his "Antiquities," particularly as he was otherwise little inclined to allude to Messianic movements. Its limits are given by him, as they are by the Evangelists, with the utmost indefiniteness. All Jerusalem and Judæa, and all the region round about Jordan, nay, even the neighbouring districts, were embraced by it.[1]

Certain is it that men of Galilee, too, entered into the baptismal covenant and received baptism. If thus the last undulations of that movement which John had aroused within men's minds are, judging by local effect, to be detected in the remote mountains of Galilee—and, according to the Acts of the Apostles, they vibrated even in the Diaspora of Asia Minor—so, judging by time, they can be detected (apart altogether from his school) after his death and Pilate's banishment, for the whole people proclaimed John's name as that of him whose death Jehovah had now avenged, on the battle-field of the year 36, where Antipas was defeated by Aretas. The Jewish people had, judging by this, been even longer occupied by the thunders of his preaching of repentance than by Jesus' Sermon on the Mount, although here, too, the voice of God was less in the storm than in the still and gentle breeze.

Most vividly has Luke described how one inhabitant of Jerusalem after the other went out in order to make his peace with the prophet—how one family after the other sought for baptism, until all Jerusalem and all the inhabitants of the Jordan region were collected at his abode. Did one ask him how repentance was to be accomplished in order to gain the kingdom of heaven, he replied, "He that hath two coats, let him impart to him that hath none; and he that hath meat, let him do likewise." To the tax-gatherers he said, "Exact no more than that which is

[1] Matt. iii. 5; Mark i. 5; Antiq. xviii. 5, 2.

appointed you." To the soldiers, "Do violence to no man, neither accuse any falsely; and be content with your wages."[1] Here, too, it was the spirit of Isaiah which was speaking in him. "Is not this the fast that I have chosen," had the son of Amos declared, "to loose the bands fastened by wickedness, to undo the thongs of the yoke, and to let the oppressed go free, and to burst in sunder every yoke? Is it not to deal thy bread to the hungry, and to bring home them that wander abroad in misery? when thou seest the naked, to cover him, and not to hide thyself from thine own flesh? Then shall thy light break forth as the morning, and thine healing shall spring forth speedily; and thy righteousness shall go before thee; the glory of Jehovah shall be thy rereward."[2]

This afflatus of the ancient prophets was also distinctly felt by the keen sense of the people in John's preaching, and they were agreed that Jehovah had in him again sent a true man of God to Israel.[3] Nay, the thought already emanated from the feeling of the great awakening which passed through the easily inflamed population of Judæa, that "the prophet like unto Moses" had arisen. John, however, rejected this thought, with the assurance that one mightier than he was coming, the latchet of whose shoes he was not worthy to unloose, whose fan was in his hand to thoroughly purge his floor and burn up the chaff;[4] although by that mightier one he may have meant Jehovah himself, or the Messiah.

But now came the all-important question, how the work which was begun was to be advanced. It seems that the Baptist, in the first place, intended to organize the covenant of the baptized more firmly. A narrower circle of disciples attached themselves to him, who shared in his strict habits, formed his permanent companions amidst the changing crowd of those who came and went, and did not desert him even in the fortress of Machærus.[5] That

---

[1] Luke iii. 11—14.
[2] Isaiah lviii. 6—8.
[3] Matt. xxi. 26, xvii. 13, xi. 9.
[4] Luke iii. 16, 17.
[5] Matt. ix. 14, xiv. 12.

he used to send out these disciples two by two, as Jesus did afterwards, we learn from the Gospels;[1] that there were twelve of them may perhaps be concluded from the fact that we afterwards find a group of twelve of John's disciples at Ephesus, after the number of the tribes of Israel.[2]

But from the manner in which the whole movement was constituted, even in forming an organized society, a dangerous crisis could not be avoided. Although the Baptist had attempted to found the kingdom of God, on the one hand, by himself, yet the external co-operation of Jehovah had also been relied upon. It was a great and strong faith in which he first put his hand to the plough, being firmly convinced that Jehovah would Himself complete the work when once it had been begun. On account of this faith was it that Jesus had called John greater than all the prophets, who had quietly left the whole of the work to Jehovah. But, nevertheless, John, as a Jew, had presented the kingdom to himself in too earthly a form. The kingdom of heaven was not to him, as it was afterwards to Jesus, a disposition of the mind; but it was a visible theocracy founded by Jehovah, of which it was certainly possible to say, Lo here! and lo there! Because *to him personally* the power was wanting of bearing the kingdom upon his own shoulders, had he relied the more confidently, according to the prophetic plan, upon the external revelation of God as not being absent. But until its appearance, a pause must occur which it was difficult to fill up. This John was not able to do. His movement was wanting in the productive thought which should maintain itself by its own weight, and external catastrophes were interposed in its place. Prophetic reminiscences, and the consciousness of being only a forerunner, or labourer, and not an originator, had referred him to this external co-operation of Jehovah. As here his dogmatic convictions were borrowed and traditional, so too, in seeking for the

---

[1] Luke vii. 19; compare x. 1.

[2] Acts xix. 7: ὡσεὶ δώδεκα. Compare Keim's Jesus of Nazara, Vol. v. p. 17, in the German edition.

means which should form the kingdom, did he unexpectedly turn back to the broad and well-travelled path of Judaism. Heroic as the beginning had been, yet here were his limits. The means of founding the kingdom of heaven was for him the repentance of the people; but repentance, the contrition of mind which the Baptist demanded as a preliminary condition of the kingdom, is an antecedent, but not the state itself. It is the gleam of the silver which precedes its solidification, the glow which announces the day; but not the metal which is coined, not the day for work which endures. John, however, attempted to extend this spiritual process to an indefinite limit; thus he found himself compelled to trust to external manifestations of repentance, and consequently he suddenly stood with both feet once more upon the ground of Judaism. The importance which John attached to baptism as to a sacramental covenant, in itself shows that he attributed a value to the external ordinance, and still, Jew-like, expected an effect from the mere ordinance itself. He believed that baptism—under whatever preliminary conditions—could as an ordinance be acceptable to God,[1] and thereby remained a Jew. To the one meritorious observance, there now, as time extended, succeeded others. His disciples manifested their repentance by fasting, already feeling that in these external religious practices they were related to the Pharisees. "Why do we and the Pharisees fast oft, but thy disciples fast not?"[2] they asked Jesus. This was the point which presented itself to Jesus for criticism, and on account of which he called the greatest born of women, the least in the kingdom of heaven. From this point of view, the work of John was to him merely as a piece of new cloth on an old garment. In fact, the great religious movement was already on the point of discharging itself into the narrow channel of an ascetic school, as developed elsewhere also by Judaism, when, just before a fall of the stream disclosed the deterioration, a violent shock from without put an end to the whole movement.

[1] Antiq. xviii. 5, 2.   [2] Matt. ix. 14.

In order to keep a popular movement like this at its height, a periodic change in the scene of action was the more indispensable, because it was necessary to fill up the time until the day when Jehovah would himself appear in action. Thus John had first left the wilderness of Judah, and had withdrawn to the Jordan. Below, near Jericho, where the river is concealed behind a forest of reeds, and its muddy waters slowly roll along between the low-lying banks towards the Dead Sea, had been his station where he baptized, and where by performing this baptism he practically inaugurated the kingdom preached in the wilderness. And now he determined to advance farther. He left Roman Judæa in order to raise his cry for repentance anew in the region beyond the Jordan in the territory of the tetrarch. It so happened that he was compelled to give it a personal application in the case of the tetrarch himself.

Antipas was at that period spending much of his time in the highlands beyond the river. Already in the early years of his reign he had converted the ancient Beth Haran, "the town in the valley,"[1] into a fortress called Livias, in honour of the empress-mother.[2] The petty tyrant loved great strongholds, and at that time even may not have had perfect confidence in his neighbour and father-in-law, Aretas. The castle commanded the very descent of the Jordan, where John, leaving his previous station for baptism, must have entered the territory of Antipas. Lying opposite to Jericho, and nearer the mountains than the river, it was probably intended, in conjunction with the fortress of Jericho, to form a barrier across the valley of the Jordan. It was directly under the eyes of the suspicious Herod that the crowds of the wilderness of Judah and the plain of Jericho now therefore continued to assemble, to the alarm of a prince who could not from his shaky throne regard such concourses of the people with the indifference of a Pilate conscious of his legion. The new camp of those desiring baptism could not have been more than from four to six miles distance from Antipas' castle. As this

---

[1] Joshua xiii. 27.   [2] Antiq. xviii. 2, 1. Livia died in the year 29 A.D.

spot had been selected with regard to the inhabitants of Peræa, the stream of people must have travelled chiefly by the great road which runs from Hesbon through Livias to the Jordan, and thus gone directly past his palaces.[1] What Josephus tells us of the feelings with which the suspicious "fox," as Jesus called the tetrarch, is supposed to have observed this movement from his fortress, is only too probable. "As the people crowded from all sides to John, for every one was greatly exalted by his words, Antipas, fearing lest the influence of such a man over the people should raise a rebellion, for all were ready to do anything he should counsel, thought it much more advisable to prevent any innovation that he might attempt by putting him to death, than after the commencement of a revolution to repent of it when too late."[2] Cautiously managing affairs, according to his wont, he had himself come to the Baptist's camping ground, if the Gospels correctly report the occasion of the arrest. Tradition has preserved only the crushing words which the man in the raiment of camel's hair hurled at the people in "soft clothing in king's houses." It seems as though the tetrarch had joined those who were inquiring about the conditions of the kingdom of heaven, for the prophet referred to Herodias, and declared, "It is not lawful for thee to have her."[3] This was an utterance which most deeply wounded the petty tyrant and yet pettier man, for it summed up his moral and political blunders. It was threatening him with the punishment of God, with the revolt of his law-abiding people, with the vengeance of his insulted Arabian neighbour. All the calamities of Antipas' life and reign sprang from his marriage with Herodias, which in its absolute perversity can only be explained by the fact that even the most prudent man, when urged by passion, can act more stupidly than even the most excessive stupidity.

These foul stories go back to a journey of Antipas to Rome

---

[1] Compare Mannert, Geographie der Griechen und Römer, vi. p. 327.
[2] See Antiq. xviii. 5, 2; Matt. xiv. 2, &c.; Luke ix. 9, xiii. 31, 32.
[3] Matt. xiv. 4.

which Josephus brings into connection with the marriage with Herodias without giving any more precise date. Antipas, when the guest of his brother Herod Boëthus, had won the affections of the latter's wife, and come to an understanding with her that, after his return from Rome, she should join him as soon as he had divorced the daughter of Aretas.

In Jerusalem there had happened to have been four sons of Herod present when the contest took place about the shields of Pilate; and the Jews had at that time addressed themselves to Tiberius in Rome in order to obtain a reversal of the acts of the procurator. It is possible that this was the fatal moment when the plot was hatched. Meanwhile, it is not known whether it was exactly *this* business which was transacted by Antipas in Rome, before taking Herodias to himself. His marriage with the Nabatæan had been dictated by policy, and perhaps "the fox" had previously obtained the consent of the emperor before venturing to put her away. Certain is it that the faithless business was agreed upon, in which Antipas, to his own injury, was as forgetful of his usual shrewdness and his own advantage, as of the law, hospitality and brotherly fidelity.

Of the wife of Herod Boëthus, all can be more easily understood. In Herodias there was mingled the blood of her grandfather Herod and of Mariamne, of Salome and Costobar. If passions can be inherited from one's ancestors, then a full measure must have fallen to her share. Moreover, her husband—of whom not even the industrious domestic chroniclers of the Idumæan family, Nicolaus and Josephus, find anything whatever to narrate—seems to have led an indolent and insignificant life as a private person, that did not correspond to the active longings of this woman. She therefore turned to her brother-in-law, who, it is true, was also fond of quiet, but could at least call a dominion his own. Measures against the Nabatæan wife were rendered unnecessary for the adulterous pair. Through the treachery which always prevailed at the courts of the Herods, information of his relations to Herodias had reached the daughter of Aretas, and she determined to fly. She asked for permission to visit Machærus, a frontier fortress that had previously belonged to Herod, where were some medicinal springs often used by invalids. These natural baths belonged at this period to her father Aretas. Perhaps, in accordance with the Oriental custom, it had been the price previously paid for the daughter. Here the Arabian king had already made preparations for bringing his daughter on. One sheikh accompanied her after the other; and when she arrived at her father's palace at Petra, Aretas declared that her marriage was annulled. Antipas received Machærus back again,[1] whether by treaty, stratagem or force, we know not. Perhaps the Arabian was afraid of the tetrarch, who then stood high in the emperor's favour; perhaps, too, Antipas made other amends at the approach of the Bedouins. Jesus says, according to Luke xiv. 31, "What king, going forth to make war against another king, sitteth not down first, and consulteth whether he is able with ten thousand to meet him that cometh against him with twenty thousand? or else, while he is yet a great way off, he sendeth an ambassage, and desireth conditions of peace." Perhaps Jesus' sovereign had acted in accordance with this maxim. In any case, the peace was not at this time broken.[2] Herodias, however, abandoned her husband, and betook herself, with her daughter Salome, to the house of the tetrarch.

This whole transaction had been developed in the immediate neighbourhood of the Baptist's present scene of action, and, intelligibly enough, it had not a little excited the population of the country beyond the Jordan, who were the most exposed to the Arabians. Politics discountenanced the repudiation of the daughter of the Nabatæan, the law and its champions the marriage with a brother's wife. For did not it stand written in Leviticus,[3] "Thou shalt not take thy brother's wife; she is thy blood relation; it is a wicked thing"? Still the first indignation

---

[1] Compare Antiq. xviii. 5, 1, with 5, 2.
[2] Antiq. xviii. 5, 1, does not agree with the later dates.
[3] Leviticus xviii. 16.

of the people may have passed away,[1] when the Baptist, by his bold words, again awoke all the terrors of conscience in Antipas. The unlawful marriage which involved him in two-fold adultery must have estranged him from his family; it was the exposed point of his otherwise so cautious government towards a people peculiarly sensitive in such things; it was the weak spot of his frontier towards the armies of the Nabatæan. The man who had referred so publicly to this crime could not be allowed to live. He caused him to be seized and imprisoned. The circumstances are not given in detail, but all accounts mention the chains and fetters of the Baptist. To leave the prisoner in Livias in the midst of the excited people was impossible. Antipas therefore commanded that he should be conveyed up to Machærus, which was inhabited by Idumæans and Arabians, and where there was no danger of a Messianic revolt. It almost seems as though there were some system at the bottom of this procedure against religious movements, since Pilate, too, not long afterwards made a most violent attack upon a popular assembly of the Samaritans at Mount Gerizim,[2] and Jesus was warned against the designs of the tetrarch.[3]

The mountain fortress of Machærus, situated upon the other side of the Dead Sea, was admirably adapted as a prison for a prophet, since it and the neighbourhood had always had in popular tradition the grim interest of an only half-known and mysterious spot. It lay upon the precipitous height of the ravine which separates Mons Abarim from Mount Pisgah, in the regions glorified by ancestral legends where the grave of Moses was sought for.[4] From the eastern shore of the Dead Sea, there runs, near the baths of Callirhoe, the narrow ravine of the Zerka Ma-în, a rapid mountain stream between blocks of rock

[1] According to Antiq. xviii. 5, 4, Herodias married Antipas after the birth of her daughter Salome, who was at the time of the Baptist's imprisonment a κοράσιον, but still no very young one, since some years after the death of Drusus (23 A.D.) Herod Agrippa was sheltered by Herodias at the court of Antipas.
[2] Keim's Jesus of Nazara, T.T.F.L. Vol. ii. p. 334.   [3] Luke xiii. 31.
[4] Deuteronomy xxxiv. 6; 2 Maccabees ii. 5.

of trapp and tuff, which lie wildly piled upwards, one on another,
towards the east. Above, on the southern side of the ravine, lies
Attaroth, a long mountain ridge some ten miles wide, running
towards the south-west. Where the wall of rock descends most
abruptly towards the Zerka Ma-în, and its edge overhangs the
valley, there cling even at the present day the walls of Machærus.[1]
There John was taken. Abrupt precipices surround the inhospitable fortress, and the barren mountain ranges of Mons
Abarim shut in the view. The tower which Alexander Jannæus
had erected here against the Arabians, had been enlarged by
Herod into a fortress, beneath the walls and trenches of which
a little town had gradually sprung up. The corner towers, some
160 cubits high, rose imposingly above the town and ravine. The
place, which contained deep reservoirs, was considered, next to
Jerusalem, the strongest in Judæa.[2] The palace had been adorned
by Herod with royal magnificence, probably similar to the
opposite one of Masada, of which Josephus asserts that the
arrangement of the apartments, with the halls and baths, was of
great variety and costly. "Everywhere there were pillars of
single stones; the walls and floors of the halls glistened with
inlaid stones."[3] In such marble halls did the tetrarch, who was
now staying here, give magnificent banquets, at which the
daughter of Herodias entertained the guests by dancing. The
people, however, told grim tales of what was done here. In the
courtyard of the castle there grew a mysterious rue of supernatural size. Not one spring in the district tasted like another
—the one was sweet, the other bitter. Out of a grotto rose two
breast-like rocks; from one there flowed hot, and from the other
cold water. Naptha and alum were also found here in abundance. The most notorious spot was the northern ravine, where
the root Baara grew, which cured diseases and cast out demons.
"The root is flame-coloured, and towards evening sends out rays
of light; and whoever tears it up, immediately dies."[4] In this

[1] Scetzen Reisen, ii. 342.   [2] Pliny, Hist. Nat. v. 15, 3.
[3] Bell. vii. 8, 3.   [4] Bell. vii. 6, 1—4.

strange place was it that this strange prisoner now passed his days.

Antipas had nothing to fear from him here. For it was useless for him to think of escaping from a fortress that was surrounded on three sides by inaccessible precipices, and to which only a single narrow path led through numerous fortified gates.[1] Nor had the Baptist any hope of finding any support in the fortress itself. Here, on the frontiers of the Arabians, Edomites and Moabites, the promises of Israel were not known.[2] The sheikhs of the neighbouring sons of the desert went in and out, and the courtiers of the luxurious Herodias busied themselves in the town, as the warm springs of the Baara valley and the cooler mountain air lent fresh elasticity to their relaxed nerves.[3] Since everything was provided here so luxuriously, these upper springs might well be preferred to their off-flow in the valley below at Callirhoe, although these lower baths also had a great reputation. For on the heights the healthy mountain air was to be found, of the good effects of which people had a really superstitious opinion. Provisions, Josephus tells us, retained their freshness in the opposite fortress of Masada for over a hundred years, "because the air at the altitude of the fortress was purified from all earthly and corrupt particles."[4] Still there was not much business done here, as the place was too remote for the purpose.[5] They are the people of kings' courts, the people "which are gorgeously apparelled and live delicately,"[6] whom Jesus contrasts with John, and the Gospels mention as being the guests of Antipas. They offered no points of contact to the imprisoned preacher of the wilderness. Rather must we think of mockery and ill-usage on their side, if any stress is to be laid on the words of Jesus over the fate of the Baptist. "They knew him not, but have done unto him whatsoever they listed."[7] Thus Antipas'

---

[1] Bell. vii. 8, 3, compare with 6, 1—4.
[2] Bell. vii. 6, 4.
[3] Mark vi. 21; Antiq. xviii. 5, 1.
[4] Bell. vii. 8, 4.
[5] Compare Bell. vii. 8, 3.
[6] Luke vii. 25.
[7] Matt. xvii. 12; Keim, Jesus of Nazara, Vol. ii. p. 340. That there was some intercourse between John and the courtiers, we learn also from Matt. xiv. 2.

fears were again lulled to sleep, and John was allowed to live.

The Gospels have given different explanations of the tetrarch's action in the matter. "And he wished to put him to death, but feared the multitude, because they counted him as a prophet," says Matthew.[1] Mark, on the other hand, has thought of the impression which that powerful presence must have made upon the uncertain Antipas. "Herodias," he tells us, "had a quarrel against him, and wished to kill him, but could not: for Herod feared John, knowing that he was a just man and an holy, and kept him safe; and when he heard him, he did many things, and heard him gladly."[2] The motives from which the tetrarch bade the executioner lay down his axe again were probably not known very clearly to any one, perhaps even to the tetrarch himself. In any case, the other narratives confirm the supposition that the imprisonment which the Baptist suffered was not a very harsh one. It resembled that which Paul endured some thirty years later at Cæsarea. His disciples were allowed to come and go; they informed him how the work stood outside; they brought word of the new preaching of the kingdom in Galilee. It seems certainly as though there were no proper cohesion among his followers after John had been taken from them. Of the Baptist's work, they, as was to be expected, had only retained the external, the ascetic side. They competed in fasting with the Pharisees, they went about mourning, for the bridegroom had been taken from them.[3] They brought to Machærus doubtful accounts of the new preacher of the kingdom from the Sea of Tiberias. Jesus' action was mighty, but his disciples did not fast. The wrathful words of the wilderness of Judah were also wanting in the new prophet. The Baptist, as though dubious about the accounts which reached him from outside, turned, the Gospels tell us, to Jesus himself for a solution of his doubts. "Now when John heard in prison the works of Christ, he sent two of

[1] Matt. xiv. 5.   [2] Mark vi. 19, 20.   [3] Matt. ix. 14.

his disciples, and said unto him, Art thou he that should come, or do we look for another?" The disciples delivered their message, and the prophet of Galilee answered the Isaiah-believing Baptist from the words of Isaiah: "Then the eyes of the blind shall be opened, and the ears of the deaf shall be unstopped. Then shall the lame leap as an hart, and the tongue of the dumb sing:"[1] and from those other words of Isaiah which he had already on another occasion[2]. applied to himself: "The spirit of the Lord God is upon me; because Jehovah hath anointed me to preach good tidings unto the meek."[3] It was a free reproduction, it is true, in which Jesus clothed these words of the prophet. "Go tell John those things which ye do hear and see: the blind receive their sight, and the lame walk, the lepers are cleansed, and the deaf hear, and the dead are raised up, and the poor have the gospel preached to them. And blessed is he whosoever shall not be offended in me."[4] Whether the answer, with its proud self-reliance and gentle censure, did actually take this exact form, whether it did actually appeal to *all* these miracles, whether it is to be interpreted symbolically, whether it satisfied John, we know not; still it is not improbable that it yet reached the Baptist. For the Baptist's imprisonment lasted over the summer. Then it came to a sudden termination. Whilst Antipas was believed to be really impressed by this mighty man, whilst popular opinion believed it could trace the influence of the Baptist in many new measures of the tetrarch, Herodias could only the more bitterly hate him, inasmuch as his proximity was a menace to her marriage and a sting to her conscience. Then Antipas, on the anniversary of his accession, gave, late in the summer,[5] a feast to the courtiers and officials of the palace, to which he had also invited the sheikhs of the neighbourhood. It

---

[1] Isaiah xxxv. 5, 6.
[2] Luke iv. 18.
[3] Isaiah lxi. 1.
[4] Matt. xi. 2—5.
[5] Compare Matt. xiv. 6 with Antiq. xv. 11, 6, and also xvii. 8, 2; 9, 3, as well as cap. 2, according to which Antipas' accession cannot have taken place before the August of the year 4 B. C. See also below.

was celebrated all the more boisterously, since it was not usually the fortune of Tiberius' vassals to celebrate the thirty-seventh or thirty-eighth year of their reign. The banquets of Antipas are of evil repute historically, both those which he inaugurated on the bridge over the Euphrates, as well as those at which he upbraided his brother-in-law Agrippa with eating the bread of charity. At the jubilee at Machærus, the young girl Salome danced before the guests and won great applause, so that the tetrarch, who could not give away a single village without Tiberius' permission, promised, in Oriental extravagance, to gratify any wish the dancer might express, unto the half of his kingdom. "Then she went out and said unto her mother, What must I ask? And she said, The head of John the Baptist. And she came in straightway with haste unto the king, and asked, saying, I will that thou give me directly on a dish the head of John the Baptist. And the king was exceedingly sorry; yet for his oath's sake, and for their sakes which sat with him, he would not reject her. And immediately the king sent an executioner, and commanded his head to be brought; and he went and beheaded him in the prison, and brought his head on a dish, and gave it to the damsel, and the damsel gave it to her mother. And when his disciples heard of it, they came and took up his corpse, and laid it in a tomb."[1] In the same mountains in which Israel sought for the grave of her first prophet was her last entombed.

One might be inclined to banish this revolting scene, on account of its ghastly colouring, to the domain of legend; but in these half-barbaric courts, deeds of horror not less grotesque than this one are not wanting. In the summer of 53 B.C., after the battle of Carræ, when the Parthian king Orodes celebrated the marriage of his son Pacorus, the actor that played the character of Agaue in the Bacchæ of Euripides, who in her madness has torn her son in pieces, bore the half-decomposed head of Crassus upon the stage, while the chorus rejoicingly repeated the well-known strophe:

[1] Mark vi. 17—29.

> We bring from the mountains
> Down to our houses
> Our noble prey, the bleeding game.¹

Why should that be impossible at Machærus which was possible at the court of Ctesiphon?² Antipas, after the death of the Baptist, once more repaired to the northern part of his tetrarchy, where we find him at Tiberias anxiously employed with memories of the prophet he had murdered.³ There Herodias married her young daughter, who as old enough for dancing seemed now old enough also for matrimony, to the aged Philip, who had already erected a sepulchre for himself at Julias, which received him indeed not long after his marriage; whereupon Salome returned to her mother's house.⁴

This unnatural marriage had probably been a speculation on

---

¹ Compare Mommsen, Römische Geschichte, iv. 331.

² Compare Herodotus, ix. 109, for the duty of kings at the royal banquets to grant even the most frivolous desires, and Suetonius, Caius, 32, for analogous cases. See also Antiq. xviii. 8, 8.

³ Matt. xiv. 1, 2.

⁴ In the chronology the following points are to be noted. The γενέσια of Mark vi. 21 and Matt. xiv. 6, which were celebrated by festivals, were, in the family of the Herods, as was usually the custom of princes at that time, the anniversary of their accession. Antiq. xv. 11, 6. Compare also Luke iii. 1, and the fact that Josephus nearly throughout reckons by *the year of the Herods' reign*. The γενέσια of Antipas would thus probably fall in August, if the limits which are given in Antiq. xvii. 9, 4, are taken into account. Archelaus departs soon after the Passover. The decision is delayed; this determines Antipas to come to Rome also. The postponement of the judgment until *after Pentecost*, 10, 2. A deputation from the popular party arrives (11, 1); Philip also arrives (11, 1); examination of their complaints; day appointed, and ὀλίγων δὲ ἡμερῶν ὕστερον finally the judgment. We must therefore look for the γενέσια late in the summer, even if Antipas did not celebrate the day of his taking possession as a festival. Mark and Matthew coincide with this date, as they make Jesus send out the twelve disciples immediately after the death of John. According to Mark vi. 7, Jesus sends out the twelve immediately after his appearance at Nazareth, at which time the death of the Baptist has just taken place. Matt. xiv. 1—12. At what time, then, did the appearance of the Baptist take place? The words of Josephus do not allow of a too prolonged imprisonment. But, according to the Gospels, too short a one must also not be assumed. Now great assemblies of the people, like those which followed him, can be kept in the Ghôr neither in summer nor in the rainy season. Thus it seems that the Baptist must have commenced his mission early in the year 34, and have been taken a prisoner while it was yet spring, just as Jesus also in all probability began his work in the spring. See below.

the part of Herodias for the inheritance of her neighbour and brother-in-law. But her plan failed: the tetrarchy was incorporated with Syria under the maintenance of a separate administration. Nevertheless, Antipas, who continued to reside at Tiberias, cast longing eyes upon it, and his ever-increasing eagerness for the prize thus spread out before him, finally brought both Herodias and himself to ruin.

5. THE GERIZIM EXPEDITION.

The watchword, that the time of God's dominion had arrived and should shortly obtain external form, had scarcely been given, when the Samaritans immediately came forward in order to claim the kingdom for themselves. In doing this they only continued to play the part they had always done. According to their own account, they, and not the Jews, possessed the actual Holy Land promised to Abraham, and where the patriarchs had pastured their herds; they had the real temple-mount; they had the true law, falsified by no prophet; so also they had the tradition that Moses had buried the real vessels of the tabernacle on their sacred mountain—vessels which the Jews pretended to have still possessed in the Solomonian temple, and, according to Jewish tradition, were miraculously concealed at the destruction of this temple by the Chaldæans. To the possession of these vessels was united, in accordance with the externality of Oriental piety, the claim to become the scene of the Messianic kingdom, on the ground that a promise, very dear to the hearts of the people, declared that at the kingdom of Messiah the ark of the covenant and the sacred vessels would once more become visible. The Jewish tradition about the matter we read in 2 Maccabees ii. 5, &c. According to it, Jeremiah the prophet, after the destruction of the temple, safely carried off the tabernacle he had rescued and the ark to Mount Nebo, where once Moses had beheld the Holy Land. "When Jeremiah came there, he found a hollow cave, wherein he laid the tabernacle, and the ark, and the altar of incense, and stopped the door. And some of those that followed him came to mark the way, but they could not find it. Which when Jeremiah perceived, he blamed them, saying: *As for that place, it shall be unknown until the time that God gather his people again together, and receive them into mercy.* And then the Lord will reveal these things, and the glory of the Lord shall appear, and the cloud also, as it was revealed under Moses."[1] Another form of the same tradition is found in the Apocalypse of Baruch.[2] There Baruch, the scribe of Jeremiah, beholds, shortly before the destruction of Jerusalem, an angel who descends to the holy city and alights in the temple in order to save the sacred things. This angel gathers together the sacred tabernacle, the high-priest's ephod, the ark of the covenant, the two tables of the law from Mount Sinai, the high-priest's garment, the altar of incense, the Urim and the Thummim, and all the sacred vessels. All these things are brought to a secret place, and then he speaks with a loud voice: "Earth, earth, earth, hear the voice of the mighty God and receive what I now entrust to thee, and preserve it until the end of the times, so that thou mayest return it when thou art bidden, in order that the stranger may not possess it. For the time is coming when Jerusalem shall arise again for all time! Then the earth opened her mouth, and swallowed all the vessels." A third and more spiritual version, finally, is contained in the Apocalypse of John, according to which the sacred vessels are concealed rather in heaven itself, and will return with the New Jerusalem. To the faithful the Messiah promises the bread of life out of the pot of manna which is hidden in heaven,[3] and at the sounding of the seventh trumpet the heavens will open "and the ark of the covenant will be seen in his temple."[4] In

---

[1] 2 Maccab. ii. 4—8.

[2] In Ceriani, Monumenta sacra et profana, Tom. i. fasc. ii.: Mediolani, 1866. Translated from the Syriac, cap. 6.

[3] Rev. ii. 17.

[4] Rev. xi. 19.

opposition to these sacred and enduring traditions, the foolish people which dwelt at Sichem asserted that the sacred vessels of the wanderings in the desert had been, on the contrary, deposited in their Mount Gerizim, and had never been at all in the Solomonian temple. It is possible that this interpretation was connected with Deuteronomy xxvii., where the twelve tribes of Israel are instructed, after their entrance into the Holy Land, some to pronounce a blessing upon the pious from the fruitful Gerizim, and others a curse upon the ungodly from the steep and barren Ebal, and to erect an altar.[1] In any case, it was here that the Samaritans sought for the sacred treasure that should become once more visible on the day of promise.

When, therefore, the Baptist movement affected the neighbouring land of the Jews, and the preaching of the approach of the kingdom caused such great agitation, the Samaritans remembered the mysterious pledge which guaranteed to their territory the commencement of the Messianic promise. "The nation of the Samaritans," Josephus informs us, "did not escape without tumults. A man excited them to it who thought lying a thing of little consequence, and contrived everything to please the multitude."[2] This was the man who, after previous intrigues, now attempted to create a movement among the mountains of Samaria similar to that which was thronging the valley of the Jordan. He therefore proclaimed throughout the valleys of Samaria that all the people were to assemble on a certain day appointed at the sacred mountain, Gerizim, where a new prophet would disclose to the faithful the place where Moses had buried the vessels of the tabernacle. According to the theology of the time, this meant exactly the same as that which the Baptist preached in the wilderness of Judah: that the kingdom of God had drawn nigh—for the vessels were to be revealed first on the day of fulfilment. And indeed nothing less was aimed at than thus snatching from the Jews the manifestation of the expected kingdom of God. The lying prophet had thus cleverly caught

---

[1] Deut. xxvii. 5, 26.   [2] Antiq. xviii. 4, 1.

the Samaritans by their most passionate desire to prove that they were the possessors of the real sanctuaries and the true Mosaism; and whether he now merely took up the watchword, or whether it was he who invented it, in any case from this time forth for centuries has it remained an article of Samaritan faith that the Messiah would once more disclose the tables of the law, the pot of manna and the sacred vessels on Mount Gerizim.[1] We can well understand that under such prospects the ravines of Ebal and Gerizim were soon as thronged as those in Ghôr. Fresh multitudes were constantly arriving at Tirathaba, where the prophet had summoned his people. As the council of elders and the "coryphæi of the country" took part in the expedition, the assembly was much more important, politically, than even the Jewish proceedings on the Jordan. The more reason had Pilate for fearing that precautions had been taken to prevent the search for the vessels proving fruitless, and that from the insignia of the kingdom they would proceed to establish the kingdom itself. In fact, measures against the arrogance of the procurator had already been set down as among the objects of the negociations on the sacred mountain,[2] and the whole movement seemed to assume a revolutionary character. Pilate, therefore, forbade the pilgrimage, and blocked up the roads to Mount Gerizim by sentinels and patrolling cavalry. But the Samaritans had already assembled in great masses at Tirathaba, and continually brought up fresh armed troops in order to force the approach. Then the procurator commanded that the place should be cleared. The troops charged. Many were killed, others perished in the crush or were trampled to death. Of the prisoners, Pilate had the most eminent executed as traitors. The Samaritan council of elders, however, was not inclined to calmly accept this ill-treatment. An appeal was made to Vitellius, proconsul of Syria, denying that there had been any intention of revolting from Rome, but acknowledging that measures had been planned against the arro-

---

[1] Peterman, Samaria, in Herzog's Real-Encyclopædie, xiii. 373.
[2] Antiq. xviii. 4, 2.

gance of Pilate. What need the Samaritans had of the vessels of the tabernacle for this purpose, was never explained. The case remained undecided for nearly two years, but ended finally in the suspension of Pilate, who arrived in Rome shortly after the death of Tiberius (March, 37), to defend his administration. What fate befell the prophet and leader of this movement, Josephus does not inform us. The Acts of the Apostles, however, has an account of a sorcerer, Simon, in Samaria, in the year of Tiberius' death, who had for some time back excited great attention, for he used sorcery and aroused horror among the Samaritans by his deeds, giving out that himself was some great one.[1] Of this same Simon Magus, the Clementine Homilies declare that he denied Jerusalem and exalted Gerizim.[2] Under these circumstances, it is natural to suppose that the prophet of Gerizim was the Simon Magus of the Acts of the Apostles, who was intriguing in Samaria in the very year 36. This also explains why Christian tradition represents this impostor as the rival and aper of the Messiah; for in fact it was in an imitation of the Messianic movement in the valley of the Jordan that he had first introduced himself. How he subsequently also was intriguing in Samaria, and was mixed up in all sorts of affairs, some of them not of the purest, will be related further on, since the Christian sources represent him as being the rival not so much of Jesus as of the Apostles. But before these movements in Samaria had led to this sanguinary catastrophe, a stronger and purer hand had succeeded in Galilee in forming a channel for the religious current of the mind, through which it henceforth flowed, whilst the flood of Jewish and Samaritan enthusiasm only too quickly again subsided.

[1] Acts viii. 9. [2] Clem. Homil. ii. 22.

6. JESUS APPEARS IN CAPERNAUM.

How great was the impression made by the Baptist upon his people and age, is proved not so much by the imitation of his activity in Samaria, as by the fact that the preaching of the kingdom from this time forth throughout the whole of this century proceeded on the outlines given it by John. Do we inquire of the Epistles to the Thessalonians or the Apocalypse, what was the kind of preaching which the Apostles of the Gentiles or of the Jewish Christians delivered to their congregations, we discern John's old discourse about the axe laid at the roots of the tree, and about the Lord who stands at the door and knocks, with this single difference, that the place of the coming mighty one is now occupied by the returning Messiah. Thus the word once pronounced did not speedily again come to rest, and in the first place was it to strike root afresh in the north of the Holy Land. The news that had hastened through the valley of the Jordan, and found an echo in the valley between Ebal and Gerizim, soon resounded also in the valleys of Galilee.

The condition of this district in the year 34 must be considered as a very excited one. Evidence of this is found in the fact that in the autumn of the year 34, probably at the feast of Tabernacles, a most sanguinary collision took place, even in Jerusalem itself, between the Galilean pilgrims to the feast and the Romans, in which the garrison of the Antonia penetrated to the inner forecourt of the sanctuary, and at the altar of burnt-offerings slew the Galileans on the top of their sacrifices, so that their blood, to the horror of the on-lookers, mingled with that of the slaughtered animals.[1] The more seething and fermentation was there among the patriots of the north. Close by Jesus had the sons of Judas the Galilean grown up, who soon after him also perished on the cross, because they in their method attempted to

---

[1] Luke xiii. 1.

save Israel.[1] If during all these anxious prospects, disturbing events and exasperating circumstances, the people, nevertheless, had only *one* thought, that of lamentation over the imprisoned Baptist,[2] this surely is a proof how mighty the prophet of the wilderness of Judah had been, and how deeply the religious character of the time had penetrated.

Into the remotest valleys did the terrible tidings spread that the Baptist had been taken prisoner.[3] Hopes were at first entertained that the mighty preacher would shake the heart of Antipas also, and that the cowardly tetrarch would not dare to attempt the life of a prophet so loved by the people.[4] Already were the credulous people ascribing the one and another measure of Antipas to the influence of the Baptist,[5] when the news came that the incredible had taken place, that Herodias had attained what Antipas had never dared upon on his own account. As the new Jezebel, the murderess of the prophet, was Herodias spoken of by the people; and it was now expected that a further attack upon the hope of Israel and her prohpets would be made by the court of Antipas.[6] "They have done unto him whatsoever they listed," was the lament in Galilee over the murdered Baptist.[7] But his downfall had not shaken their faith in him. Whoever spoke of his baptism otherwise than as a gift of grace from Heaven, might expect the vengeance of the people.[8] "If we say of men, we have to fear the people," declared the Pharisees in their deliberations on his baptism as late as the Passover of the year 35. It was not believed by all that he really was dead. "Some say thou art the Baptist," the disciples of Jesus informed their Master; and even in the newly erected palace at Tiberias, at the celebrated tables and candelabra of Corinthian brass, the question arose whether the Prophet of

---

[1] Antiq. xx. 5, 2.
[2] Antiq. xviii. 5, 2.
[3] Matt. iv. 12.
[4] Matt. xiv. 5, 9.
[5] Mark vi. 20.
[6] Luke xiii. 31.
[7] Matt. xvii. 12.
[8] Matt. xxi. 26.

Capernaum was not John risen from the dead, since his mighty powers were working in him.[1]

It was at the time of the Baptist's imprisonment—according to our chronology, therefore, in the spring of the year 34—that the first two Gospels place Jesus' appearance in the synagogues of Galilee. Jesus was descended from a religiously-minded family of the little town of Nazareth, whose tendency towards strictness can be recognized in the Essenic-coloured ascetic life of his brother James. He himself had been among those who had received the baptism of John at the Jordan.[2] When he heard the news, in his native town of Nazareth, that the Baptist had been dragged off to Machærus, he left his home and betook himself to the district by the lake, in order that the preaching of the advent of the kingdom of God which the tyrant had silenced in Peræa might be the more emphatically repeated by him in this forum of Galilee.[3] Isaiah, the son of Amos, had in former times been seized by the hand of the Lord, while in the temple the choirs of Levites rushed upon him, and the clouds of incense rolled above him, and the ground seemed to tremble at the sound of the sacred trumpets.[4] Amos, the herdman, had been taken by the Spirit while on the lonely hill-side, when, busied with his sycamore fruit, he learned how the Syrians had threshed Gilead with threshing-wains of iron, and how the Tyrians had sold Israel's sons to Edom; then he heard Jehovah roar out of Zion and thunder out of Jerusalem, and he deserted his herds in order to be a shepherd to Israel.[5] Thus it became a sign to Jesus to begin, that everywhere there was lamentation for the Baptist. When he saw Israel without a shepherd, the shepherd's heart within him impelled him to action.[6]

---

[1] Mark vi. 14, viii. 28; Vita, Jos. 13.   [2] Mark i. 9.

[3] According to Matthew iv. 12. According to Mark, he had already come out of the wilderness to Capernaum; according to Luke, he came first in consequence of the unbelief of his native town.

[4] Isaiah vi. 1, &c.   [5] Amos i. 2, vii. 14.   [6] Matt. ix. 39, xi. 9.

The cry which he raised was that of John: "The time is fulfilled, and the kingdom of God is at hand: repent ye, and believe the gospel."[1]

According to Mark, Jesus in Nazareth had been a carpenter by trade;[2] and that he was in fact sprung from the labouring class of the population is confirmed by the language of his discourses and parables, which everywhere refer to the antecedents and relations of the ordinary workman's life, and betray a knowledge of it which no one could have gained merely by observation. He is at home in those poor, windowless Syrian hovels, in which the housewife must light a candle in the day-time in order to seek for her lost piece of silver;[3] he is acquainted with the secrets of the bakehouse,[4] of the gardener[5] and the builder,[6] and with things which the higher classes never see—as "the good measure, pressed down and shaken together and running over," of the corn-handler;[7] the rotten, leaking wine-skin of the wine-dealer;[8] the patchwork of the peasant-woman;[9] the brutal manners of the upper servants towards the lower;[10] and a hundred other features of a similar kind are interwoven by him into his parables. Reminiscences even of his more special handicraft have been found, it is believed, in his sayings. The parable of the splinter and the beam is said to recall the carpenter's shop;[11] the uneven foundations of the houses, the building-yard;[12] the cubit which is added, the workshop;[13] the distinction in the appearance of green and dry wood, the drying-shed;[14] but from the pregnancy of expression peculiar to him, it would be possible to find similar evidence for every other handicraft. Nevertheless, the circumstance that his discourses always move in this sphere of the

---

[1] Mark i. 15.
[2] Mark vi. 3.
[3] Luke xv. 8.
[4] Matt. xiii. 33, xvi. 6; Luke xiii. 21.
[5] Matt. xv. 13.
[6] Luke vi. 49.
[7] Luke vi. 38.
[8] Matt. ix. 17.
[9] Matt. ix. 16
[10] Luke xii. 45.
[11] Matt. vii. 3.
[12] Matt. vii. 24.
[13] Matt. vi. 27.
[14] Luke xxiii. 31.

ordinary man's activity, has contributed to establish their exceptional popularity.

By the removal of Jesus from Nazareth to Capernaum, the preaching of the kingdom of God was transferred from the wilderness of Judah to the most populous district of the thickly inhabited and intellectually active Galilee.

Let us examine this world-historic stage, upon which an idyll so dear to humanity was now being performed, somewhat more closely.[1] The western shore of the Lake of Gennesareth is about fourteen and a half miles long,[2] and is divided into a narrow southern and a broader northern half. The whole southern half, about ten miles long from the outflow of the Jordan, consists of a narrow strip of land between the lake and the declivities of the limestone plateau, which descend precipitously to the lake. Only in the middle of this strip of shore did room remain between the mountains and the surface of the water for a fair-sized town, the new Tiberias, which was built a mile and a half to the north of the warm springs of Emmaus.[3] The wall-like mountains then run for a good three miles towards the north, close along the lake; then they suddenly recede far back at Magdala (el Mejdel), and allow room for a fresh green plain, three miles long and a mile and a half broad. This meadow-land, running three miles along the lake, is the celebrated plain of Gennesareth.[4] At the present Khân Minîyeh (which is identified by some with Dalmanutha, by others with Capernaum), the limestone mountains again project to the lake,[5] and follow the north-western bend of the shore

---

[1] Compare Bell. Jud. iii. 10, 7; Robinson's Palestine, Vol. ii. 380, &c.; Van de Velde, Reise nach Syrien und Palaestina, ii. 336, &c.; Furrer, Wanderg. durch Pal. 306; Ebrard, die Lage von Kapernaum, Stud. u. Krit. 1867, 4.

[2] See Robinson, Pal. ii. 417.

[3] Antiq. xviii. 2, 3.

[4] Bell. iii. 10, 8; Matt. xiv. 34; Mark vi. 53.

[5] The country which Matt. xv. 39 calls the coasts of Magdala, is termed in the parallel passage, Mark viii. 10, the parts of Dalmanutha. The boundaries, therefore, touched one another, and we must in any case look for Dalmanutha between Capernaum and Magdala.

to the plain of Julias, through the marshy ground of which the Jordan flows into the lake.

Upon this northern, narrower strip of shore, lay CAPERNAUM, close to the lake, according to the Gospels, and on the great caravan road.[1] If the latter is to be identified with the yet visible Roman road, which runs from Jacob's-bridge by the shortest way through the mountains towards the lake, then Khân Minîyeh would indicate the site of Capernaum, since this road first touches the lake there. But since the shorter road is usually the more modern, the road, at the time of Jesus, may have led down the more convenient valley of the Jordan, across Julias, to Capernaum; and only under this supposition can the numerous band of tax-gatherers in Capernaum be explained, as well as the garrison which was situated there, because then we have to look for the town on the frontiers of the territories of Philip and Antipas.[2] In this case, however, we should have to identify the present Tell Hum with Capernaum, and Khân Minîyeh, on the other hand, with Dalmanutha. To the north of the little town, there immediately began the marshy ground which the Jordan had deposited before it ran into the lake.[3] When Josephus on one occasion sprained his hand here by falling from his horse that had stuck in the marsh, Capernaum was the nearest spot to which the wounded general was borne. As the enemies' troops had entrenched themselves at Julias, it seems from this notice also that the nearer Tell Hum is to be identified with Capernaum rather than the more distant Khân Minîyeh.[4] The places Chorazin and Bethsaida must also be sought for in the neighbourhood of this battle-field; Chorazin on this side, and Bethsaida on the other, of the mouth of the Jordan;[5] the former up on the heights of a side valley, the latter down on the lake bank. Jesus also speaks of them as neighbouring towns to Capernaum.[6] Impor-

---

[1] Matt. iv. 13, 15, ix. 1. The caravan road is also proved by Matt. ix. 9—11.
[2] Matt. viii. 5, ix. 9; Luke vii. 5.   [3] Jos. Vita, 72.   [4] Jos. Vita, 72.
[5] See the Map of Van de Velde: Bir Kerazeh and el-Mesadîyeh.
[6] Matt. xi. 20, 23.

tant places which lay further on were Julias, Arbela and Tiberias. Julias lay to the north on the Jordan, before it flows into the lake. Pliny reckons this town among the most pleasant of this district. It was a new creation of the tetrarch Philip, who during his own lifetime built his sepulchre here, in which he was just laid in the year 34.[1] To the south, upon the steep limestone rocks where numerous hawks built their eyries, did Arbela, the robbers' nest of evil fame, menace, with the caves of Herod in the heights of the valley opening out at Magdala, which formed the sally-port of the robbers towards the lake.[2] Of the ostentatious Tiberias we have already spoken. Probably, more frequently than here, the fishermen of Capernaum visited Tarichæa in order to sell their fish, which, pickled in barrels, were thence sent far and wide.[3]

The appearance of the lake as a whole is not without charm. The blue surface of the water lies deeply depressed between the yellow walls of limestone. To the north, the mountains of Upper Galilee rise, and in the background Hermon majestically rests. The western bank, with its fruitful terraces, sloping stepwise, and the green meadow carpet of the plain of Gennesareth, is the scene of Jesus' ministry to which the dense population thronged. On the eastern bank the waves wash a narrow strip of level strand, behind which rise barren precipices of rock and steep mountain walls, outworks of the inhospitable Gaulanitis. There is Jesus' asylum from the throng of people, where he sought and found solitude when the obtrusive curiosity of the Galileans drove him away from Capernaum. At the time of Jesus, the plain of Gennesareth especially was a smiling garden. "On account of the luxuriant fertility," says Josephus,[4] "all kinds of plants grow here, and everything is cultivated in the best manner possible. The mild air suits the plants. Walnut-trees, which need cold, grow in immeasurable abundance near palms, which require heat, and fig and olive-trees, which a more mode-

---

[1] Antiq. xviii. 2, 1.   [2] Compare Vol. i. 236, 237.
[3] Strabo, iii. 2.   [4] Bell. iii. 10, 8.

rate temperature suits. It is as though there were a contest in nature to unite the contradictory at one point, or a happy contention of the seasons, each of which claims the land as its own. The ground produces the most various fruits, not once a year alone, but at the most various times. The royal fruits, grapes and figs, are supplied continuously by it for ten months in the year, whilst the other sorts ripen the whole year through."

The plain owed this fertility to the numerous water-courses flowing from the neighbouring declivity. The spring Capharnaum, especially, bubbled up here, which much exercised the imagination of the natives, and, according to one tradition, was said to be connected with the Nile. Even at the present day there is a copse-surrounded pool, in the crystal-clear waters of which numerous fish dart about, and that, flowing down through several channels, waters the lower lying meadows,[1] which is admired as the alleged spring Capharnaum. To this spot upon the lake-bank the inhabitants of Capernaum frequently resorted.[2] Here, too, is the natural market of the district.

Even from Josephus' description, the pride of the Rabbinical school, that afterwards settled here, in this corner of the earth becomes intelligible. "Seven seas, spake the Lord God, have I created in the land of Canaan, but only one have I chosen for myself, the sea of Genesar," did they declare. More than was suspected by these scribes had this lake been chosen by the Lord God, and favoured above all the lakes of the earth.[3] How well known to mankind are these shores, these valleys and these fields! These are the slopes with the vineyards about which the householder set an hedge, and digged a wine-press, and built a tower.[4] These are the sunny hills upon which the old wine had grown and the new wine is growing, for which the householder carefully provides the new skins.[5] This is the meadow-carpet of the plain of Gennesareth, with its thousand upon thousands of

---

[1] Jos. Bell. iii. 10, 8.
[2] Matt. xiv. 34.
[3] Midrash Tillim, fol. 4, 1 b, Sepp. 2, 170.
[4] Matt. xxi. 33.
[5] Luke v. 37.

lilies, which in the spring are arrayed in the glory of Solomon, and in winter are cast into the oven.[1] These are the pastures where the shepherd leaves the ninety-and-nine sheep in order to seek for the one that is lost on the mountains, and when he has found it layeth it on his shoulders rejoicing.[2] These are the ravens which hover around the rocks of Arbela, which have neither storehouse nor barn, and yet find their food on the shore below.[3] These are the mountains from which the hawks fly upwards, terrifying the hen's chickens.[4] These are the gardens where the fig-trees grow, on which the gardener found no figs for three years,[5] where the mustard-seed becomes a great tree, so that the birds of the air lodge in its branches.[6] Yes, how well known to us is the whole of this valley![7] Yonder are the mountains of Gaulanitis, above which in the mornings the red mist stood, and the leisured scribes said, "It will be foul weather to-day; for the sky is red and lowering;" or the hills of Magdala, behind which the sun sank glowing, and the idle Rabbi declared, "It will be fair weather;"[8] or the clouds drifted from Tarichæa to the mountains of Safed, where the experienced declared, "There will be heat to-day."[9] Just as in every similar valley, here, too, there are rapid changes in the sky, and not seldom sudden storms occur, which fall like a whirlwind upon the lake,[10] or else as torrents of rain sweep down the houses.[11] The business life, too, which the discourses of Jesus frequently take into the circle of their observations, is due to the situation of the little town. Here comes the rich merchant along the commercial road, having exchanged his heavy load of Babylonian carpets for the light produce of the foreign pearl fisheries;[12] here fishermen, tax-gatherers and vine-dressers move too and fro. Above in Julias, below in Tiberias, dwell the people in silken garments, and are

---

[1] Luke xii. 27, 28.
[2] Luke xv. 4.
[4] Luke xii. 24.
[4] Matt. xxiii. 37.
[5] Luke xiii. 7.
[6] Luke xiii. 19.
[7] Matt. xvi. 3.
[8] Matt. xvi. 2.
[9] Luke xii. 55.
[10] Matt. viii. 24.
[11] Matt. vii. 24.
[12] Matt. xiii. 46.

called "gracious lords."[1] The youthful Salome dwells in one, her mother Herodias in the other neighbouring castle; so that even the intercourse of the friendly courts would not escape the observant eye of the inhabitants of Capernaum.[2] This town, on the frontiers of two princes, on the military road of the nations, on the bank of the lake, in the midst of numerous hamlets, had been sought out by Jesus in order that from this spot he might begin to preach the kingdom of God. The little one-storied[3] house, surrounded by a court-yard,[4] of his disciple Peter, who dwelt here, together with his brother and mother-in-law, was Jesus' usual place of abode.[5] Peter and his brother were fishermen, and their house lay below on the strand.[6] They had both been called by Jesus when managing their boats and mending their nets, in that he promised, "I will make you fishers of men."

The little town itself lay close to the lake. As the low-lying grounds of the Jordan were in the immediate neighbourhood, the town seems to have had the reputation of being a fever-nest, on account of the marshes which extended to the north. When Josephus, after the battle of Julias, had been carried to Capernaum with a sprained wrist, the physicians ordered him to be taken for the night to Tarichæa, in order that the fever might not be increased in Capernaum.[7] Peter's wife's mother, too, lay sick of a fever[8] when Jesus on one occasion came back from the synagogue, and to the present day the surrounding districts complain of the same evil.[9] The population consisted in part of fishermen, for the Gospels make us acquainted with an active fisherman's and sailor's life upon the lake. Many tax-gatherers were also employed in the place,[10] whose presence, and that of the garrison situated here, can be accounted for by the proximity of the frontier, or the caravan road which ran from Damascus to

---

[1] Luke xxii. 25. [2] Mark x. 42; Luke xxii. 25, xiv. 31; Matt. xxii. 11.
[3] Mark ii. 4. [4] Mark ii. 3, iii. 20. [5] Mark i. 16, 30.
[6] Mark ii. 13, iv. 1. [7] Vita, Jos. 72. [8] Mark i. 30.
[9] Compare Furrer, 315. Dr. Robinson also was attacked by fever here; see his Palestine, iii. 362.
[10] Matt. ix. 9.

Ptolemais. This was the Gentiles' road, which was as unholy as the towns of the Samaritans: on this road, too, stood the custom-house of Matthew.[1] Owing to the rich and fruitful soil in the valley, and the sunny slopes of the limestone mountains, however, agriculture and the cultivation of the vine were the chief occupation of the inhabitants. The wheat of Capernaum and Chorazim is celebrated in the Talmud; the cultivation of the vineyards is accurately described by Jesus; and no very good opinion is entertained of the vine-dressers.[2] A "wine-bibber," on the other hand, is the name given to the master of Capernaum by the Pharisees. A place thus situated could not be insignificant; it had, too, its own synagogue.[3]

That the ministry of Jesus had the relations of such a little country town for its background, can be deduced indirectly from his discourses also, which everywhere reflect the rural condition of Galilee. There is in these discourses a constant attention to the state of the season, of the weather, of the field work, of the harvest, which is thus familiar only to the circle of ideas of an agricultural population. At the season of the fig-tree, Jesus points out to his disciples how its branches become full of sap and its buds swell, showing that it will soon be spring. He marks how the ploughman follows the plough,[4] that the attentive make even furrows, while those whose eyes turn back mar the field. Again, he watches the sower sowing corn, and sees the corn falling upon the field or beyond the field into the road, and the sparrows fly from the roofs and the fowls run from the barns in order to pick it up,[5] and he is grieved about other grains which are trodden under the wayfarer's foot or crushed by the passing waggon. Then he returns to the field, and now here and there the corn has sprung up and stands joyously clothed in green. But when he came back along the path in the evening, he found the stalks withered, and, trying the soil, found stony ground.[6] The year

---

[1] Matt. ix. 9.
[2] Menachot, 85, 9; Grätz, iii. 360; Matt. xx. 1, xxi. 33, xi. 19.
[3] Mark i. 21.   [4] Luke ix. 62.   [5] Mark iv. 4.   [6] Mark iv. 5.

advances: then he points to the blue and red flowers which the wicked enemy has sown among the wheat, but he is concerned for the good stalks trodden down in pulling out the tares.[1] Then the summer comes; the field grows white for harvest. He sees the workers at sultry noon; the children bind the tares in bundles in order to burn them;[2] after the midday heat comes the evening's repose, when the labourer is paid his scanty earnings.[3] Other illustrations are given him by the activity and bustle of the kindred fishery on the lake, when he regards the work, how the fish follow after the destructive bait and entangle themselves in the net—how the fishermen sort them on the beach, gathering the good ones into casks and casting the bad on one side.

These discourses not only give us a thoroughly living and brightly coloured picture of the conditions of Jesus' life in Capernaum, but also do not leave us altogether without a clue to his personal activity. The Gospels prove to us that Jesus preached the kingdom of God publicly to the Galileans, as well as entered into their synagogues to teach them there.[4] Thus in Luke iv. 16, he is presented to us as he rises before the collected congregation and mounts the platform which stands in the midst of the house of God. The synagogue attendant hands him the roll. The reading of the Thorah has already taken place, and he reads the prophetic words, "The Spirit of the Lord Jehovah is upon me, because Jehovah hath anointed me." Thereupon there follows his Midrash. Many of our discourses of Jesus betray by their form and contents that they were delivered in the synagogue, like the antitheses in the fifth chapter of Matthew, which, in the language of the synagogue, regularly commence, "Ye have heard that it was said.... but I say unto you." The discourse in Luke iv. 25 is similar. "But I tell you of a truth, many widows were in Israel in the days of Elijah, when the heaven was shut up three years and six months;.... and unto none of them was Elijah sent, save unto Sarepta, a city of Sidon, unto a woman

---

[1] Matt. xiii. 26.
[2] Matt. xiii. 30.
[3] Matt. xx. 8.
[4] Mark i. 39, iii. 1, vi. 2.

that was a widow. And many lepers were in Israel in the time of Elisha the prophet, and none of them was cleansed, saving Naaman the Syrian." There are other discourses, again, which, from their connection with the events and incidents of out-door life, were manifestly delivered to collected crowds; thus most of the parables, with their allusions to the fate of the seed-corn, to the beauty of the field flowers, to the habits of the fisherman's life, to the secrets of the bales of goods, still allow it to be discovered whether their circle of hearers was gathered on the blooming pastures, on the wave-rocked boat, or on the thronged military road. The discourses delivered at table in the wanderings from farmstead to farmstead also are not wanting—those of bread and salt, of old and new wine, of rotten and sound wineskins, of higher and lower places, of the boisterous or quiet hospitality—which offer occasion for the deepest sayings, just as the thinker of the East loves them. Those most easily to be recognized, finally, are the words spoken to the more intimate circle treating of the duties of imitation and discipleship, and have been preserved with especial accuracy.[1]

The inquiry was made at an early date, how Jesus had attained this great eloquence. "What wisdom is this which is given unto this man?" the people at Nazareth immediately demanded. "Is not this the carpenter, the son of Mary, and brother of James, and Joses, and Judas, and Simon? and are not his sisters here with us?"[2] This testimony that he did not belong to the Rabbis of the country is confirmed by the thoroughly original form of his discourses, which owe nothing certainly to the schools, and without a trace of pedantry everywhere give the most simple expression of the human perception of the divine.

Under these circumstances, certainly, we are altogether without information as to the course of his development; for the narrative of Jesus' early knowledge of the law which astonished even the scribes of Jerusalem, is rather a traditional feature of Jewish his-

---

[1] Weizsäcker, Unters. über die evang. Gesch.: Gotha, 1864, pp. 355 ff.
[2] Mark vi. 3.

torical narratives that appears to have adorned the youth of others also. Thus Josephus, for example, informs us about himself: "Even as a boy of fourteen, I was commended by all for my love of learning, on which account even the high-priests and principal men of the city came to me in order to know my opinion about the accurate understanding of points of the law."[1]

In order to ascertain the materials of the education received by Jesus, we must go back therefore once more to his own discourses. And here, certainly, he does not disown acquaintance with the best part of the education of the time, in that he has a marvellous knowledge of the Old Testament. This is shown, not so much by the many quotations which he has always at hand, as by the numberless Biblical reminiscences out of which in many cases his discourses are woven together.[2] He knows "what is said,"[3] and what again and again "stands written." The mild outpourings of blessing, like the rolling rhetoric of denunciation,[4] are uttered in the words, now of the Law, now of the Psalms, now of the Prophets; and even the most brilliant sayings of the new doctrine are not seldom dug out of the mine of Old Testament revelation. Instead of many another, we will merely call to mind the parable of the wise and foolish builder, taken from Ezekiel xiii. 11, and the various discourses on the vineyard, taken from Isaiah v., in which the motive given by the prophet is in part briefly used and in part further elaborated. The parable of the Last Judgment, when the Messiah separates the sheep from the goats, is in like manner woven together from Isaiah lviii. 7, where the pious feed the hungry, clothe the naked, bring the poor that are cast out to their house, and hide not themselves from the suffering; from the proverb of Solomon, xix. 17, that he that hath pity upon the poor lendeth unto the Lord; and from Isaiah lxvi. 24, where the everlasting torment is described, the worm of which shall not die, nor the fire be quenched. To what

---

[1] Jos. Vita, 2; compare for Moses, Antiq. ii. 9, 6; for Samuel, Antiq. v. 10, 4.
[2] Compare Holtzmann, Synopt. Evang. p. 459.
[3] Matt. v. 43.   [4] Mark ix. 43.

the ancients, however, could only imperfectly stammer forth, Jesus, in his divine command of the moral world, gives the only right expression. When Jesus the son of Sirach[1] says of the power of wisdom, "Put your neck under the yoke, and let your soul receive instruction; she is hard at hand to find: behold with your eyes, how that I have had but little labour, and have gotten unto me much rest,"—Jesus recasts this sentence into his eternal saying of the easy yoke and light burden which he will lay upon those who will learn of him. Many other of his sayings can in a similar manner be analyzed into free, ingenious combinations taken from the treasures of illustration and thought in the Old Testament; and his polemical discourses, especially, not seldom pour a shower of the most crushing passages from the Scriptures upon the heads of his opponents. But they are not merely citations from memory; he has himself experienced the whole spiritual world of the prophets. The pathos of an Isaiah, the melancholy of an Hosea, the meekness of a Jeremiah, the joy in nature of an Amos, the power of observation of the proverb-writers, the whole world of feeling of the psalmists, have been transferred to him, and contradict the assertion that it is impossible that an idea in all its fulness can be concentrated in one individual.

7. The New Preaching of the Kingdom.

What Jesus proclaimed in these discourses in the synagogue and in his public addresses, was the preaching, so familiar to the people, of the future of the kingdom of God. The greater emphasis of proclamation, the fuller description of the coming judgment, the multiplicity of illustration and symbol in which he clothed this great idea of the time, distinguish his promises for the future in form alone from those of the book of Enoch and

---

[1] Ecclesiasticus li. 34.

contemporary Apocalyptics, the thoughts of which are otherwise everywhere re-echoed. Jesus, too, speaks of a coming day of harvest, and just as the Baptist beheld the axe which was laid at the roots of the trees, so Jesus heard the clinking of the divine sickle. "The harvest is the end of the world and the reapers are the angels."[1] As the Baptist had discoursed in Judæa of the purging of the threshing-floor and the burning of the chaff, so Jesus speaks on the lake of the separating of the good and bad fish;[2] as the former preached of the day of Jehovah coming with thunder and lightning, so according to Jesus would the judgment come in whirlwind and storms of rain, and make manifest which house was built upon the rock and which upon sand.[3] If the former demanded fruits meet for repentance, so the latter foretold a strict account which would not allow even an idle word to escape,[4] and would enter into judgment for every look and thought.[5] While these predictions of the approach of the great day of judgment which the prophets had foretold, connect him immediately with the Baptist, yet there are others which call to mind Jesus' patriotic countryman, Judas the Galilean. Whilst the latter demanded adhesion to himself as prophet in order to establish the true dominion of God, he bid his followers esteem death of no account and serve Jehovah. They should throw away their lives and then God would be with them, for the souls of the pious were preserved for ever, the wicked alone depart to Gehenna. To hold Jehovah as the Lord, that was Israel's freedom.[6] In similar tones do the words of Jesus reach those whom he demands shall follow him. "He that findeth his life shall lose it; and he that loseth his life for my sake shall find it." "Whosoever shall confess me before men, him will I confess also before my Father which is in heaven; but whosoever shall deny me before men, him will I deny also before my Father which is in heaven."[7] "For what shall a man be profited, if he shall gain

[1] Matt. xiii. 39. [2] Matt. iii. 12, with xiii. 49. [3] Matt. vii. 24.
[4] Matt. xii. 36. [5] Matt. v. 28. [6] Antiq. xviii. i. 1, 4.
[7] Matt. x. 32—39.

the whole world, but lose his soul?"[1] As the coming kingdom, finally, is described, from the days of the book of Daniel downwards to those of the fourth book of Ezra, as a great and joyous festival, so Jesus also places before his disciples a joyous period of recompence into which the pious will enter as virgins to a marriage,[2] when the cup shall circulate at the marriage-feast,[3] when "the righteous shall shine forth as the sun in the kingdom of their Father."[4]

But on closer examination it is found that, on the other hand again, this kingdom is spoken of as one which, invisible indeed and spiritual, is yet already there. John had spoken of the commencement of the kingdom and the taking it by force; Jesus went a step farther, in that he proclaimed the actual presence of this kingdom: "Behold, it is among you."[5] It is there as the grain of mustard-seed which grows up into a tree, as the leaven which leavens all the dough, as the pearl which the buyer has acquired, as the treasure in the field which the digger can seek.[6] Thus the kingdom of God appears to him as a mystery of the Divine grace, already working in secret. Already is the upper world sinking down into the lower; already is the spiritual world bursting through the earthly veil; already is the precious purity of this existence purging itself and removing the earthly dross. A kingdom of the other world, it is already becoming one of this; a kingdom of the future, it is already present.

That Jesus could present this conception of the kingdom of God as a divine growth that has already struck its roots down into the lower world, rests upon the fact that for him the kingdom consists essentially in a spiritual constitution of humanity. We are therefore at once struck by one thing in this new preaching of the kingdom, that it opens quite new doors into the kingdom of God, which John had not found and which the Pharisees had even shut. John, too, had demanded that the divine kingdom

[1] Matt. xvi. 23.   [2] Matt. xxv. 1.   [3] Matt. xxvi. 29.
[4] Matt. xiii. 43.   [5] Luke xvii. 21.   [6] Matt. xiii. 31—44.

should be taken by storm, not by the weapons of the Galilean, it is true, but by works of asceticism and God-pleasing performances. Thus he had fallen back into the usual path of Judaism, which strove to restore the purity of the people in a merely negative manner, so that the circle of the impure from which man had to abstain was always being extended, always being more sharply defined.[1] To fast more, to pray more, to repent more than all who had gone before, was the way on which the Pharisees, Essenes and disciples of John had travelled one after the other. A new way into the kingdom of God could only be found by him who had a new revelation of God. The others had refined over-much concerning the constitution of the kingdom; Jesus thought first of all about God.

Those have been called geniuses and God-sent prophets who "once again go back to the beginning," and present a *new* question to the world. The new question which Jesus presented was the word directed to the God of the Jews: Art Thou truly a God of wrath, and is the world truly miserable only because Thy curse rests upon it? The law answered Yes to this question, but the whole world answered a thousand times No. This it was which appeared to the people so surprisingly new and comforting in his preaching, the word new to Israel, that God was the loving Father of men. The fundamental presupposition of all Judaism, and the motive power of all Pharisaic laboriousness was, in fact, the conviction that God was a jealous God, visiting the sins of the fathers upon the children unto the third and fourth generation. If the Pharisee busily troubled himself about fulfilling a thousand minute scrupulous precepts, if the Essene afflicted himself in circumspect loneliness, if the Sadducee made himself of importance in the temple service and sacrifices, if the people were filled with anguish at the sense of their estrangement from God and God's desertion of them, it was because, as the pivot of their whole theory of life, stood the belief in an angry and avenging God, who inexorably

[1] Compare Weizsäcker, 419.

demands a righteousness for which He has nevertheless made man much too weak. Even John had not risen above this conception. More terribly indeed than the others had he spoken of the descending axe and the wrath to come.[1] Then, in the very face of all the signs of Divine wrath which weigh upon the people and set the activity of the masters in Israel in motion, there comes a new prophet with the message never heard before, that God is the Father of men, and that He has loved them from the very beginning of the world, and in proof of this he points to the lilies of the field and the birds of the air.[2] That an eternal compassion is poured upon the world,[3] that an eternal love watches over the turmoil of human life as much as over the stillness of the lonely hill-side,[4]—this had his heart first discovered in that secret communion with God which caused him to say, "No man knoweth the Father save the Son."[5] The old wrathful God of Israel was to him a Friend and Father. Did others see how God was jealous of His right, and visited the sins of the fathers upon the children to the third and fourth generation,—he saw how this same God sendeth rain on the just and on the unjust, and maketh His sun to rise on the evil and on the good, how He tends the birds in their nest, and inclines to hear the prayers of the troubled hearts of men. This, none before him had felt. This was his work.

For certainly we have now come to a point at which the new that is coming into existence can no longer be derived in any way from existing conditions, but springs immediately from the personal spiritual life of Jesus. How Jesus came to recognize God as the Father, is a question which men have already attempted to answer on purely contemporary historical grounds. From contemplating the errors into which Judaism fell when seeking to reconcile her angry God, say some. But then others had also seen these aberrations, and yet had not cried, Abba, Father. Was it from contemplating the glory which God has poured over His world?

---

[1] Matt. iii. 7—10.   [2] Matt. vi. 28.   [3] Matt. v. 45.
[4] Matt. vi. 30.   [5] Matt. xi. 27.

But the lilies of Galilee have bloomed for others also, and the heavens were equally blue for Pharisee and Sadducee. Consequently all such attempts at derivation are futile. It is the personality which is the source whence the historical antecedents immediately spring, and where the interpretation of the operating conditions ends. Here is the thread which leads immediately to the region of divine creating, and not even can a secular genius, nor a true individuality, be demonstrated to be the mere resultant of antecedent circumstances. This, however, we can say: this strength of the filial consciousness could have been developed only in a mind which was pure, blameless and sinless in the sight of the Deity, in which all human restlessness and discontent were removed, upon which lay no anguish of a finite world, no tormenting consciousness of being only a mere fraction of that which it ought to have been. The sinful man—the stained or even the merely disturbed conscience—must always see God opposed to himself as wrathful and avenging, as a jealous God; but the revelation that God is the Father of men could only arise in a mind in which the image of God was reflected undisturbed, because the mirror was without blemish. The revelation of God as the Father is the strongest proof of the absolutely normal state of the human nature in Jesus.

From this new conception of God, however, there proceeded an absolutely new religious world. If the God whom mankind reveres be wrathful and avenging, then the task of religion is to appease this wrath. It is the inculcation of various sacrifices, prayers and ascetic practices. If, on the other hand, God be the Father of mankind, then the only religious duty is the duty of love, and the kingdom of God will consist in the filial relation of mankind to God. It is a spiritual kingdom of filial affection, of aspiration after Him, of unconditional obedience to His commands. The poor in spirit, the meek, the merciful will inherit it; those who hunger and thirst after righteousness will be filled; the pure in heart are those who shall see it; the peacemakers those who shall be called its children; and when distress and persecution arise, the righteous shall inherit it.[1]

The kingdom, according to Jesus' own exposition, exists in doing God's will upon earth just as it is done in heaven by the sons of God, the angels. It was consequently an essentially spiritual kingdom that occupied the place of the hopes of a kingdom of the Pharisees. They had turned the ancient prophetic promise into a political programme, which was to be carried out by means of ordinary punishments against the people, battles won against the Romans, and zealous agitation against the aristocracy. Their idea of the kingdom needed first of all a revolution in the sense of the Maccabean wars for freedom, and then a miracle of God from on high in addition. Jesus, on the other hand, declared that they would not establish the kingdom of God like a state; they would not be able to say, "Lo here! or, lo there! for lo, the kingdom of God is in the midst of you." This change followed necessarily from the new revelation of God. The idea of the kingdom could no longer be founded on the ancient covenant between a jealous God and a wearisome people. Men stand to God in the relation of children. They do not serve Him, therefore, for the sake of reward, but out of love, "that they may be the children of their Father which is in heaven." God loves them, not on account of their performances, but from His own Fatherly goodness and mercy, which makes His sun to rise on the evil and on the good, and has more joy over one sinner that repenteth than over ninety-and-nine just persons. From this view, it is true, the ground generally was taken from under the feet of Judaism, and with the presuppositions the consequences fell also. Where remained any necessity for sacrifice, for the temple service, washings, fasts, tithes, if the Father ask nothing from His children save the heart? Where remained the Rabbis' hope of keeping God, according to contract, to the fulfilment of His promises, as soon as the Mosaic pattern-state had

[1] Matt. v. 3—10.

been actually established? Where remained the exceptional position of the Jews and their claims to be the chosen people? One part of the theocracy after another collapsed, for its foundations had given way. The thought which, from blunting custom, passes by to-day like a dull sound on the ear of the multitude, was for that world a word of new creative power.

With the new heaven there came also a new earth. If the kingdom of God be a filial relation to God, then it is for men a kingdom of brotherliness. They are brothers because they have *one* Father; and among them it is not law and statute which prevail, but the commandment of love, which does more than it is obliged, more than is demanded. It yields the cloak as well as the coat; it goes two miles with him who demands one; it forgives unto seventy times seven, and accuses none save oneself. And this love prevails not only among the members of the covenant, of the rank, of the party. The man is to be loved because he is a man, because he is a brother. While the ancient world in general paid little heed to the thought that the poor, the lowly and insignificant had also hearts to feel pain and pleasure, that they also had been born for freedom, love and happiness,—Judaism had completely limited all sympathy to the sons of Abraham. This foundation of the Jewish theory of life also crumbled away. " Ye have heard that it hath been said, Thou shalt love thy neighbour, and hate thy enemy. But I say unto you, Love your enemies; bless them that curse you; do good to them that hate you, and pray for them which despitefully use you and persecute you; that ye may be the children of your Father which is in heaven; for He maketh His sun to rise on the evil and on the good, and sendeth rain on the just and on the unjust. For if ye love them which love you, what reward have ye? Do not even the tax-gatherers the same? And if ye salute your brethren only, what do ye more than others? Do not even the heathen the same?" This was a new tone in this discordant Jewish world, that, in its suspicious anxiety about its law, produced hardly anything else than hatred. It seemed a duty, indeed, to this race to hate the

Gentiles, to hate the Samaritans, to hate the tax-gatherers; and then, in addition, the Rabbi hated the priest, the Pharisee the Sadducee, and both hated the lawless common people. Jesus, on the contrary, loves all—some because they, too, are the children of Abraham, and the others because they, too, are the children of God; for from the belief that God is the Father proceeded love, and nothing but love, towards this world so full of hatred. And as soon as this consequence of the proper conception of God is accomplished, is not the kingdom of God already here? It is in this time of God's peace and brotherly love that the promised Messianic kingdom consists; and in order to create it, in the very sense of John, all that is necessary is to put this new heart in the place of its stony one; then, without the naked sword of the Gaulonite, is the kingdom of heaven given to the world, just as it already encompassed Jesus with its peace. Therefore, in place of the observer of the Jewish law, the citizen of the kingdom of God ought to appear, from whom would be demanded, not the fulfilment of external ordinances, but compassion, purity of heart, peacefulness, meekness, humility, sorrow for the present condition of the world, and hunger and thirst after righteousness.

These are the commandments, the fulfilment of which was not to be rewarded with the kingdom of God, as the Pharisees believed, but the fulfilment of which is itself at once the beginning of the kingdom. This it was, too, which distinguished Jesus from John. The latter had desired to prepare for the kingdom in the dim expectation of a succeeding theophany, in the hope that God would bestow the kingdom as a reward for the faithful work. Jesus brought the kingdom itself, and knew that he possessed it. Not upon any external means of help, not upon the legions of angels for which he could have prayed the Father, did he count. Without contradicting the hopes of the pious—nay, on the contrary, confirming them—he could yet at once rest the kingdom that was to be founded on its own importance; he could found it upon the internal truth of its thought, upon its own nature. This preparation for the kingdom was its actual presence. It was in the disposition of the mind which he bore within himself that the kingdom of God, as his own experience taught him, lay. It needed only that there should be the same disposition in others, and the kingdom of God was there for Israel as it was already there for himself. "Seek ye first the kingdom of God and its righteousness, and all these things shall be added unto you."[1] In order to unite the people to such a spiritual kingdom, he certainly could not establish any kind of new custom or usage, like the Essenes or John had done. There were no external means beyond his word and attachment to his person. Whoso believed on him could attain to the kingdom, but no one else. The first task of his word and preaching, consequently, was to arouse a consciousness in the people of the difference between the external righteousness of the law with which the Pharisees would win the kingdom of God, and the internal justification which is in itself God's kingdom. "Except your righteousness shall exceed the righteousness of the Scribes and Pharisees, ye shall in no case enter into the kingdom of heaven."[2] The "greater righteousness," the "new commandment," the "great commandment" which includes all the rest, is ever an inward state of mind. It is not the outward action, but the source of the action, which is the chief thing. "Ye have heard," he declares—and the manner of the words compels us to believe that they were uttered in the synagogue—"that it was said to them of old time, Thou shalt not kill, and whosoever shall kill shall be in danger of the judgment; but I say unto you, that whosoever is angry with his brother shall be in danger of the judgment. . . . . Ye have heard that it was said, Thou shalt not commit adultery; but I say unto you, that whosoever looketh on a woman to lust after her hath committed adultery with her already in his heart. . . . . Ye have heard that it was said to them of old time, Thou shalt not forswear thyself, but shalt perform unto the Lord thine oaths; but I say unto you, Swear not at all. . . . . But your manner of speech shall be, Yea, yea ; Nay,

---

[1] Matt. vi. 33. [2] Matt. v. 20.

nay; for whatsoever is more than these cometh of evil."[1] Everywhere in these new commandments does Jesus go back from the action to its ground, from the mere expression of the disposition to the disposition itself. Upon the disposition does all depend, in it does the injury lie. "Do men gather grapes of thorns, or figs of thistles? Even so every good tree bringeth forth good fruit; but a corrupt tree bringeth forth evil fruit." Whilst the law demands fruit, Jesus demands before all else healthy roots. Morality is not a sum of performances, it is a disposition of the mind. The separate commandments of Judaism, therefore, recede beside this demand on the state of the whole man. The utterance of the prophet Hosea, "I will have mercy and not sacrifice," often fell from his lips;[2] and a scribe who placed the love of God above burnt-offerings and sacrifices, he declared was not far from the kingdom of God.[3] To be so disposed to others as to oneself, "that is the law and the prophets."[4] It is not the food which defiles, but the depraved thought. To Jesus, who opposed the way of righteousness followed at the time and by "them of old," none, consequently, seemed farther from the kingdom of God than those who content themselves with fulfilling the works of the law. Those who are satisfied, for whose needs the external service of the law suffices, will never understand the claims of the kingdom of God. And therefore does he declare those blessed who hunger and thirst after righteousness, who sorrow, who are poor in spirit, for theirs is the kingdom of heaven. Here does the word prevail throughout, that only those who really exert themselves can be saved. And therefore does it seem to him, as his praising the scribe who spoke wisely proves, that the recognition of the subordinate value of ritualistic ordinances is the first step towards the kingdom of God. Thus he places before his followers tasks of a far different character than the fulfilment of a definite number of separate formulative ordinances. "Be ye perfect, even as your Father in

[1] Matt. v. 21. [2] Matt. ix. 13, xii. 7.
[3] Mark xii. 33, 34. [4] Matt. vii. 12.

heaven is perfect," his only commandment declares; according to which, striving and aspiration, hungering and thirsting, exertion and anxiousness will never cease; according to which, too, the mind conscious of self-content, and with the satisfied words of that young Pharisee, will never again be able to declare, "All these things have I kept; what lack I yet?"[1]

Whilst it remains for ever true that the natural man as a rule understands nothing of the tidings of a spiritual world, yet this spiritualization of the idea of the kingdom of God found in this very Judaism, accustomed to more material performances and anxious for more substantial rewards, its scholars that were especially dull in hearing. It was necessary for Jesus, therefore, to never tire of presenting this kingdom of a higher sphere as an entirely supersensual one to his contemporaries, in ever new illustration and ever new attempts at elucidation. The Pharisees, according to Luke,[2] demanded "when the kingdom of God should come." "The kingdom of God," Jesus answers, "cometh not with observation; neither shall they say, Lo here! or, lo there! for behold, the kingdom of God is in the midst of you." It is a spiritual process which has already begun—although none can seize it with hands. It is the awakening of love to God, of love to man, the visitation of peace from above, that disposition of the mind in which it is God that rules.

Not even does Jesus announce, once for all, how the kingdom of God is to be attained *by the individual*. He knows of no method of salvation, and offers no assistance to mere externality by describing the symptoms of conversion. The kingdom comes in one way to one, in another to another. It is for one like one thing, and again for another it is like something else. While it can fall like an inheritance to the Israelite, as the dowry of a pious house,[3] yet another can find it like a treasure in a field, to his own surprise,[4] and while grovelling in the affairs of earth, the true meaning and purport of life will suddenly disclose itself to him.

[1] Matt. xix. 20.
[2] Luke xvii. 20, 21.
[3] Matt. viii. 11; Luke xv. 12.
[4] Matt. xiii. 44.

As a merchant seeking the noblest and best, another will obtain it like a pearl, in comparison with which all other splendour fades away.[1] In turning his pound to good account, a fourth learns how best to put it out at usury, and makes his stake in the kingdom of heaven.[2] "The wind bloweth where it listeth"—thus does the Gospel of John describe the same fact—"and thou heareth the sound thereof, but canst not tell whence it cometh and whither it goeth: so is every one that is born of the Spirit." Does the eye, however, scan the full number of those who become the citizens of the kingdom, then is the kingdom of God "as if a man should cast seed into the ground, and should sleep, and rise night and day, and the seed should spring and grow up, he knoweth not how. For the earth bringeth forth fruit of herself: first the blade, then the ear, after that the full corn in the ear. But when the fruit is brought forth, immediately he putteth in the sickle because the harvest is come."[3]

Thus Jesus was most fond of comparing himself to a sower who sows the word, and then carefully looks for the fate of the scattered seed.[4] The seed is good, the crop will soon sprout. It is upon an internal development, consequently, that he places everything, upon a constant, internal, organic growth. But in this, too, does he firmly believe. The kingdom will increase as surely as the seed sprouts, as surely as the grain of mustard-seed becomes a tree, as surely as the leaven leavens the whole lump, as surely as the spark spreads into a flame. There is no need of any victorious battles, of any violent revolutions; for Jesus knows that the world he bears within himself has of itself force enough to transform the external world. Nevertheless, this thought of the kingdom did not stand before Jesus' consciousness merely in this abstract form, but at the same time it had a concrete and practical one. He believed in an ethical kingdom that is already here; he believed at the same time, however, in a better world that was just on the point of appearing, as fore-

[1] Matt. xiii. 46.   [2] Luke xix. 16.
[3] Mark iv. 26—29.   [4] Mark iv. 10.

told by the prophets and by John; and the kingdom which he announced did not lie in a far-off time, but, like John, did he believe that it would assume shape immediately.[1] The kingdom of Jesus is to be the kingdom which Israel is expecting; it is therefore, when regarded from this side, yet again the belief in an immediately approaching theophany that will also change the external condition of the world. From the parables of the grain of mustard-seed, of the leaven, of the seed growing secretly, it could certainly be believed that Jesus already sees in the idea the kingdom itself, which as a thought in itself sure of victory, calmly leaves the realization to the centuries. But, in fact, Jesus had not contemplated such a far-off termination, and did not contradict the prophecies of the Fathers and the faith of the pious that it was God himself who would complete and finish the holy work.[2] In itself, certainly, his kingdom had need of no such assistance, and consequently it has survived its absence. But this interference of God was a part of the tradition of the Scriptures in which Jesus believed, and of the most sacred convictions of all the best of his contemporaries. His preaching, therefore, is now to the effect that the kingdom is nigh, that it will come, that the day of judgment is approaching; now that it is, ideally, already amongst men, and that its entrance took place without men being aware of it. In profound and presageful manner, however, are the kingdom that is come and that that is to come—the constant development and sudden catastrophe—so interwoven, that the living and future generations were both of them enabled to think of it in this form. The material kingdom of God, the in-breaking judgment of God, the glorious time of mercy, were the constant forms of the belief of the pious,—the horizon of the people, of the Baptist, of the prophets, that embraced Jesus also. Only first when the opposition of Israel to his thoughts of the kingdom was confirmed, when the change of this evil world into the better one was ever being accomplished more and more slowly, when the Lord of this world won more

---

[1] Thus Keim, Jesus of Nazara, T. T. F. L. Vol. iv. pp. 145, 146. [2] Ibid.

victories than the Son of Man, did Jesus begin to speak more explicitly of the coming deeds of God, of the wrath of the judgment, of the forcible subjection of Satan.[1] This, however, was the result and not the starting-point of his preaching. When he began in the joyous spring-time of Galilee, the happy anticipations swelled his breast that the time of salvation has commenced, the kingdom is here, the heavens touch the earth, and the seed of the word, the net of the Son of Man, the leaven of preaching, the spark of discourse will, without the axe of John and the devouring fire of Isaiah, introduce a condition of the people worthy of the God who will visit them.

In accordance with this confidence in the energizing powers which dwell within the good seed of the word, Jesus did absolutely nothing in order outwardly to establish the kingdom. Neither the phylactery of the Pharisee, nor the baptism of John, nor the communal life of the Essenes, was to distinguish the children of the kingdom from the children of the world. It was not to be outwardly recognized who belonged to the kingdom and who not. "Let both grow together until the harvest," he declared; and there was nothing he more dreaded than the separation of his own followers, as being the putting of the light under a bushel, and removing the salt of the earth.

---

8. External Points of Contact.

Religious ideas have a future before them proportionate to their capacity for transfiguring the passionate interests of the present into those that are universally human, so that in these ideas each generation finds its needs satisfied. It is only as they relate to the living questions of the present that these ideas attract the living to them, and only as they are reduced to their purely human contents that they remain dear to those who come

---

[1] See Keim, Jesus of Nazara, Vol. iv. p. 146.

afterwards. This spiritualization of that which is determined historically into the ideal is, however, the work, not of cleverly thought-out formulæ, but of genius, which shares indeed in the interests and ideas of its age, but yet, according to the elevation of the individual perception, purifies them from their accidental constituents. It was thus that Jesus stood related to the doctrine of the kingdom of God. He remains a Son of his century, in that he sees that this kingdom is everywhere being prepared for, in that to him all the signs of the times point to the coming of this kingdom, in that he observes the throes which accompany the kingdom bursting through its earthy shell; but, on the other side, he portrays the kingdom in such a purely spiritual manner, he places it so exclusively upon the permanent needs of the human heart, that this thought of the kingdom remains unaffected although all to whom he promised the kingdom have tasted of death. This attachment to the hopes of his contemporaries was in a high degree the expression of the fervent bond of affection which united him to his people. In a certain sense, it is true, genius is always solitara and homeless in the age in which it lives. But Jesus was not a solitary thinker who preconceived of theories equally adapted to humanity in any century, but he went along hand in hand with his people, wholly given up to the little flock at his feet. Not thinking, but *saving* was his task.

As the characteristic feature of his relation to God was his consciousness of being His child, His son, so in his attitude towards humanity, the pitying love, the true shepherd's heart, was the fundamental character of his mind, the key-note to which all else was attuned. It is told how mightily this genius was stirred within him when he beheld the spiritual destitution of his people. This pity is the impulse from which he acts, and that is aroused with double strength within him in face of the condition of Israel as it presented itself to him. The priesthood sat in Jerusalem, and the Scribes disputed in the schools. About the masses of the people no one troubled. "But when he saw the multitudes, he was moved with compassion on them, because they fainted, and were scattered abroad as sheep having no shepherd."[1] He himself describes the feelings which seized him when he thus beheld the people, as the welling up of a mother's heart.[2] At the same time he had the blessed consciousness of being able to help them all if only they would allow him; and it was from this full consciousness of the blessedness of giving and of being able to give, and from the conviction that he knew how they could find rest for their souls, that the cry proceeded, "Come unto me, all ye that labour and are heavy laden, and I will give you rest."

As Jesus, however, throughout expected and desired that inward normal condition of the relations of human existence, in which alone he saw help—only in the concrete, national form, the form, that is to say, of the Messianic age, or of the kingdom of God which was expected to appear immediately—it would have been natural for him to remain in contact externally with the historical relations of that community of the people which was first of all to be led into the path of peace. The less that Jesus thought of breaking away from the national basis of the ancient covenant with God, the more concrete the form under which he thought of and strove for the new kingdom, as being the Messianic kingdom prepared for by the past history of his people, so much the more expedient was it to connect that kingdom with the historical threads of the present, effecting respectively the reform of the theocracy through the theocracy, the conception of God through the schools, and the state of public affairs through the public authorities. The first thing, in view of such an end as his, was to turn to official Judaism as organized in the theocracy, the teachers and the schools, in order to bring in the amendment through their agency, and not to the separate atoms of the community. There was, moreover, in Jesus' position to his people from the first, no impediment to his entering on the path of national life as it presented itself to him. On the contrary, a very strong *patriotic*

[1] Matt. ix. 36.　　　　　[2] Matt. xxiii. 37.

feature in him is not to be ignored. He, too, burned with ardent zeal for his people, and, in the words of the most patriotic of all the Psalms, he termed Jerusalem the city of the Great King.[1] He did not disdain to give instructions as to the spirit of mind in which the altar in the temple-court ought to be approached,[2] and sent lepers that had been healed to the priest to fulfil the ordinances of the theocracy.[3] The Sanhedrin is to him the highest court, above which there alone stand the fires of Gehenna,[4] and temple and altar are for him a holy place where the honour of God abides.[5] Even the negative side of all patriotism is not wholly wanting. When first sending forth his disciples, he forbids them to carry their tidings to the towns of the Samaritans and the countries of the Gentiles;[6] and in his parables, in accordance with his people's manner of speaking, dogs and swine represent the outside nations.[7] On the other hand, he knows that even the least of his people shares, by birth, in a great promise, because he is a son of Abraham;[8] and during the last days of his life the deep anguish of a patriotic heart finds utterance in the lamentation, "O Jerusalem, Jerusalem, ... how often would I have gathered thy children together, even as a hen gathereth her chickens under her wings, and ye would not!"[9] The question, consequently, why Jesus did not open the way for his kingdom of God from the seat of the theocracy and with the means it put into his hands, finds its answer, not in any sort of reason founded on principle, but in the simple fact that Jesus was a Galilean, and that the spiritual kingdom which he had to proclaim could begin from any point. Jesus simply remained among those relationships in which God had placed him. He did not reject theocratic ways, but yet he did not seek them. Within the settled arrangements of the Galilean synagogue, he proclaimed

---

[1] Psalm xlviii. 2; Matt. v. 35.
[2] Matt. v. 23.
[3] Matt. viii. 4.
[4] Matt. v. 22.
[5] Matt. xxiii. 16—22, 35.
[6] Matt. x. 5.
[7] Matt. vii. 6, xv. 26.
[8] Luke xix. 9.
[9] Matt. xxiii. 37, 38.

his tidings of the kingdom, until the synagogue became too narrow for his needs or itself rejected him. On the other hand, he was as one having authority, and not as the Scribes,[1] in this respect also, that he did not desire the alliance of the Sanhedrin at Jerusalem, and, as a matter of course, still less enter into relations with the then rulers of Galilee. On the contrary, he avoided Antipas, who was living only two leagues distant from Capernaum; and if we find no mention of the splendid Tiberias in the Synoptics, it proves, not indeed that Jesus shared the prejudices of the Rabbis against this unclean spot, but rather that he gladly avoided its worldly, half-Gentile life.

His preaching of the kingdom of God, moreover, in that it was directed to the inward man, had few external points of contact. The absence of reference to contemporary events is a sure sign, rather, that the political world only very occasionally offered him a basis on which to rest his preaching of the kingdom. For the parable of the Talents he has borrowed his background from the time of Archelaus, a time that may have been freshly recalled to mind by the contest of the Herods for the inheritance of Philip. The occasion for the saying about the slaughtered Galileans and the tower of Siloam was given by Pilate. Those who like can find, in the builder who has spent his money and the king who is short of troops,[2] Antipas, the indefatigable builder and cautious diplomatist; but we never find Jesus receiving an impulse from any of the potentates of that time, or his action determined by any events of the day. Much, certainly, is said about the signs of the times that so clearly proclaim the nearness of the kingdom, just as the red sky in the evening proclaims a fine morrow, and that only those permanently blind fail to interpret.[3] "Ye hypocrites," does he assert of the Pharisees, "ye can discern the face of the sky and of the earth, but how is it that ye do not know how to discern this time?" But it is not his intention in any way to dwell upon those signs that just at this time were rising above the political horizon. As the statesman understood the

---

[1] Matt. vii. 29.   [2] Luke xiv. 28—32.   [3] Luke xii. 54.

age, nothing had place in it which did not refer to the great contest of the nation against heathenism. Before this great question that was pressing on to a sanguinary decision, all other interests must remain silent. Certainly it was in the very relations of the age that the demand lay to attach himself to these movements. Others had been shipwrecked by this temptation. Judas the Gaulonite also had been seized by Satan, and taken up into an exceeding high mountain, where all the kingdoms of the world could be seen:—the Arabians at war with the Romans, the swarming troops of the Parthians, the wild sons of Peræa contending against the legions, and the prospect of victory. He and others had succumbed under the temptation; they had mingled the Messianic idea with worldly interests; they had worshipped the prince of this world and had died. Nay, it is probable enough that in the year 34, when the hoof-tramp of the Parthian under Artabanus sounded through the steppes, and Aretas—his pride as father being insulted—was calling his Bedouins to arms, the thought of effecting Israel's salvation by the sword was more in the air than ever. Jesus, however, replied to this thought: "Get thee hence, Satan; for it is written, Thou shalt worship the Lord thy God, and Him only shalt thou serve." If the second temptation, as it is now often understood, mean this, that at some time or other the demand came to Jesus to make himself at first serviceable to the powers of this world in order that he might afterwards make them subject to himself, then certainly this impulse, as we gather from the whole tone of Jesus' mind, did not proceed from himself, but was thrust upon him by external circumstances. In fact, it was no mean resolve to appear before a people chafing under the yoke of the foreigner, and goaded on to the utmost blood-thirstiness, with the message: "Blessed are the peacemakers, for they shall be called the children of God; blessed are the meek, for they shall inherit the earth." But Jesus was able to do this. The peculiar sharpness, however, with which he repels every attempt to draw him into contemporary movements, shows that, nevertheless, he regarded this thought as a temptation. Did the pilgrims from the festival at Jerusalem return nome with the exciting news that Pilate had mingled the blood of the Galileans with that of their sacrifices, and with this passionate word expect him to utter the signal for rebellion against the oppressors of Israel, he ignores entirely the accusation against the Romans, and speaks not about the guilt of those who had met with the accident, but about the sins of the people which burdened them all so heavily. "Suppose ye that these Galileans were sinners above all the Galileans because they suffered such things? I tell you, Nay; but except ye repent, ye shall all perish in like manner. Or those eighteen upon whom the tower in Siloam fell and slew them, think ye that they were sinners above all men that dwelt in Jerusalem? I tell you, Nay; but except ye repent, ye shall all perish even thus."[1] The question, too, which agitates all Israel, as to whether the people of God might pay taxes to the Gentile emperor without destroying the sanctity of their land, does not touch him. "Show me the denarius. Whose is this image and superscription? Render, therefore, unto Cæsar the things that are Cæsar's, and unto God the things that are God's."[2] Without personal participation in these contests of the time, he knows nothing, too, of the aversion to the tax-gatherers or of the hatred towards the Samaritans; nay, he even presents to the orthodox the unheard-of spectacle of a teacher in Israel sitting at table with tax-gatherers and requesting shelter in Samaritan cottages.

If Jesus, consequently, could have nothing to do with the impelling motives of the time and the sympathies and antipathies of his people, still far less could he find union with one of the schools serviceable in advancing the kingdom of God.

From the ESSENES his whole conception of the world sepa-

---

[1] Luke xiii. 2—5.

[2] Matt. xxii. 15 f. This answer tells on every side; although were the inscription Gentile, on account of the imperial name, and the image sinful, on account of the law which allowed of no image or likeness, yet the giving of this coin could no longer destroy any consecration, since God claims other things than the revenue of the Israelitish ground.

rated him. This world was not to him impure, but the perfected creation of the Heavenly Father, and therefore he did not think of escaping its contact by prudent solitariness and anxious asceticism, and compensating for its contamination by still more frequent washings, still stricter fastings, and for this purpose adding a new order to those already existing. In the great market-place of life was the gospel to be preached, for the light had not been given in order to be put under a bushel.[1] Thus, too, he had no secret doctrine to communicate, like the masters of the Essenic covenant; no long registers of angels and strange revelations of the other world, which were confided to the adepts as secrets under the seal of awful oaths. His fundamental principle was the exact contrary; that which had been heard in the darkness was to be spoken in the light, that which had been spoken in the ear was to be proclaimed upon the house-tops, for the light ought to be set on a candlestick and not put under a bed.[2] All that can be truly said of any friendly relations to the Essenes, of whom the rationalistic age had so much to narrate, is, that whilst the Sadducees and Pharisees are directly attacked by Jesus, towards the Essenes he observes a benevolent silence, and indirectly, perhaps, he recognizes some of the principles by which they lived. If, for example, he finds those worthy of mention who for the sake of the kingdom of God remain unmarried, such praise is a commendation also of the Essenes;[3] and so, too, will it have been counted to their honour by him that they had long recognized that God had more pleasure in mercy than in sacrifice.[4] But this exhausts all his relations to the Essenic covenant.

So much the more zealously must that party have offered itself to Jesus which he met in the market-place of the life of the people, and that worked wholesalely upon the ecclesiasticism of the masses. This common work at once created relations between them, and the PHARISEES were at first in no

---

[1] Mark iv. 21.
[2] Luke viii. 17, xii. 2, 3.
[3] Matt. xix. 12.
[4] Matt. ix. 13.

way hostile to him. Jesus may have appeared to them as a herald of that expected kingdom, which they too proclaimed, and we do not find that they offered any difficulties at his first appearance. The synagogues, which were entirely under their influence, were open to Jesus, and he proclaimed his glad tidings in them unhindered. And naturally so, for his watchwords were the same as theirs, in so far that the significant words, "kingdom of heaven," "kingdom of God," "kingdom of the Great King," were to them, too, stars to which they looked upwards, and that shone and sparkled in their favourite books of Daniel, Enoch, the Sibylline Oracles, the Psalms of Solomon and in the Targums.[1] That his tidings were good, they could not therefore deny; they were only doubtful as to whether he were a worthy messenger. When they demanded a sign from him in order that they might attach credence to the fact that he had been sent, it was still an open question with them whether they might not be able to unite with him. Several Pharisees even invited him as a guest to their houses;[2] and in opposition to the hated tetrarch, who had erected his palace upon a former place of burial, there were still many, at a yet later period, upon his side, in order to prevent the blood of a prophet of the kingdom of God being shed anew by the hands of the Herods.[3] Certainly the opposition in principle between the kingdom of God proclaimed by Jesus and the theocracy which they represented was so great, that Jesus appeared to them to be one of the worst seducers of the people, as soon as the consequences of his thoughts were apparent. To Jesus, on the other hand, this state of affairs must have been evident from the first, for this simple reason, that he had evidently closely observed the Pharisees before his entrance on his public ministry; for a criticism like his can only be exercised when there is an accurate knowledge of the object of which it treats. In fact, it is proved by that decisive rebuff of the Pharisees in connection with the tribute-money that Jesus was well acquainted with the

---

[1] Keim, Jesus of Nazara, Vol. i. p. 348; compare the passages there given.
[2] Luke vii. 36.   [3] Luke xiii. 31.

theory of the Gaulonite; but the finer distinctions of the school also, as to which oath was valid and which not valid,[1] the theory about the various degrees of sanctity,[2] and the relations of purity and impurity in vessels and their contents, were thoroughly familiar to him ;[3] and with regard to the subject introduced by the schools, as to which was the chief commandment, he assumed a thoroughly decided position.[4] From this debate he was even able to appropriate a positive precept, that, namely, of Hillel: "What is hateful to thyself, do not to thy fellow; this is the whole law; all the rest is commentary."[5] It is this exact knowledge, however, which makes Jesus from the first assume that repellent attitude towards the Pharisees that shows that he is determined to keep his work from being mixed up with theirs.

Thus Jesus declined *all* external connections—for of the temple nobility in Jerusalem there could be no question whatever—and placed his tidings, singly and alone, in continuance of the revival effected by JOHN in Judæa. When John's voice behind the walls of Machærus grew silent, he came forth; and when in the autumn the news of the Baptist's death spread through Galilee, he sent out his messengers to the twelve tribes of Israel. The re-assumption of John's words, "Repent, for the kingdom of heaven has drawn nigh," was to make the people immediately aware of the identity of the new preaching with that of John; and in his words about the Baptist, Jesus comprehended his activity and that of the Baptist under one category as the preaching of the kingdom, and contrasted it with the expired prophetic age as the age of action.[6] It is in the same sense that he calls the Baptist the precursor of the kingdom foretold by Malachi, and assures the disciples "that Elijah is come already and they knew him not, but have done unto him whatsoever they listed."[7] It is in this connection that the oldest account of the evangelical history already sees the work of Jesus: "The

---

[1] Matt. xxiii. 16, v. 33.   [2] Matt. xxiii. 17.   [3] Matt. xxiii. 25.
[4] Matt. xxii. 37.   [5] Matt. vii. 12; compare Grätz, iii. 226.
[6] Matt. xi. 12.   [7] Matt. xvii. 12.

beginning of the gospel of Jesus Christ was John baptizing in the wilderness and preaching the baptism of repentance for the remission of sins." How far these words were true to Jesus himself, and what was the motive-power of the incitements which he brought back from the Jordan to Galilee, it is difficult to determine. There cannot, however, be any doubt but that the mighty personality of the Baptist had made a great impression upon him also. He has expressly testified that John had come in the way of righteousness,[1] that his baptism had been of heaven and not of men.[2] Nay, he even compared him to the most mighty of the witnesses to the covenant.[3] What reverence this age had for Elijah! The son of Sirach knows no second like him. "Then stood up Elijah," he declares, "a prophet like fire, and his word burned like a lamp. He brought a sore famine upon Israel, and by his zeal he diminished their number. By the word of the Lord he shut up the heaven, and three times brought down fire. O Elijah! how wast thou honoured in thy glorious deeds, and who may glory like unto thee! Who didst raise up a dead man from death, and his soul from the underworld by the word of the Most High: who broughtest kings to destruction, and honourable men from their seat: who heardest the rebuke of the Lord in Sinai, and in Horeb the judgment of vengeance: who didst anoint kings to take revenge, and prophets to succeed after him: who wast taken up in a whirlwind of fire and in a chariot of fiery horses: who wast ordained for reproofs for future times, to pacify the wrath before the Lord's judgment, and to turn the heart of the father unto the son, and to restore the tribes of Jacob. Blessed are they that saw thee!"[4] We see that all the majesty of prophecy was believed to be incorporated in the Tishbite, and yet the comparison with Elijah hardly sufficed for Jesus to describe the greatness of John: "If ye will receive it, this is Elijah, which is to come." It is not a prophet that he calls him, but more than a prophet, for "among those

---

[1] Matt. xxi. 32. [2] Matt. xxi. 24.
[3] Matt. xi. 14. [4] Ecclesiasticus xlviii. 1—11.

that are born of women there has not arisen a greater than John the Baptist."[1] When Jesus thus spoke of him, all the images of that time again became living to him,—the flags whispering on the river-side, and the prophet thundering forth his denunciations; the reed shaken by the wind, and the mighty, heroic man; the well-clad courtiers of Antipas, and the dweller in the desert on whom the camel's skin hung,[2]—a proof that the impressions which the speaker had brought back with him from the place of baptism at Jericho were deep.

But at the same time there remains the fact that Jesus declared the least in the kingdom of God greater than this same John. And we have already seen why. For John, in fine, had also attempted to form the kingdom of God merely by the worn-out means of Judaism. Repentance and fasting, watching and rough clothing, and the blessing of the waters of Jordan, were yet the only means of winning the kingdom which his disciples possessed when he left them behind in the world, sorrowing like mourners. Jesus, consequently, can see in this Baptist movement only the *beginning* of the kingdom of God, a first attempt at assault, in which the mighty besieger falls while still before the gates, and beholds the kingdom itself only afar off, like Moses, beside whom he is buried.[3] His attempt to found the kingdom of God had at last led merely to outward asceticism instead of inward regeneration. The Baptist movement at its commencement had not been so intended, it is true; but as the Baptist had chosen the water of Jordan and the wilderness, fasting and rough clothing, as means for arousing the multitude, the fault was his that his disciples, following the example of the Essenes, made the means into an end, and sought the kingdom of God in outward usages. Therefore was it that Jesus reproached the school of John, in that it had put the new wine into the old bottles, the bottles burst and the wine was spilled. It had put the patch of unfulled cloth into the old garment, and the rent had been made worse. With their fastings

---

[1] Matt. xi. 11.   [2] Matt. xi. 7—14.   [3] Matt. xi. 12.

and countenances soured by asceticism, the followers of John resembled mourners; just as though the coming of the kingdom were a funeral; whilst *his* disciples are like the marriage guests who greet the bridegroom.[1] The position of Jesus to John is most clearly declared in these expressions. The Baptist had a knowledge of the kingdom of God, and attempted to form it, but his means had been perverted ones. The kingdom of God could not be established by these old means and forms. The attempt only destroyed the old without founding the new. The decayed and rotten theocratic forms fall to pieces when it is attempted to infuse a new spirit and meaning into them; but the new thoughts also are lost, in that they are pressed into forms that are foreign to them. The repentance which the kingdom of God requires is not to be shown in the penitential forms of Judaism; the wine is spilled, the rent is made worse. From this it follows, therefore: put not the new wine into old bottles, turn away from tradition, and let the new spirit seek such vesture and form as are suited to it.

The gloomy tone of the Johannine school, moreover, seems to have met with little sympathy from Jesus. He sees no reason why the children of the kingdom of God should go about sorrowing like mourners. The disposition in which he greets the kingdom of God on its descent from heaven, has nothing in common with the penitential psalms and terrible words of the prophets so familiar to John. His mind is full of exultation and festive joy at the love of the Father, which he beholds everywhere poured out over the world; and to become perfect as He is, is the only rule, precept, prayer and asceticism which he enjoins on his disciples. But in doing this, he has drawn such a definite boundary between his field of labour and that of John, that even the most explicit connection with John's efforts, so magnanimously recognized by him, is not able to make him appear as the continuator of the Baptist movement.

Of all the points of contact which the age offered, Jesus

---

[1] Matt. ix. 14—17; Mark ii. 18—22; Luke v. 33—39.

accepted only the most customary of all: he entered into the customs of the Galilean teachers, which could astonish no one, as it was of daily occurrence, spoke in the synagogue and taught in the congregation. He preached the kingdom of God, yet not between the sublime precipices of the wilderness, but from the homely platform of the synagogue. He appeared before the people, not in the prophet's mantle, but in the usual dress of the Jewish man, at the four ends of which the customary tassels were not wanting.[1] While the Pharisees, Essenes and John had summoned to their aid the rhetoric of countenances worn by asceticism, broad phylacteries and an impressive nature, in order to touch the heart, Jesus did the most customary thing of all, he came forward to give the Midrash when the Thorah had been read.

9. THE FIRST MESSIANIC COMMUNITY.

In founding that which, as a matter of history, Jesus has founded, a circle of communities, namely, in which the principles of the kingdom of God are realized, and out of which the great kingdom of God is finally to be built up, cell by cell, he pursued a method so inconspicuous, that it can be well understood how to the more distant portions of the people—as the circles of the historian Josephus, for example—the whole ministry of Jesus could remain unknown. For the world, however, in which he lived, his activity, limited at first to speaking, must yet have made a powerful impression. The spiritual barrenness of the synagogue at that time, and the meagre sustenance afforded by its preaching of the law, best elucidates the saying, "They were astonished at his teaching; for he taught them as having authority, and not as the scribes."[2] We are acquainted with those discourses of the scribes with which the synagogues re-echoed, for example, from the Book of Jubilees. There the most minute

---

[1] Matt. ix. 20; Mark vi. 56; Luke viii. 44. [2] Matt. vii. 28, 29.

precepts regarding the Sabbath are inculcated as though they were the very foundations of the moral order of the universe; there the sorts and qualities of the sacrificial wood, the range of the tithes, the perniciousness of eating blood, the indispensability of being circumcised on the eighth day, are discoursed upon with as great a zeal as though the right conditions of an existence really worthy of man were contained in them. This was the morality and religion of his contemporaries; so that certainly the word of Jesus, drawing from the deepest depths, in itself explains that movement of the spirit which now awoke in Capernaum. The Synoptics tell of a mighty concourse of the multitudes,[1] which, it is true, never attained the height of the Baptist movement, and was essentially confined to Galilee, but yet is so important, that Jesus could be plainly called the Prophet of the Galileans. As soon as it is noised abroad that Jesus is in Capernaum, so many throng to the little house of Peter that the narrow court-yard is unable to contain them.[2] He has to direct his disciples to have a small boat ready for him, in order that he may withdraw from the throng of the people,[3] or he escapes through the back door to the mountains, in order to pass lonely nights there in prayer.[4] Even a quite peculiar feature of the confluence of the people at this time is preserved by Mark: "And they went into a house, and the multitude cometh together again, so that they could not so much as eat bread."[5]

The reason for this concourse was certainly not only the news of his preaching, but still more that of his deeds. It is a fact testified to by the collective branches of the evangelical tradition, that the cures and casting out of devils—which were at that time expected by Judaism from its Rabbis, and which the Essenic prophets and Qabbalists were accustomed to practise by means of nostrums, exorcisms and all kinds of sorcery—were performed on his side by Jesus also, but through the mere force of his

[1] Mark i. 32, 33, 45, ii. 2, 4, 15, iii. 3, 7, 10, ix. 15, &c.
[2] Mark ii. 2.   [3] Mark iii. 9.   [4] Mark i. 45.   [5] Mark iii. 20.

personal influence and the power of his word. The same curative excitement which the Rabbis produced by incantations and enchantments, by wonderful manipulations and mysteriously awful formulæ, was here obtained simply by the mere presence of the Master, whose word assured the sick that he had authority from God. Should he, who drew his disciples from their nets or the plough, before whom the woman that was a sinner melted into tears, whose visit converted Zacchæus and the yet harder natures of tax-gatherers, whose look kept Mary motionless in devotion, and at whose feet hundreds found rest unto their souls,—should he not exercise the same spiritual effect as the magic wand of the Qabbalists and the charm of the Rabbis? Nay, rather was this activity of a prophet so self-evident to his contemporaries, that they did not wait until *he* offered help, but came of themselves to him. Some pressed to him themselves, others were carried. Ashamed, did the woman secretly ill stretch forth her hand from behind to his garment, while another publicly confessed his sins and their penalty. Did one not venture to beg Jesus to visit his house, another is brought into his own house in order that he cannot avoid helping him. The blind cry by the way-side, "Thou Son of David, have mercy on us!" and the Canaanitish woman follows him even after he has repulsed her with hard words. Especially do those sick from demoniacal possession feel the greatness—sustained by the enthusiasm of the whole neighbourhood—of this prophetic figure. They tremble in every limb; they strive to fly, and feel that they are held fast; they cry out against their tormentor, and yet in his will become conscious of their own will, which alone has power over the evil spirit. Jesus appears in these cases generally in a state of emotional exaltation. "He is beside himself," said his mother and brethren when they saw him thus for the first time. "He casts out devils by the greater demon which is in him," declared the reviling Pharisees; and his disciples speak also of his *threatening* the evil spirits. Thus it is now a word of command that he directs towards the sick: "Hold thy peace and come out of him, thou unclean spirit!" "I say unto thee, arise!" "Take up thy bed and walk." Now, according to the state of the case, it is a word of consolation, which redeems the faint-hearted and attains by warm emotion what in the other case was effected by sudden fright: "Be it unto thee, as thou hast believed;" "Woman, thou art loosed from thine infirmity;" "Son, be of good cheer; thy sins are forgiven thee." The magic chain which exists between him and the sick is the faith, which manifests itself in some as terror and in others as trust. Where thousands believe, he who needs help believes a thousand-fold. Thus his will was in a condition for again arousing so much will as was, above all, necessary for recovery.[1] How far the miraculous accounts related are historical, can no longer be positively determined from sources the oldest of which is thirty years later than the events narrated, and which in details often contradict each other. On the whole, the picture presented by the Synoptical Gospels of this miraculous activity will be a faithful one. Thus have the eye-witnesses described Jesus, and assuredly this is what he was to them. There are, moreover, more concrete remembrances in existence of how Jesus became a worker of miracles, and some narratives have better credentials than others.

In the account presented by the most ancient of the Gospels,[2] Jesus' miraculous action on the possessed and suffering appears, on the first occasion, to have been in consequence of a great spiritual revival, which, through him, had taken hold of Capernaum. His first appearance took place on the Sabbath in the synagogue. Whilst Jesus was speaking and a feeling of astonishment ran through the assembly at his words, a man possessed suddenly screamed out, "What have we to do with thee, Jesus of Nazareth? Thou art come to destroy us. I know thee who thou art, the Holy One of God. And Jesus rebuked him, saying, Hold thy peace, and come out of him: and the unclean spirit tare him, and cried with a loud voice, and came out of

---

[1] Keim, Jesus of Nazara, T. T. F. L. Vol. iii. 226—249.   [2] Mark i. 21—34.

him." Then the assembly broke up in unmeasured astonishment. "It is a new teaching," the people of Capernaum declared. "With authority he commandeth even the unclean spirits, and they obey him. And immediately his fame spread abroad throughout all the surrounding region."[1] As Jesus now returned to his house, Peter's wife's mother, who lay sick of a fever, stretched out her arms towards him and he took her by the hand; "and immediately the fever left her and she ministered unto them." The news of the Master's fresh deed spread like wild-fire in Capernaum. The people collected in crowds, in the evening, at the door of Peter's house. All those in the little town that are possessed, diseased or sick, are brought to him. "And Jesus healed many that were sick of divers diseases, and cast out many devils; and suffered not the devils to speak, because they knew him."[2] Then, however, he withdraws from the people, and escapes before the break of day to a solitary place, in order that he may there pray in solitude. From morning until evening has Mark's Gospel in its narrative followed this memorable day, for the very reason, indeed, that it remained in remembrance as one especially decisive to the witnesses of this time. The first cures appear, according to this tradition, consequently, as the immediate sequence of the great religious commotion which had taken hold of Capernaum;[3] and just as Jesus himself is most deeply moved whilst healing the people—"rebuking," "looking round with anger," "being moved with compassion," "looking up to heaven, and sighing"—and however else Mark may express it[4]—so, too, a similar frame of mind in the people is requisite for success; for when this exaltation does not run through the people, and the individual does not feel, from contact with Jesus, the electric spark of faith or a holy thrill of adora-

---

[1] Mark i. 23—28.

[2] Compare the amplifications in Weizsäcker, Unters. über d. ev. Geschichte, p. 364. Holtzmann, Synopt. Ev. p. 480. Ewald, Gesch. Israel, v. 218.

[3] Before this event, Jesus had only preached; compare Weizsäcker, p. 364.

[4] Mark i. 25, 43, v. 40, vii. 34, v. 9, 25.

tion, then the miraculous power is also wanting. Thus the primitive historical account plainly and openly records how there were unsuccessful attempts at healing in unbelieving Nazareth. "And he could there do no mighty work, save that he laid his hands upon a few sick folk, and he healed them. And he marvelled because of their unbelief."[1]

Between the former wonderful results and the latter failures just recorded, there stand, however, those cures and casting out of demons which pass away again with the relaxation of the tension and exaltation of the mental life. Jesus explains this fact as the incapacity of the sick person to protect himself against fresh attacks of the evil one. "When the unclean spirit is gone out of a man, it goeth through dry places, seeking rest, and findeth none. Then it saith, I will return into my house from whence I came out; and cometh and findeth it empty, swept and garnished. Then goeth it, and taketh with itself seven other spirits more wicked than itself, and they enter in and dwell there; and the last state of that man becometh worse than the first."[2] Whilst Jesus here finds the origin of the phenomenon of the return of the disease in the sick person's state of mind, it seems to have been a usual explanation that in such cases the sick person was tormented by more than one demon, so that a single expulsion did not suffice. The diseased Gadarene had even a legion of evil spirits in him, which means that he seemed incurable by all the means that had been tried in vain upon him. In the same manner, one may suppose that the disease in Mary of the neighbouring Magdala had returned seven times, since Jesus cast seven evil spirits out of her.[3] Otherwise Jesus himself puts his cures under the same category as those of the Rabbis. "If I by Beelzebub cast out the devils, by whom do your sons cast them out?"[4] does he demand of the

---

[1] Mark vi. 5; compare Mark v. 34, ix. 24, Matt. ix. 28.
[2] Matt. xii. 43—45.   [3] Mark xvi. 9; Luke viii. 2.
[4] Matt. xii. 27. So Keim, d. gesch. Chr.: "He did on a great scale what they did on a small one." For the cures of the Rabbis, compare Bell. Jud. vii. 6, 3; Antiq. viii. 2, 5; and Dial. cum Trypho, 1.

Jews. The presumption which he claims for his deeds is only that made by the other teachers for themselves, that it is *God* who is operative in them, especially as one devil would not hurt the other.[1] In the same manner, in the circle of his disciples, healing is not his prerogative merely, but he instructs his followers that they are to cast out devils, to anoint the sick with oil, to lay their hands upon them and to pray over them, promising them that the devils will be subject to them. Nay, even those who did not follow Jesus made these attempts *in his name*—just as mighty names generally played an important part in the exorcisms of the Rabbis; and Jesus said to his disciples, who were indignant at it: "Forbid him not: for there is no man which shall do a miracle in my name and shall be able lightly to speak evil of me."[2] The consciousness of this power remained with the followers of Jesus throughout the whole of the primitive age of the Church, but it was always considered to be a gift which was possessed by one, and not by another; which was mighty at one time, and at another withheld.[3] But it was just because Jesus does not ascribe these cures to some mysterious power operative in himself, but to the state of mind of the sick, that it does not occur to him, in case of failure, to be himself disconcerted, but is then simply astonished at their unbelief. Nothing else certainly could have produced such an effect upon the people; and contributed to the concourse of the multitudes, as the news that the Prophet at Capernaum has power over all diseases and all evil spirits. The besieging of Peter's door, too, is to be for the most part thus understood; and wherever Jesus appears, there the sick throng to him in crowds in order to touch the border of his garment,[4] for simply from this touching did many a one expect to recover. That centurion of Antipas could even think, soldier-like, that Jesus commanded the demons like a guard which comes or goes as it is commanded.[5]

---

[1] Matt. xii. 26.
[2] Mark ix. 39.
[3] Matt. xvii. 20; Mark ix. 18, xvi. 18; 1 Cor. xii. 10, 28, 29.
[4] Matt. ix. 20, xiv. 36.
[5] Matt. viii. 9.

To the miracle-seekers of the time, especially among this superstitious people, would it seem proper enough to make their recognition of Jesus as a credible messenger of the Messianic kingdom dependent upon some palpable, thorough-going miracle which should exclude all doubt. We have credible witnesses to the fact that this demand, "Show some sign," was a temptation to many a man at this period, because hoping that Jehovah would not deny his prophet. When proof was demanded, they did not hesitate a moment in promising the people all the deeds of Moses and Joshua, and they had confidence enough in their mission to venture the attempt. Thus, under the procurator Fadus, a certain Theudas commanded the people to assemble at the Jordan, in order that he might lead Israel through the river dry-shod.[1] Under Felix, a prophet even promised to overthrow the walls of Jerusalem, as formerly Joshua had done those of Jericho, and collected 30,000 men for the purpose on the Mount of Olives; others summoned the people into the wilderness, where they promised them to bring the signs of the kingdom of God.[2] The more firmly a man believed in his mission, the more natural was the thought of compelling the belief of the people by *one* great deed, and so putting all the unwilling to silence. When, therefore, it happened, that Jesus himself saw results proceeding from his words, his prayers, his rebukes, which he could not ascribe to any natural connection of things, the thought of superadding to the internal truth of his preaching an external attestation by some unequivocal miracle, and thus assuring its willing and credenced acceptance, may very well have gained, for the moment, a seductive power. In fact, we do find in that parabolical narrative, in which Jesus seems to have clothed the history of the temptations which met him on his difficult path—that after the first temptation, to use his gifts in order by their aid to make bread—after the second, to worship the spirit of this world in order to obtain the more certain power and influence for himself—as the third temptation, there was

---

[1] Antiq. xx. 5, 1.   [2] Bell. Jud. i. 13, 4.

the thought of performing some sign which should exclude all doubt. The thought became doubly natural when justified from the Scriptures, and thus the Gospel represents Jesus as really standing upon the roof of the western porch of the temple, where Jerusalem, with its roofs and cupolas, lay at a precipitous depth below him. "If thou art the Son of God, cast thyself down," does the evil one say to him, whilst he refers to the words of the 91st Psalm, "For He shall give His angels charge over thee, to keep thee in all thy ways. They shall bear thee up in their hands, lest thou dash thy foot against a stone."[1] Jesus heard this voice, as Theudas and others had heard it, but he declared to it, "It is written again, Thou shalt not tempt the Lord thy God."[2] How far a real occurrence lies at the bottom of this symbolical narrative, and how much of it belongs to the parabolical vesture, cannot be decided. It is a fact, however, that this temptation from without occurred to him more than once. If he on every occasion repelled it, without doubt that luminous passage of Scripture, "Thou shalt not tempt the Lord thy God," was his guiding star. But here, too, the unusual sharpness of his rejection of the demand whenever it occurs seems to mean just this, that he recognizes it to be a temptation. For this reason also does he forbid people to mention his cures,[3] and in nowise recognizes it as a proof of a true faith when any one is able to perform signs in *his* name. Many who prophesy and perform signs in his name will nevertheless be denied by him at the last judgment. It is wholly on the inward possession of the kingdom of God that he places everything. Neither is the power of working miracles, so wondered at by the people, the ultimate proof to him of his mission, nor is the adjuration of demons in his name by others a proof of their discipleship. He who receives the kingdom of God is his disciple, and no one else. Therefore, also, does he regard the greater influx of a curious multitude as in no way an advancement of the kingdom

---

[1] Psalm xci. 11, 12.   [2] Deut. vi. 16.
[3] Mark i. 34, 44, v. 43, vii. 36, viii. 26.

of God; he forbids his cures to be noised abroad, and endeavours to escape as much as possible from the concourse produced by them, so that we find him at last constantly engaged in retreating from the people. Although he wished, finally, to be recognized by the whole of the people, yet it was nevertheless without any appeal to the stormy fanaticism of the people. A proportionately important part of his discourses assumes, on the contrary, a smaller circle of true followers, disciples and learners as his hearers; so that, in addition to his activity in public, his power is, even with preference, dedicated to the instruction of a little community. Josephus has, at a later period, spoken with the bitterness of a renegade of these little Messianic flocks, which sprang up at that time on every side, and which he—whether they joined the patriotic movement of the Gaulonite or the prophetic one of the Baptist—terms robbers or deceivers, and whom he verbosely accuses of being the cause of the feverish commotion in Judæa. Here, now, are we able to look into the internal life and external activity of such a flock, which—led by a Prophet whom the Pharisaic apostate doubtless reckoned also among the numerous " deceivers " of the time—lives in hopes of the coming kingdom.

The first and MORE INTIMATE CIRCLE had been, as it seems, an accidental one. We see in Capernaum, at first, certain friendly families flocking around Jesus. The house most intimately connected with him is that of the fisherman Jona,[1] relatively that of his two sons Simon and Andrew, under whose roof Jesus found shelter. Simon was married, and his wife, who at a later period accompanied him on his missionary journeys,[2] had her mother living with her, so that we have to think of Jesus, in Capernaum, as an inmate in a numerous family.[3] Another believing family was that of the fisherman Zebedee, who, it has been attempted to prove, was Jesus' uncle.[4] The religious

---

[1] Matt. xvi. 17.   [2] 1 Cor. ix. 5.   [3] Mark i. 30.
[4] By identifying the mother of the sons of Zebedee, mentioned in Matt. xxvii. 56, with the sister of Jesus' mother, mentioned in John xix. 25.

tendency of this family had its source in Salome, his wife, who sometimes accompanied Jesus himself on his journeys,[1] and on one occasion threw herself vehemently at her Master's feet, with her sons, desiring for James and John the highest places in the kingdom of God.[2] Zebedee himself is never mentioned except in connection with his nets. "They left their father Zebedee in the ship with the hired servants, and went away after Jesus."[3] A fifth disciple, besides these two pairs of brothers, was found in the tax-gatherer Levi, the son of a certain Alphæus [Cleopas], who must also have belonged to the friendly circle.[4] Levi, who was called Matthew, had a place in the toll-house on the neighbouring frontier, as collector of tolls. His duties, consequently, were to search the transports of merchandize travelling to and fro on the *via maris* between the territories of the two tetrarchs, to make a note of their value on the table of tolls, to levy the toll, and book and deliver the proceeds to the tax-farmers.[5] That he was the first among the disciples of Jesus who wrote down the sayings and discourses of the Master, agrees well with the fact that he, from his previous occupation, was more accustomed than the others to use the style. Besides this older circle of disciples, there are certain women mentioned, "which had been healed of evil spirits and infirmities, Mary called Magdalene, out of whom had gone seven devils, and Joanna the wife of Chuza, Herod's steward, and Susanna, and many others, which ministered unto him of their substance."[6]

---

[1] Mark xv. 40, xvi. 1; Matt. xxvii. 56.
[2] Matt. xx. 20.
[3] Mark i. 20.
[4] Mark ii. 14.
[5] The action of the minor toll-officials is clearly portrayed in Philostratus, Apollon. i. 20. On his entrance into Mesopotamia, the toll-collector at Zeugma led him to the table of tolls, and asked him what they brought. Apollonius answered, "I bring frugality, righteousness, virtue, temperance, manliness and endurance," and in this way gave a series of names which are of the feminine gender. Whereupon the toll-collector, who had only his gains in view, said that he had consequently entered these female servants. Apollonius, however, rejoined, "Not so; for it is not servants that I am bringing, but mistresses." That tolls were levied on the frontiers of even the most insignificant territories is made clear from Plin. Hist. Nat. xii. 32, 6, according to which the freight for incense between Gaza and Thauma, on account of the numerous tolls, came to 688 denarii.
[6] Luke viii. 2, 3.

Before Jesus, however, had called his fifth disciple, he had again left Capernaum in order to avoid the influx of the masses as much as possible. When, in consequence of that day of miracles, his house was not empty until nightfall, "in the morning, rising up a great while before day, he went out, and departed into a solitary place, and there prayed. And Simon and they that were with him followed after him and found him; and they said unto him, All men seek for thee. And he said unto them, Let us go elsewhere into the neighbouring towns, that I may preach there also; for therefore came I forth. And he preached in their synagogues throughout all Galilee, and cast out devils."[1] His short absence, however, had in nowise abated the curiosity of the multitude. When he returned to Capernaum, and the people heard that he was in the house, "straightway many were gathered together, insomuch that there was no room to receive them—no, not so much as about the door; and he spake the word unto them."[2]

A new cure, that of a man sick of the palsy, marks this visit also. Jesus' reference to the man's consciousness of sin, and his words of consolation, "Thy sins are forgiven thee," now, however, excite the opposition of certain scribes, who from the first do not accept the new Prophet with the immediate confidence of the believing multitude. Whilst he now, not in the synagogue, but on the shore of the lake, is addressing the people, and, proceeding farther, enters into the house of Levi at the toll-house, the dissension of the Rabbis of Capernaum breaks out into open opposition. "Why doth he eat and drink with publicans and sinners?" is their first question; to which they soon add other reflections on the neglect of fasting, on the plucking by the disciples of the ears of corn, and on the healing on the Sabbath-day by their Master. From this we learn that Jesus from the first, in accordance with his preaching of the kingdom of God, put the Jewish ordinances aside as things indifferent, yet without taking up any polemical action against them; but from the publicity of Oriental

[1] Mark i. 35—39.   [2] Mark ii. 3.

life, such an untheocratic attitude must have become in the shortest time an object of public discussion. Was the question, however, once suggested, then the Pharisees and the officials of Antipas had a common interest with regard to Jesus in opposing his ministry; and as, for the sons of the southern sun, the distance between thought and action is only a very short one, they were already credited with designs upon his life. Thus we see Jesus, after a very short period of action, driven out of Capernaum.[1] In order to avoid being condemned by the synagogue and put to death by Antipas, he speedily withdraws to some part on the lake not more definitely described, but situated probably on the coast of Philip's dominions. A small ship which belonged to one of his disciples is always kept in readiness, in order that he may be able to change his place of abode quickly, "because of the multitude, lest they should throng him. For he had healed many; insomuch that they pressed upon him to touch him."[2]

From this time, Jesus' life is a wandering one, and many allusions in the Collection of Sayings call to mind the toilsomeness of the journeys in the heat of the sun, when the corn is standing high,[3] on the stony paths of Judæa, where corn-fields alternate with thorn-thickets and debris of rock,[4] or along the glaring walls of the vineyard,[5] or on the parched limestone plateau, where the traveller accepts the cup of cold water as a benefit to be repaid in the kingdom of God.[6] "Sufficient unto the day is the evil thereof,"[7] Jesus declares to his disciples; and a sad picture of his privations is presented when he dissuades a young man who desires to join the not yet completed circle of his disciples with the words: "The foxes have holes, and the birds of the air have nests; but the Son of Man hath not where to lay his head."[8] The primitive document [Grundschrift] has

---

[1] Mark iii. 7. [2] Mark iii. 10. [3] Mark ii. 23; Matt. xii. 1, ix. 37.
[4] Matt. xiii. 2—8, iv. 6. [5] Matt. xxi. 33, xx. 12.
[6] Matt. x. 42. [7] Matt. vi. 34.
[8] Matt. viii. 20; Luke ix. 57. These words are taken from the Collection of Sayings, and are put by Luke in the journey through Samaria; by Matthew at the beginning of

comprehended this period of Jesus' wanderings, which preceded the completion of the circle of disciples in the twelve, in the words contained in Matthew: "And Jesus went about all the cities and villages, teaching in their synagogues, and preaching the gospel of the kingdom, and healing every sickness and every disease. But seeing the multitudes, he was moved with compassion for them, because they were harassed and scattered abroad, as sheep not having a shepherd. Then saith he unto his disciples, The harvest truly is plenteous, but the labourers are few; pray ye, therefore, the Lord of the harvest, that He will send forth labourers into His harvest."[1] The picture which Jesus uses is manifestly suggested by the aspect which the fields of Galilee presented to him on his return. The corn, which was half-ripe when he departed, so that it could be plucked, has now been gathered in by the reapers. It is the time of year which the book of Ruth so charmingly describes. The bound-up sheaves have been piled together, and wherever the reapers have finished, the poor glean the stalks that remain.[2] The passing traveller cries, "The blessing of Jehovah be upon you;" and the reapers reply, "We bless you in the name of Jehovah."[3] Jesus also found that it was now time to hire reapers for the coming harvest. We find him again in Capernaum at his accustomed work; there he summons "whom he would," the mutually-related families, "to the mountain;" without doubt the same place where he was accustomed to pray in solitude.[4] In any case, "the mountain was well known to the Christian community, and by it piously revered;—more probably it was one of the hills between Capernaum and Chorazin than Tell Hattin, lying three leagues to the south in the valley of Magdala, which is now pointed out as the "Mount of Beatitudes."[5]

Jesus' ministry, before calling the twelve. Certainly, after the circle had been completed, a thirteenth could not well offer himself.

[1] Matt. ix. 35—37. Mark has generally abbreviated the commencement of the calling of the twelve. Compare Holtzmann, Synopt. Evg. 74.

[2] Ruth ii. 3, 15. [3] Ruth ii. 4; Psalm cxxix. 8.

[4] According to Luke; compare Mark iii. 13, Matt. v. 1, Luke vi. 12.

[5] Stanley, Sinai and Palestine, 5th edition, p. 368.

Here, in view of the lake and mountains, Jesus once more laid before his companions the principles of the kingdom of heaven; and so deeply has this "Sermon on the Mount" impressed itself upon the remembrance of his followers, that two Evangelists undertook afterwards to re-construct it, and this significant name includes in our Matthew a great part of the Collection of Sayings.[1] It is, moreover, quite possible that the eight blessings on those for whom the kingdom is appointed, the exhortations to his followers to be as salt to the strengthless world, to enlighten the darkness, and his lamentations over the schools which heighten the letter and neglect the spirit, were spoken at this very time. After this address, Jesus chose twelve men from those present in order "that they should be with him, and that he might send them forth to preach, and to have power to heal sicknesses and to cast out devils."[2]

The five who had accompanied Jesus up to this period were re-chosen. Most of the others also probably came from the believing families of Capernaum. Thus there were the sons of Cleopas and Mary, James and Judas; the latter, to distinguish him from the betrayer, was called "Lebbæus," the man of heart, or "Thaddæus," the man of mind.[3] Philip, according to an account of uncertain origin, lived in the neighbouring Bethsaida.[4] Thomas, too, according to the same tradition, was a Galilean.[5] Simon is designated by his surname, the Zealot, as a participator in those movements which, a generation before, had originated in the neighbouring Gamala, but that now found a home in every part of the land.[6] Only of one of those chosen by Jesus is it certain that he was not a Galilean, but a Judæan; and this solitary man from Judah, who had found admittance into this circle of Galileans, was the one who betrayed him.

To this narrower circle from this time forth was the work of

[1] The primitive document contains them also. Compare Ewald, Evangel. p. 208; Holtzmann, Synopt. 76.

[2] Mark iii. 14, 15.

[3] Mark iii. 18, xv. 40; Luke vi. 16; Acts i. 13; Eusebius, Hist. Ecc. iv. 22.

[4] John i. 44.   [5] John xxi. 2.   [6] Antiq. xviii. 1. 6.

Jesus most especially directed. The twelve he calls henceforth his companions, friends and brethren, his servants[1] and labourers,[2] or his children and little ones. They are the salt of the earth, the light of the world,[3] the inhabitants of the city that lieth on a hill,[4] the exemplars for whose good works men will glorify God,[5] his fellow-labourers at the plough,[6] the fishers of men,[7] who catch souls for the kingdom of God. The name Apostle (Malachim, Sheluchim) itself shows that the circle in which the principles of the kingdom were first to be realized had been from the very beginning intended to be the commencement of a mission which should set ever-widening wave-circles in motion; and that Jesus chose exactly twelve apostles was an unmistakable sign that the preaching of the kingdom was destined for all Israel. On the whole, tolerably individual outlines of at least the heads of this first little community which Jesus gathered around himself have been preserved for us.

Its recognized head is SIMON, the son of Jona, whom Jesus called his Peter, or Cephas, that is, his rock, probably more because Simon was a true support of the affairs of the kingdom from the first, than to designate any peculiarity in the character of the oldest of the apostles. For with all the fidelity and warmth of his genuinely Galilean heart, Peter was yet of a thoroughly sanguine disposition, with all the amiabilities and weak peculiarities belonging to this temperament. He it is who, as spokesman of the disciples, always finds the answer most quickly, but occasionally also incurs the strongest censure on its account;[8] who is the first to draw the sword for Jesus, but also first to deny him.[9] His whole life long did he act from the impulse of the moment, and more than once boldly assume a position of which he despaired sooner than became an apostle, when once he had recognized its danger.[10]

---

[1] Matt. x. 24. [2] Matt. ix. 37, xx. 1. [3] Matt. v. 13, 14.
[4] Matt. v. 14. [5] Matt. v. 16. [6] Luke ix. 62.
[7] Matt. iv. 19. [8] Mark viii. 29—33. [9] Luke xxii. 50, 57.
[10] Gal. ii. 12; Luke xxii. 54, 57. So symbolically in Matt. xiv. 29, 30.

The characters of the SONS OF ZEBEDEE, to whom Jesus, on account of their impetuosity, added the name of Sons of Thunder,[1] appear to us to have been not without an alloy of sharpness and passionateness. They had brought with them, when they came to Jesus, hopes of an earthly kingdom;[2] and when the Samaritans had on one occasion dared to deny Jesus hospitality, they had reminded their Master of the angry Elijah, and demanded vengeance from heaven for the insulted dignity of the kingdom of God. "But Jesus turned and rebuked them; and they went into another village."[3] Characteristic is it also that John, returning from an expedition, informed Jesus, "Master, we saw one casting out devils in thy name, and we forbad him because he followed not with us;" and now, too, did Jesus rebuke him for this harsh exclusiveness, with the significant words, "Forbid him not; for he that is not against us is for us."[4] Next to them, the tax-gatherer MATTHEW was probably the most important member of this enlarged circle. At any rate, he was the first of them all who took up the style to preserve Jesus' words for succeeding generations.[5] What we know of the rest is little, but the characteristic expressions used about them confirm the feeling of confidence which we spontaneously repose in those chosen by Jesus. That JUDAS received the surname of LEBBÆUS, or THADDÆUS, shows that one feature of his mind which characterized him was faithfulness, benevolence. But the surname, too, of the Zealot which SIMON bore was at this period a title of honour, for those were not the worst who burned with zeal for the law, and with the dying Mattathias declared, "Now hath pride and correction gotten strength, and the time of destruction, and the wrath of indignation. Now therefore, my sons, be ye zealots for the law, and give your lives for the covenant of our fathers."[6] How, finally, JUDAS from Karioth became included in this circle, remains a mystery, like all else concerning this man. That he got the surname, "the man from Karioth," a name

---

[1] Mark iii. 17.   [2] Mark x. 35.   [3] Luke ix. 55, 56.
[4] Luke ix. 49, 50.   [5] Euseb. Ecc. Hist. iii. 39.   [6] 1 Maccabees ii. 49, 50.

telling nothing of his nature, can be explained either from the simple fact that there was nothing else to remark about him, or that the distance of his home was at first worthy of observation to the people on the lake-side who were so well known to each other. His love of money is throughout the most conspicuous feature that is related of him; but if even the oldest accounts are not agreed as to the end that is said to have overtaken him, this is a proof that the other apostles knew little about him, and that, finally, he remained as impenetrable to his contemporaries as to us.

All the disciples, however, were not included in the circle of the twelve. Even up to the time of the last journey, calls to discipleship were made, and rejections necessary, as Jesus called those whom he did call without any participation on their part, and rejected many who offered themselves.[1] The motives from which Jesus separated just these twelve from the great body of disciples are never given us. Nevertheless, it was a living circle which Jesus had gathered round himself, one in which striking individuality was not in any case wanting. Yet it was some time before the Master found his newly-called disciples competent and ready to undertake the mission assigned them;[2]—nay, during the whole period of his intercourse with his disciples there are signs that Jesus was dissatisfied with the worldly and feeble understanding of those who had been the first called, who were not able to comprehend the spiritual nature of the doctrine of the kingdom of God. He calls them worldly-minded and "without understanding," "fearful," "hard of heart," "of little faith;" and on one occasion he even utters the sharp words to them, "O faithless generation, how long shall I be with you? how long shall I suffer you?"[3]

The preponderating impression which we receive of the intercourse between Jesus and his disciples, is, however, in spite of

---

[1] Matt. viii. 18; Luke ix. 61, viii. 38.   [2] Mark iii. 20—vi. 7.
[3] Mark ix. 19; compare, too, Mark iv. 13, 40, vi. 52, viii. 17, 18, 21, 33, ix. 6, 19, 32, 34, x. 24, 32, 35, xiv. 40.

such decisive rebukes, that of a loving condescension to their weakness, and of patient endeavour to raise them, as far as possible, to his own level. Of formal instruction and discipline, like that we read of as forming the relation between the Rabbi and his pupil, in this intercourse there is not a trace. That the disciples are constantly with Jesus, listen when he speaks to the people, and ask him if they have not understood him, are its principal features.[1] His instruction is rather the formation and development of their character, than an introduction into the Scripture or the intellectual basis of the new doctrine.[2] Exhibitions of moral weakness, too, he knows how to make them aware of with mildness and earnestness, as when he playfully terms the sons of Zebedee, בְּנֵי רְגֶשׁ, Sons of Thunder, on account of their vehemence;[3] or warningly puts before them as the reward of their service for the kingdom of God, instead of honourable seats beside the throne of Messiah, the cup of suffering and the baptism of blood;[4] or when he set a child in the midst of the disciples, and answers their question, "Who is the greatest in the kingdom of heaven?" with a reference to its innocence: "Verily, I say unto you, except ye become as the little children, ye shall not enter into the kingdom of heaven!"[5]

If we find in the history of this social life few instances, relatively, in which the disciples exercised any determining influence, this is to be accepted as a proof that their intercourse with Jesus was of a purely receptive character; which was the impression entertained by the Church, even from the very first, of this relation of the disciples to Jesus. When giving us their report, too, the disciples have not, in the usual manner of witnesses, emphasized what *they* had done at such or such an important occasion; from the Synoptical sources, at least, very few instances have been handed down. True reverence is silent about itself, and the impression received by every one from the three Gospels is, that those who gave the accounts to which our sources are to be ultimately traced, forgot all about themselves in the presence

---

[1] Mark vii. 17.   [2] Mark x. 35.   [3] Mark iii. 17.
[4] Mark x. 35—45; Matt. xx. 23.   [5] Matt. xviii. 2.

of this Man from Nazareth. Thus in reality the Messianic kingdom had appeared in the communion of the Messiah with child-like, willing minds. Although the disciples might remain weak and erring men, yet they were themselves conscious that the few months lived in his companionship had elevated them above thousands who had wandered with them and before them under the palms of Judæa.[1] The very fact that after Jesus' death they waited for a whole life-time for his return, is the most sufficient testimony to the fervour of their adoring love.

Besides this intensive action upon a small circle, however, the extensive action upon the whole nation was not in any way neglected. Jesus' mission was directed, not to a few houses at Capernaum, but to Israel. The kingdom he was preaching concerned all the children of the Father; above all, those to whom belonged the promise. Was this promised kingdom in its external form the peculiar purport of Jewish worship and Jewish morality, then he would explain to the people its true meaning; nay, he did not shrink from the idea of gaining this nation, so hardened in its usages, proud of its law, factious and in part degenerated, as free citizens of the kingdom of God. That he put these wide limits to his work, and that in so doing the enormous labour of such an undertaking stood clearly before his eyes, is proved by the images under which he spoke of it. Like a ripe harvest-field of endless extension did it stand before his eyes when he declared to the five disciples, "The harvest truly is plenteous; pray ye, therefore, the Lord of the harvest that He send forth labourers into His harvest."[2] Then, again, the image of leaven presented itself, with which he is to work through and so leaven the masses;[3] or the bare stubble-field into which he is about to cast the fire-brand. "I came to send fire on the earth," he declares to the people, "and what desire I more than that it be already kindled!"[4]

How his contemporaries would bear themselves with regard to this kingdom, was now the all-important question.

[1] Luke x. 24.   [2] Matt. ix. 38.   [3] Luke xiii. 20.   [4] Luke xii. 49.

10. THE KINGDOM AND THOSE TO WHOM IT WAS PROCLAIMED.

The selection of the twelve apostles had taken place some time about Pentecost. The ears of corn were ripening when the disciples had plucked them, and that contest with the Rabbis taken place which occasioned Jesus leaving Capernaum. When the fields were white to harvest, he, too, had determined to call additional labourers to his aid. At the time of the harvest thanksgiving, the feast of Pentecost, therefore, was the Sermon on the Mount delivered and the apostolic community founded. Now followed the sultry summer, necessitating somewhat longer retreats and occasional cessation from work. Nevertheless, the contest did not stand still.

Certain is it, on the contrary, that as the formation of a regular circle of followers betokened a farther step in establishing the large community that was to be founded, the opposition of the synagogue that had appeared at the calling of the first five disciples must inevitably have been awakened afresh to prevent the realization of any new measure—a thing which the neighbourhood could endure without objection only so long as it was confined to the purely ideal spheres of exposition and promise. At first, the primitive document states,[1] the concourse of the people was doubled, but at the same time scribes from Jerusalem appeared in Capernaum in order to observe Jesus' actions. From their very nature were the schools jealous of every movement of the spirits that they did not originate, and their emissaries were accustomed to thrust themselves wherever they had not been invited.[2]

Here, moreover, their appearance may be connected with their alarm at the preaching of the kingdom, an alarm inspired in the Pharisees by John the Baptist. In Judæa, the Baptist movement

---

[1] Mark iii. 20—30; Matt. ix. 32—34, xii. 22—32; Luke xi. 14—23. On the original text, compare Holtzmann, Synoptische Evangelien, 78.

[2] Compare Antiq. xx. 2, 4. Who is not reminded, when reading these passages, of the circumstances in the Epistle to the Galatians?

had come to an end; the more necessary was it to prevent its finding an entrance into turbulent Galilee. The synagogues of Jerusalem, therefore, sent teachers down to Galilee in order to keep a watch on Jesus. The emissaries mingled among the crowd when Jesus appeared in public, and when they became witnesses of the healing of one possessed who was prevented by the demon from speaking, one of them, exasperated, exclaimed, "He casteth out devils by Beelzebul, the prince of the devils." Jesus discusses the point with them in the court-yard of Peter's house,[1] and asks them, "How can Satan cast out Satan? And if a kingdom be divided against itself, that kingdom cannot stand. And if Satan has risen up against himself and is divided, he cannot stand, but hath an end. And if I by Beelzebul cast out devils, by whom do your children cast them out? Therefore they shall be your judges. But if I with the finger of God cast out devils, no doubt the kingdom of God is come upon you."[2] In other words, therefore, it is his opinion that the casting out of devils by the Spirit of God proves the actual advent of the kingdom of God, and this assumption Jesus supports by the farther reference, that his breaking into the house of the strong man—the devil—and taking away his goods—diseased mankind—clearly show that the strong man had been previously bound, and that consequently the kingdom of the devil had come to an end. As the people, who had throughout remained under the impression caused by casting out the demon before their eyes, seized with astonishment, thronged impetuously about the house, the interference of the Rabbis produced no farther results; but another interruption taking place at the same time, Jesus decided once more to leave Capernaum. As in Jerusalem, so simultaneously in Jesus' home in Nazareth, had a watch been kept upon his actions, and the doubts cast upon his mission here were felt by Jesus in a way that was much more painful. It was just to those who were most nearly related to him that his work had become more and more incomprehensible; and when they understood that he considered

---

[1] Mark iii. 23.   [2] Matt. xii. 22—32; Mark iii. 20—30; Luke xi. 14—22.

himself to be a prophet, if not indeed more than a prophet, they imagined that he was beside himself.[1] His brothers, accompanied by their mother and sisters, travelled to Capernaum, which was distant two short days' journey,[2] in order that they might personally ascertain their relative's state of mind. According to Mark, they arrived at the moment when the excited crowd were thronging around Peter's house, and Jesus was discussing with the Pharisees whether devils could be cast out by the help of the devil. "He hath Beelzebul," the stronger demon, had the Pharisees declared, "and by the prince of the devils casteth he out devils." This declaration was now taken up by his own friends also, and thus the confusion was increased. "They went out to lay hold of him; for they said, He is beside himself." True, they were not able to force their way through the crowd thronging around the door that listened to Jesus' controversy with the Pharisees; but those around Jesus interrupted his discourse, on their account, with the message, "Behold, thy mother and thy brothers and sisters without seek for thee. And he answered them, saying, Who is my mother, or my brethren? And he looked round about on them which sat about him, and said, Behold my mother and my brethren! For whosoever shall do the will of God, the same is my brother, and my sister, and mother."[3] Nevertheless, he immediately breaks off, and goes down to the shore of the lake. From the prow of a ship he uttered parables to the multitude that had collected, about the various results of the word of God and the destiny of the kingdom of God. It is the time following the harvest. Corn-sheaves and fruits have been brought home, the bundles of weeds shoot out flames of fire on the hill-tops, while fresh furrows, for the second sowing, are formed by the plough; all these pictures are interwoven by the speaker into his discourse, and not less pictures of the lake which he observes around him from the gently-rocking boat.[4] When, however, the fall of evening at

---

[1] Mark iii. 21.
[2] The distance is about thirty miles.
[3] Mark iii. 20—35.
[4] Compare Keim, Geschichte Jesu, 1873, p. 218.

length brought this exciting day to a close, Jesus did not return to Peter's house, where, perchance, fresh scenes of pain might have awaited him, but directed that he should be carried across to the lonely shore on the other side of the lake, where he would be far removed from the tumult and commotion of Capernaum. It was in this passage that, according to Mark, whilst Jesus, wearied out, was sleeping on the cushion at the stern, the boat shipped so much water that the disciples awoke him with the words, "Master, carest thou not that we perish?" But he rebuked the storm and chided the disciples: "Why are ye so fearful? have ye not faith yet?" Thus Cæsar among the breakers on the Acroceraunian coast said to the desponding helmsman, "Be of good cheer, thou carriest the Cæsar."[1] The certainty of a vocation which is a factor in the history of the world, and that cannot be wrecked in a leaky boat, is proclaimed in both utterances. He remained at first in the country on the farther side, and next we find him in the half-Gentile Gadara, one of the cities of the Decapolis, the territory of which extended down to the lake. Ruins of temples, theatres and colonnades bear witness, even at the present day, to the splendour of this Gentile city, that had been rebuilt by Pompeius, the precincts of which were destined to afford rest to the Galilean Prophet when escaping from the throng occasioned by Galilean curiosity. His purposed retreat, indeed, was soon disturbed by his meeting with a demoniac, to whom the news of the proximity of the great exorcist had penetrated. To the present day, tombs cut out of the mountain are to be seen,[2] in one of which the possessed took up his abode, as is so impressively described in the Gospel according to Mark. "When Jesus was come out of the ship, immediately there met him out of the tombs a man with an unclean spirit, who had his dwelling among the tombs; and no man could any longer bind him, no, not with chains; for he had been often bound with fetters and chains, and the chains

---

[1] Cass. Dio, 41, 46.
[2] Burkhardt, Reise, i. 434; Antiq. xiii. 13, 3; Bell. i. 7, 7.

had been plucked asunder by him, and the fetters broken in pieces: neither could any man tame him. And always, night and day, he was in the mountains, and in the tombs, crying and cutting himself with stones."[1] However mythical the narrative in its further course may be, nevertheless it presents us with a true picture of Oriental life. Thus Robinson saw the insane sitting, rattling their chains, before the walls of Jerusalem; and the tombs in the rock of the Gadarenes were well known to the source of our information, so that it is quite possible that some actual reminiscence forms the basis of this narrative; at the least, it took its rise on the very spot where its scene lies.

From the territory of the Gadarenes we find Jesus once more returning to the other side, and, as before, working among the multitude by his word and healings.[2] Without doubt, the little towns close to Capernaum, Chorazin and Bethsaida, Dalmanutha and Magdala, were those where Jesus chiefly stayed.[3] During this ministry in Capernaum and Gadaritis, the summer had passed away. The course of the narrative now takes us into western Galilee. Over well-cultivated hills and fruitful valleys runs the road from Magdala to Nazareth on which we meet Jesus. Between the level lines of hills which border the plain of Esdraelon on the north lies Jesus' native town, built terrace-wise on the more or less precipitous cliffs of the cavernous limestone mountains. Above the eastern heights Tabor was visible, towering aloft and crowned with roofs and towers.[4] This was the impression of his youth which had suggested to Jesus the words, "A city that is set on a hill cannot be hid."[5] In spite of Jesus' experience with regard to his own family, he did not pass his native town, but, on the contrary, even used the opportunity for speaking to the congregation in the synagogue. The very passage of Isaiah which, according to Luke, he made the basis of his address, proclaimed the avowal of his Messianic mission for him; and before his friends, brothers and sisters did

---

[1] Mark v. 2—5.   [2] Mark v. 21.   [3] Matt. xi. 20—24.
[4] Bell. iv. 1, 1, 8; Renan, Vie de Jésus, chap. ii.   [5] Matt. v. 14.

he avow that the Spirit of the Lord was upon him, that he was sent to preach the gospel to the poor, to heal the broken-hearted, to preach deliverance to the captives—so that they should become free—and recovery of sight to the blind, to set at liberty them that were bruised, and to preach the acceptable year of the Lord.[1] But his words fell to the earth without striking any roots. True, they wondered at the wisdom which proceeded out of his mouth, but the worthy townsfolk of Nazareth could not comprehend how he could be a Prophet whose brothers and sisters they knew. "Is not this the carpenter," they asked, "the son of Mary, the brother of James and Joses and Judas and Simon? and are not his sisters here with us? And they were offended at him." In the presence of this disposition, his miraculous powers, too, failed him. The narrowness of the provincial mind paralyzed even Jesus' energy. "And he could there do no mighty work, save that he laid his hands upon a few sick folk, and he healed them. And he marvelled because of their unbelief."[2] "But he said unto them, Ye will surely say unto me this proverb, Physician, heal thyself: whatsoever we have heard done in Capernaum, do also here in thy country!"[3] It is in this connection, therefore, that the warning speech is to be taken, that it is possible for the kingdom of God to pass away from not only the home of the Prophet, but even from Israel itself. "But I tell you of a truth, many widows were in Israel in the days of Elijah when the heaven was shut up three years and six months, when a great famine was throughout all the land; but unto none of them was Elijah sent, save unto Sarepta, a city of Sidon, unto a woman that was a widow. And many lepers were in Israel in the time of Elisha the prophet; and none of them was cleansed, saving Naaman the Syrian."[4] Under any circumstances, to the ear of the Jews these words, that it was possible for a prophet of the house of Israel to turn even to the Gentile proclaiming the Messianic kingdom, must have had an impious sound. The effect of these words is depicted by Luke as being very violent; they thrust

---

[1] Luke iv. 18.   [2] Mark vi. 3—6.   [3] Luke iv. 24.   [4] Luke vi. 25—27.

him out of the city, attempt to stone him, and he is miraculously saved. Mark and Matthew, on the other hand, merely state that he made the memorable remark, "A prophet is not without honour but in his own country, and among his own kin, and in his own house."[1] And he left Nazareth, "and went round about the villages teaching." It is possible that, at this time, he directed his steps from Nazareth straight across the wide and magnificently extensive plain of Jezreel to Nain, which lay upon the other side of the undulating, green expanse on Little Hermon,[2] and then farther on to the villages of the Samaritans—remembered by Luke, who relates a rich cycle of traditions of his work there.

At this time was it that Antipas again made his appearance in Tiberias. The precious head of the Baptist had already fallen, and it is possible to interpret the fact that, just at this point of time, Jesus sent out his disciples as an answer to this strongest blow against preaching the kingdom of God.[3] He himself had begun preaching the kingdom on that day on which the seizure of the prophet had been announced; now also does he send forth his messengers in the hour when the blood-stained murderer of the prophet returns from Machærus under the delusion that he has cut off the head of the movement. Anew are they to repeat the war-cry, Repent and be converted, for the kingdom has drawn nigh, throughout Galilee, from the lake to the frontiers of Phœnicia, from the highlands down to the boundaries of Samaria.[4] Just as the disciples are enumerated in the list of the apostles in pairs, so now, too, did they start on their way two and two.[5] Simon and his brother Andrew, James and his brother John, Philip and the son of Talmai, the melancholy Thomas and the practical Matthew, James and his brother Thaddæus, and, finally, Simon the Zealot and Judas of Kerioth; the brother with the brother, the friend with the friend, the ardent with the cold.

---

[1] Mark vi. 4. [2] See Keim, Jesus of Nazara, T. T. F. L. Vol. iv. p. 115.
[3] Mark vi. 7, compare verses 29 and 30; Matt. xiv. 1, 2, 14.
[4] Matt. x. 7. [5] Mark vi. 7, δύο δύο.

With exactness did their Master prescribe their method of procedure for them. They were to stand forth singularly simple in appearance amidst the splendidly and voluminously clothed Orientals; no purse in the girdle, no shoes on the feet, not even a scrip for their journey. As preachers of peace and friends of mankind, they were even to lay aside the staff, allowed to the Essene, on their wanderings; and since, owing to their being forbidden to provide money for travelling expenses, they had to seek for hospitality, neither the school nor market-place, but the house and chamber were to be the place of their communications, as was in keeping with their degree of maturity.[1] Whilst it was the custom for every traveller to ceremoniously greet his acquaintance, by putting his hand from his heart to his forehead and then placing it in the other's right hand, or bowing, according to circumstances, three or seven times, they in their haste were to salute no man by the way,[2] but when they came into a house they were to pronounce the Shalom, and if the house were not worthy of it, then their Shalom would return to them again. Not everywhere, as previous experiences had already taught Jesus, would they be well received. "And into whatsoever city ye enter, and they receive you, eat such things as are set before you; and heal the sick that are therein, and say unto them, The kingdom is come nigh unto you. But into whatsoever city ye shall enter, and they receive you not, go out into its streets, and say, Even the very dust of your city, which cleaveth to us on our feet, we do wipe off against you; notwithstanding, be ye sure of this, that the kingdom of God is come nigh."[3] The prophecies of blood, certainly, which have been introduced here by Matthew, have their origin in a later age, and are in part a

---

[1] Keim, Geschichte Jesu, 1873, p. 200.

[2] Luke x. 4; compare also 2 Kings iv. 29. On the other hand, compare Abraham's greeting: Jubilees 19, and Gen. xviii. 2, xxxiii. 3. For the present mode of greeting in the East, see Furrer, Wanderung in Pal. p. 119.

[3] Luke x. 8—11. Luke, as well as Matthew, has made up the precepts for the missionary journey from the Collection of Sayings; Luke, however, has apportioned the contents of the latter in part to his account of sending out the seventy disciples.

reflection of persecutions which arose first after the death of Jesus. Nevertheless, the primitive document points to an ill-usage of the Messianic messengers also, on account of which is it to be ascribed that it will be more tolerable on the day of judgment for Sodom and Gomorrha than for many a village in Galilee, the dust of which the rejected messengers had to shake from their feet. So loweringly had the clouds already gathered. Under such circumstances, Jesus might well compare his disciples to sheep sent out amidst wolves, and point out the two-fold character of the gospel, which to-day is a palm of peace and to-morrow a sword. Well could he remind them of the hour when the Pharisees had recently called him Beelzebul: how much more would they thus call those of his household! Nevertheless, he did not now contemplate carrying out that threat he had uttered in the synagogue at Nazareth. On the contrary, he held that the tidings of the kingdom were to be proclaimed to *that* nation only to whom the promises had been made. The disciples were to go neither by the *via maris* northwards to Syria, nor westwards to Phœnicia, nor were they to set foot on the ground of Samaria. "Go not forth into the way of the Gentiles, and into any city of the Samaritans enter ye not; but go rather to the lost sheep of the house of Israel."[1] "And they went out and preached that men should repent. And they cast out many devils, and anointed with oil many that were sick, and healed them."[2]

When the disciples thus appeared two and two in the villages of Galilee, and, commissioned by Jesus, began to preach the near approaching kingdom of God, the name of Jesus was made known not only in the cottages of the villages of his native land, but also in the palace of Antipas at Tiberias, and every one sought in his own way to come to terms with this new phenomenon.[3] Especially were the eyes of John's murderer fixed with suspicion on the new Prophet, who in his preaching and actions reminded the tetrarch most uncomfortably of the murdered Bap-

---

[1] Matt. x. 5, 6. [2] Mark vi. 12, 13. [3] Mark vi. 14.

tist. It was in his newly-built residence, the Hellenic palace so hateful to the Jews, that he first heard of Jesus, and mockingly said to his courtiers, "This is John the Baptist, risen from the dead; and therefore the mighty powers work in him."[1] But in this mockery there was a murderous threat. Thus had the old Herod often brooded over some gloomy thought, mocked about it, threatened, and then again let it rest, until suddenly he dealt the fatal blow. Similar conduct was now feared from the tetrarch. Suspicion and watchful caution were features of his character. News of what was occurring in the palace could very well reach Jesus, for there, too, he counted followers like Joanna the wife of Chuza, Herod's steward, and Menahem the foster-brother of the tetrarch. Yet it was not from his friends, but from the Pharisees, who would so gladly have removed him from Galilee, that he received warning of Herod's designs. They came to him with the hurried advice, "Get thee out and depart hence; for Herod desireth to kill thee!"[2] Jesus, however, quietly replied, "Go ye and tell that fox, Behold, I cast out devils, and I perfect cures to-day and to-morrow, and the third day I shall be completed." And with an ironical side-glance at the Pharisees, who were so anxious about his life, he added: "Nevertheless, I must walk to-day and to-morrow and the day following; for it cannot be that a prophet perish outside of Jerusalem." Thus did it take place. "He departed thence by ship into a desert place apart."[3]

It is in the tetrarchy of Philip, at the upper end of the lake, where Jesus was safe from the designs of Antipas, that we must look for this place of refuge. There his disciples found him.[4] The plain of Batihah, which is not inferior in its magnificence to the plain of Gennesareth, and commanded by the newly-built town of Julias, harboured for a time the citizens of the "kingdom." The people sought for them in this asylum, and it was related how Jesus, like the prophet Elisha of old, had miraculously fed the multitudes that were constantly coming and going.[5]

---

[1] Matt. xiv. 1; Mark vi. 14; Josephus, Vita, 13.
[2] Luke xiii. 31, 32, 33.   [3] Matt. xiv. 13.   [4] Mark vi. 30.
[5] Mark vi. 34; Matt. xiv. 14; compare 2 Kings iv. 42.

When, afterwards, he once more appeared in the neighbourhood of his home, he is greeted with joy as one whose absence had long been felt. Perhaps to avoid notice, he had not gone to Capernaum, but remained in the neighbouring district, in the fields and by the numerous brooks of which lay scattered villages and hamlets that afforded shelter to him and his followers.[1] But here, too, he could not prevent the concourse of the people. "And when they were come out of the ship, straightway the people knew him, and ran through that whole region round about, and began to carry about in beds those that were sick, where they heard he was; and withersoever he entered, into villages or into cities or fields, they laid the sick in the public places and besought him that they might touch if it were but the border of his garment; and as many as touched him were made whole."[2]

Forthwith we find that the scribes, too, prepared for contest, appear upon the scene. They have not lost sight of their opponent, for they have a message from the Sanhedrin to the false prophet. Just as we found them even before Jesus' retreat to Gadara, before his journey to Nazareth and the sending out and return of his disciples, that is, several weeks ago in Capernaum, so now, too, do we still find them at the post of danger in order that they may oppose Jesus' actions and repair the mischief which his untheocratic position and his discourses—weakening allegiance to the law—threaten to establish among the communities on the lake; in case of need even, they are ready to put in action the strict law against the seducer of the people. From the publicity of life in Galilee, it was easy for them to catch the disciples in the very act of eating with unwashed hands, and from this moment did their competency to establish their charge begin. "Why," they demanded of Jesus with all the earnestness of judges conducting an examination, "do thy disciples transgress the tradition of the elders, for they wash not their hands when they eat bread?" The more abruptly

---

[1] Bell. iii. 3, 2; Mark vi. 55.   [2] Mark vi. 54—56.

their question was put before the people, the more regardless was the tone of Jesus' answer. "Why," demands he, "do ye transgress the commandment of God for the sake of your tradition?" and, instead of justifying himself, brings a mass of accusations against them of washing cups instead of keeping their hearts pure; of enriching the Corban and allowing their parents to starve; of neglecting the most ancient commandment of the Scriptures, "Thou shalt honour thy father and thy mother," for the latest ordinance, and thus making the saying of Isaiah applicable to them, "This people honoureth me with their lips, but their heart is far from me."[1] What they had been fearing would be the consequence of his preaching, he now did expressly. He released the people from the commandments concerning food. He called the people to him and said, "Hear and understand: not that which goeth into the mouth defileth the man: but that which cometh out of the mouth, this defileth the man." The disciples were alarmed as to the results of this violent collision, and when Jesus retired into Peter's house, they said to him, "Knowest thou that the Pharisees were offended when they heard this saying?" But he answered and said, "Every plant which my Heavenly Father did not plant shall be rooted up. Let them alone: they be blind leaders of blind men. And if a blind man lead a blind man, both shall fall into the ditch."[2] By the plants which God has not planted, he meant ordinances, the hedge around the law, which overshadowed the word of God; and by the ditch, the great catastrophe of the people to which, foreboding disaster, he here refers for the first time. Thereby is the breach between the men of the schools and the Prophet of Galilee for ever complete. To them he is now the enemy of the law, the associate of sinners and tax-gatherers; to him they are a wicked and adulterous generation, hypocrites and vipers' brood.

How very different this contest was from those of all previous occasions, is proved also by Jesus' determination to leave Galilee

---

[1] Isaiah xxix. 13.   [2] Mark vii. 1—23; Matt. xv. 1—20.

altogether. "And Jesus went thence and withdrew into the parts of Tyre and Sidon."[1] The twelve accompanied him in his flight. Its direction, which is given by the notices contained in the historical source, takes us up the steep slopes of the mountains above Chorazin, and then across the barren plateau of the limestone range to the north.[2] On the other side of Safed the summits of Hermon appear.[3] Leaving Gischala on the right, the way leads into a table-land, intersected by many valleys and ravines. It was a journey of two days before they could reach the declivity at the feet of which extended the plain of Tyre. The yellow streak of the coast separates the green plain from the blue sea, far out into which stretches the tongue of land whereon the proud Tyre is built. Strictly confining himself to intercourse with his followers, and curtly, nay even sharply, repelling any chance recognition,[4] Jesus wandered on through the fruitful plain of Phœnicia, always green from the proximity of the sea, to the borders of Sidon. Manifestly he purposed a somewhat extended wandering life in order to allow the hatred of his enemies to fall asleep; and this choice of a GENTILE place of refuge is in itself evidence of the increased danger of his position. In the throng of the mercantile and manufacturing district of the coast, would it be most difficult for his enemies to trace him. Making a wide circuit through the territory of Paneas and Ulatha, Jesus then turned back towards the mountains of his home. But when, after long wandering, he approaches the neighbourhood of the lake, he does not go to Capernaum, but crosses the Jordan, and wanders through the territory of Philip, who now probably was already at rest in his sepulchre at Julias, in order to gain repose in the peace of the Decapolis.[5] Here, too, is it impossible to determine how long this absence from Capernaum was continued.

It was at Dalmanutha, a town of the plain of Gennesareth, to the north of Magdala, where Jesus, returning homewards across

---

[1] Mark vii. 24. [2] Matt. xv. 21. [3] Furrer, Wanderung in Palestine, p. 332.
[4] Mark vii. 27. [5] Mark vii. 31—viii. 10.

the lake from the Decapolis, again trod the ground of his first activity.[1] Perhaps it was at this time that the Pharisees uttered the scoffing words to Jesus returning with empty hands: "When the kingdom of God should come?" Jesus replied: "The kingdom of God cometh not with observation: neither shall they say, See here, or there; for, behold, the kingdom of God is among you."[2] They certainly could perceive nothing of this kingdom, that had already come, and so they demanded a sign as proof that the kingdom was there. But what sign was it possible for him to give after they had ascribed those which he had done to Beelzebul? "This evil and adulterous generation," he continues, "seeketh after a sign: and there shall no sign be given unto it, but the sign of the prophet Jonah;"[3] that is, that preaching of repentance by which the Gentile Nineveh was warned, without any external authentication of the prophet. The signs of the times are as manifest as the red glow in the morning or evening sky; and referring the weather-wise to these signs, Jesus turns his back upon them.[4] Now also does he seek safety on the farther shore, and in his discourses to the disciples, who were afraid of entering into the towns belonging to Antipas, he, according to Mark, classes the Pharisees and Herod together as like-minded,[5] and utters a warning against the leaven of the pious that has spoiled the bread of Israel.

If this repeated retreat into solitude may be explained positively by the given necessity of fitting the disciples for their vocation in quietness and apart from the distractions of the Galilean life, and negatively by the necessity of avoiding any premature catastrophe, nevertheless this course of life, considered externally, still appears to have been a repeated but fruitless attempt upon the same ground. The lamentations of Jesus over Capernaum and the neighbouring places present the matter in

---

[1] Mark viii. 10.   [2] Luke xvii. 20, 21.
[3] Matt. xii. 39.   [4] Matt. xvi. 1—4; Mark viii. 11—13.
[5] On the re-duplication of the account of the miraculous feeding at this place, see Holtzmann, Synopt. Evangelien, p. 85.

the same light, and there can probably be no doubt but that the scribes from Jerusalem regarded *themselves* as the victors in this contest. Crowds, applause, cries of Hosanna, were, in spite of all the Pharisees had done, as little wanting as at an earlier period. On the contrary, the concourse of the masses had rather increased than diminished. Whole villages, some from long distances, followed him. Did he cross over to the other shore, then multitudes followed him round by the land; did he return to the plain, he was again received by those who had waited for him. According to the stories of the miraculous feeding of the multitude, the crowd at times amounted to between four and five thousand men. Women surrounded him with their children, the sick were brought on their beds, and even between the Gadarene graves or on the distant Phœnician military road, one or another ever appears, who recognizes him who is known to all, and either is terror-striken or else beseeches him for help. Antipas' dread of a repetition of the Judaic movement in Galilee, consequently, was not without grounds, for it was just this very concourse of the multitude in the wilderness which so strongly called well-known Messianic precedents to mind. But for the aim which Jesus had in view, it was this concourse which had little value. He finds more curious glances and empty homage than obedience to his commands. Thus it was a genuine expression of this popular homage when a woman cried, after one of the discourses of Jesus, "Blessed is the womb that bare thee, and the paps which thou hast sucked;" or when another breaks out with the words, "Blessed is he that shall eat bread in the kingdom of God."[1] Jesus, however, answered, correcting them, "Yea, rather, blessed are they that hear the word of God and keep it;" and yet more strongly on another occasion did he rebuke the empty reverence they proffered him with the indignant words, "Why call ye me Lord, Lord, and do not the things which I say?"[2] In a similar key, that other speech asserts, "By

---

[1] Luke xi. 27, xiv. 15.
[2] Luke vi. 46; compare Keim's Jesus of Nazara, T. T. F. L. Vol. iv. p. 210, &c.

your fruits shall ye be known. Not every one that saith unto me, Lord, Lord, shall enter into the kingdom of heaven, but he that doeth the will of my Father which is in heaven. Many will say to me in that day, Lord, Lord, did we not eat and drink in thy presence, and didst not thou teach in our streets? And then will I confess unto them, I never knew you; depart from me, ye that work iniquity."[1] Thus the Galilean movement remained, apparently, as fruitless as the Baptist movement. People felt themselves exalted by his words, Josephus declared, at a later period, of the preaching of John, and the people of Galilee had nothing more for the preaching of Jesus. The demand to be in earnest about the commandments of the kingdom of God fell upon that dull resistance of indifferentism which the most idealistic demands are the soonest in experiencing. There is no doubt—and the alarm of the Pharisees and Antipas is the best proof of it—that the Galileans loved Jesus; but where Jesus now wished to bring individuals into obedience to the demands of the kingdom of God, where he required a closer union with the community founded by him, there ever intervened moral indifference and the trivial hindrances of the daily life which most unconditionally hold back the better classes in particular. One, who seems impressed by the glad tidings, must first attend a funeral; another must still put his house in order;[2] and even the most zealous retire when the demand is made that they shall imitate the example of the twelve and follow after Jesus by the surrender of their possessions.[3] Thus Jesus compares the invitation to the kingdom of God to an invitation to a feast for which no one finds time: "The first said, I have bought a piece of ground, and I must needs go forth and see it: I pray thee have me excused. And another said, I have bought five yoke of oxen, and I go to prove them: I pray thee have me excused. And another said, I have married a wife, and therefore I cannot come."[4] To this dull opposition of the children

---

[1] See Matt. vii. 20—23; Luke vi. 46 and xiii. 26.
[2] Matt. viii. 21; Luke ix. 59.   [3] Matt. xix. 22.   [4] Luke xiv. 18—20.

of the world there was now added the heightened opposition of that customary piety which missed everything in Jesus that it deemed a due observance of the fear of God. His knowledge of God had raised him and his disciples above the Jewish forms of worshipping God, and this little circle, consequently, gave offence to every pious Israelite, in that it was lax in observing the precepts concerning the Sabbath, the hours of prayer, and prescribed purifications; more especially, however, from the fact that neither the Master nor his disciples fasted, but, on the contrary, instead of mortifying themselves, cultivated a cheerful companionship with circles that were in part theocratically of ill repute. The very people who had found John too much like the Essenes and mocked at his strict asceticism, found Jesus' life too worldly and were offended at his companions. "Whereunto shall I liken this generation?" he consequently exclaimed. "It is like unto little children sitting in the markets, and calling unto their fellows, and saying, We piped unto you, and ye danced not; we mourned, and ye lamented not. For John came neither eating nor drinking, and they say, He hath a devil. The Son of Man is come eating and drinking, and they say, Behold a man gluttonous, and a wine-bibber, a friend of publicans and sinners."[1] It is the same knowingness, too, which will have nothing to do with the new wine out of the new bottles, but mockingly declares that the old is better.[2] But why, then, Jesus asks, had they gone after John at all? Did they expect to find one like themselves, a reed shaken by the wind? Or had they gone, as they had run lately, when the tetarch and his wife entered Tiberias? Did they expect to see a man in rich clothing? but they that wear rich clothing are in kings' houses. But such rebukes could only serve to complete their change of feeling, and we soon see how the same district which a few months before had idolized Jesus, now renounced him. Like a panorama does the country around the lake lie extended before us in that rebuke which Jesus, according to Matthew, at that time uttered. "Then began he to

---

[1] Matt. xi. 16—19.   [2] Luke v. 39.

upbraid the cities wherein most of his mighty works were done, because they repented not. Woe unto thee, Chorazin! woe unto thee, Bethsaida! for if the mighty works which were done in you had been done in Tyre and Sidon, they would have repented long ago in sackcloth and ashes. But I say unto you, It shall be more tolerable for Tyre and Sidon in the day of judgment than for you. And thou, Capernaum, shalt thou be exalted unto heaven? Thou shalt be brought down to hell; for if the mighty works which were done in thee had been done in Sodom, it would have remained until this day. But I say unto you, that it shall be more tolerable for the land of Sodom in the day of judgment than for thee."[1]

It is from this point of time that Jesus distinguishes between the called and uncalled. "Many are called, but few chosen." "Wide is the gate and broad is the way that leadeth to destruction, and many there be which go in thereat: because narrow is the gate and straitened is the way which leadeth unto life, and few there be that find it."[2] The thought of a divine predestination, the view that it was the Father's will to save only a part, throws its shadow across the sunny, bright field of his religious conception of the world, and as he had proclaimed, Come unto me, *all* ye who labour and are heavy laden, so now he learned to acquiesce in the fact that only a *few* choose the narrow way and find rest unto their souls. The year which he had just gone through had been *to him* no acceptable year of salvation, but had called far different prophecies of Isaiah to mind. The Scripture recounted how this people had always been hard of heart, and had drawn near to Jehovah only with its lips and not with its heart. It recounted how, though Israel were as the sand on the shore of the sea, yet only a remnant should be saved. But he found consolation for this gloomy lot in the love of his disciples, whom he recognized as the light of the world, the salt of the earth. Another change, however, occasioned a state of affairs, which soon made him appear to the teachers

[1] Matt. xi. 20—24.   [2] Matt. vii. 13, 14; Luke xiii. 24.

and leaders of the country in a far more dangerous light. In the parable in which he enumerates the trivial hindrances that keep the well-to-do out of the kingdom of God, he himself announced this change. When none of the invited guests would come, "Then the master of the house was angry, and said to his servants, Go out quickly into the streets and lanes of the city, and bring in hither the poor, and maimed, and blind, and lame, ... and go out into the highways and hedges, and compel them to come in, that my house may be filled." There was a complete breaking away from official Judaism and the circles which represented it. "Come unto me, all ye who labour and are heavy laden," was now the watchword. To the poor is the gospel preached, and, in contrast with the riches of the wisdom of the schools, the simplicity of the poor in spirit is declared blessed. During the whole of this later period, Jesus never enters a synagogue, and makes no farther attempt to work by the aid of theocratic institutions. In place of the discourses in the school, there is a thoroughly public ministry. "Thou didst teach in our streets," do the Galileans declare, according to Luke.[1] It is, consequently, no longer those who walk respectably in the theocratic ordinances and the circles representing the pith of the community, to whom the promises of the kingdom are offered. The king seeks for his guests wherever he can find them. The satisfied have shut their doors against the preacher of the kingdom. Therefore he turns with two-fold love to the poor, oppressed, suffering people. Oriental misery in its most terrible shape becomes the dearest object of his care. It is presented to us in the Gospels in all its forms: the disfigured leper, who with piercing cry implores the compassion of the passer-by;[2] poverty in the most ghastly degree of want, lying beside the ownerless dogs in expectation of the broken meats that are thrown away before the door;[3] the beggar whose exposed sores the dogs come and lick;[4] the possessed who, naked like an animal, crying and

---

[1] Luke xiii. 26.   [2] Luke xvii. 13.
[3] Luke xvi. 20.   [4] Luke xvi. 21.

cutting himself with stones, takes up his abode among the tombs.[1] Never did his love, thus seeking out and finding, beam forth more divinely than here, where it stooped even to the most wretched, to those whom Judaism, in the wisdom of Elihu, had passed by, because either they or their parents had sinned, else they had never been thus punished by Jehovah.

It is not, however, earthly destitution alone that especially claims Jesus' compassion, but, in even a higher degree, spiritual wretchedness, so far as it is really conscious of its wretchedness. Had the theocratically respectable section of the people shown themselves as a whole unsusceptible to the gospel of the kingdom of God—on the other hand, the very persons who were proscribed by the theocracy were the more enthusiastic in their reception of Jesus. It had been already noticed in the revival under John that the tax-gatherers and harlots were the most eager in thronging to hear the new tidings.[2] The pariahs of the nation, for whom the theocracy had no more indulgence, and those whose consciences were more deeply seared—those to whom the empty forms of Pharisaism offered no consolation—listened eagerly to the tidings that God was a Father of love, of compassion, who pardons all who from the heart beseech Him for it. Here Jesus found a faith and love which a satisfied and self-righteous Judaism would have ever denied him; and in his own nature, the fundamental feature of which was everywhere revealed as compassionate love and desire to help and save, this state of things found a response from the bottom of his heart. "The Son of Man is come to seek and save that which is lost," did he more than once declare; and when the Pharisees wondered that he could sit at table with tax-gatherers and notorious sinners, his answer is, "They that are whole need not a physician, but they that are sick. But go ye and learn what that meaneth, I love mercy, and not sacrifice; for I am come, not to call righteous men, but sinners."[3] It becomes a favourite theme of his parables that the saving of the lost is the chief aim of religion.

[1] Mark v. 3.   [2] Matt. xxi. 32; Luke vii. 29.   [3] Matt. ix. 10—13.

This was the original meaning of the parable, among others, of the Prodigal Son, a parable which the Pauline Gospel afterwards referred to the Gentile and the Jew. According to Jesus, the younger son, who rebels against the discipline of his father, dissipates his inheritance, and sinks so low as to become a tender of swine, is the Jew who has neglected all his theocratic duties, forfeited the blessing of Abraham and associates with the unclean, but who now repents and returns to his father's house, one who is alive again from the dead, and as such received by his father. The pious Israelite, however, who has worked in the vineyard of the Lord, hears the sounds of rejoicing at the welcome-home, and angrily refuses to come in. He recounts to the lord how many years he has served him, and how he has never yet been honoured, as is this sinner, with drums and cymbals. The lord of the house even condescends to excuse himself. "Son," he replies, "thou art ever with me, and all that I have is thine. It is meet that we should make merry and be glad: for this thy brother was dead, and is alive; and was lost, and is found."[1] But soon the words of justification take a sharper tone, like words of accusation; the Pharisees are no longer the blameless and the whole, the tax-gatherers no longer the lost and sick. "Which," he demands, "did the will of his father, he who said, I go and went not, or he who said, I will not, but afterwards repented and went?" Verily, the tax-gatherers and the harlots may well go into the kingdom of heaven before you."[2] And thus, in the divine parable of the Pharisee and the Tax-gatherer in the temple, does he contrast the two types. "The Pharisee stood and prayed thus with himself: God, I thank thee that I am not as other men are, extortioners, unjust, adulterers, or even as this publican. I fast twice in the week; I give tithes of all my increase. And the publican, standing afar off, would not lift up so much as his eyes unto heaven, but smote upon his breast, saying, God be merciful to me a sinner. I tell you this man went down to his house justified rather than the other."[3] By

---

[1] Luke xv. 11.   [2] Matt. xxi. 28—31.   [3] Luke xviii. 9—14.

such speeches, certainly, did he break with the powerful party of the people. As his eyes thus critically rest upon this party, it, too, is challenged to measure his position by the standard of the law. "Why eateth your Master with tax-gatherers and sinners?" the disciples are asked. "This man, if he were a prophet, would have known who and what manner of woman this is that toucheth him," muttered the Pharisees. They pointed with the finger to the adherents whom he had picked up at the custom-house.

So much the more did this development, once begun, pursue its course, and of necessity lead finally beyond the limits of Judaism. To the Jewish nation had the kingdom of God been offered, and it was as a nation, as a corporate community, that it had rejected the call. It was to the assemblage of individuals that Jesus saw he had to address himself, and when they came, they came just because the theocracy had not sufficed for them. Jesus found in his mission and in his idea of the kingdom of God no ground for rejecting them because they had fallen out with the priesthood. But the same was true of the Gentile. Certainly it was not that Jesus, rejected by the Jews, had himself turned to the Gentile, but it was the Gentile which came to him.[1] He held himself as rather repelling than inviting them; but there were occurrences which forced him to exclaim, "Verily, in no man in Israel have I found so great faith."[2]

A prelude to this change is found in his relations to the Samaritans. Apart from the fact that Jesus took no interest whatever in the burning questions of the times, there was no room in his bosom, as revealed to us, for any antipathy towards those who stood outside of the community. Even when, in his journey towards Sidon, he declared to the Phœnician woman, "Let the children first be filled; for it is not meet to take the children's bread and to cast it unto the dogs,"[3] he seems to have been more moved by the thought of seeing the children starving

---

[1] Compare Keim, Der geschichtliche Christus, p. 51.
[2] Matt. viii. 10.   [3] Mark vii. 27.

than annoyed by the demand of the Gentile woman. So from the
first there was probably no aversion felt by him for the Samaritans,
although at this very time there was a very hostile feeling against
them, because, under the protection of Rome, they had assumed
a strong position in opposition to the Jews, and often also
behaved with insolence.[1] On his journeys, Jesus had unhesitatingly gone through the villages of the Samaritans, whilst the
orthodox Jew made a wide circuit round the defiled territory.
He even did not scruple about asking for shelter in a Samaritan
dwelling, whilst the teachers were yet insisting that "he who
takes the bread of a Samaritan is like unto him who eats the
flesh of swine."[2] Thereby could it happen to him, certainly,
that the shelter was refused him "because his face was as though
he would go to Jerusalem."[3] Rejected with contumely, the sons
of Zebedee, like the Tishbite, were desirous of calling down fire
from heaven, but Jesus rebukes them and corrects their Jewish
zeal.[4] Such isolated experiences did not in any way disturb his
appreciation for the comparatively milder side of the Samaritan
character; and it was not forgotten by him that the tenth leper
who alone had thanked him for being healed was a Samaritan.[5]
Challenged by the national pride of the Jews, he narrated the
parable of the man who, between Jerusalem and Jericho, passed
by the robbers' caves and fell among assassins. Priests and
Levites left him lying, whilst a Samaritan took pity upon him.
So Jesus informed the virtuous Rabbi, "willing to justify himself," and bade him "Go and do likewise."[6] There were similar
experiences, however, which soon urged him forward to promise,
to the greatest indignation of the Rabbis, that the kingdom of God
would be opened to the Gentiles also, and that there was a danger
of its being lost to the Jews. Had not a Gentile—Antipas' centurion at Capernaum, who declared that his house was not worthy
of receiving him—by his reliance on him compelled him to
exclaim, "Verily, in no man in Israel have I found so great

---

[1] Antiq. xviii. 2, 2.   [2] Pirq. R. Eliezer, c. 38.   [3] Luke ix. 53.
[4] Luke ix. 55.   [5] Luke xvii. 16.   [6] Luke x. 29—37.

faith;"[1] and similarly the Phœnician woman, who clung fast to him in spite of his harsh saying about the dogs to whom it was not meet to cast the children's bread, forced the confession from him, "O woman, great is thy faith!"[2] Similar occurrences must have been previously experienced by him when he gave offence to the people of Nazareth by his assertion that God had already by means of the prophets addressed himself to the Gentiles.[3] There had been no friendly leave-taking offered him then in return for these words, but, nevertheless, when he sent out his disciples he had still confined the preaching of the kingdom throughout to the sheep of the house of Israel. Now, however, he goes much further, in that he not only speaks of the admission of the Gentiles, but even of the exclusion of the Jews. "Many will come from the east and from the west, and shall sit down with Abraham and Isaac and Jacob in the kingdom of heaven. But the sons of the kingdom shall be cast out into the darkness without; there shall be weeping and gnashing of teeth."[4] It was the result of Jewish unbelief. Jesus could not help perceiving that even Tyre and Sidon must needs be more believing under the impression of his deeds than this Judaism.[5] In addition to the remembrance of Naaman the Syrian and the widow of Sarepta, he thought of the Gentile people of Nineveh and the queen of Sheba, who had also listened to revelation at a time when in Israel there had been a people with deaf ears and dimmed eyes. That this perception, however, was the result of a progress, a development, is shown, as by two boundary-stones, by his two declarations on sending forth the disciples; the first of which is, "Go not forth into the way of the Gentiles, and into any city of the Samaritans enter ye not;" and the other, "Go ye into all the world, and preach the gospel to all nations."

Whilst Jesus, during the course of this development, had drawn nearer and nearer to those elements which were excluded

---

[1] Luke vii. 1—10; Matt. viii. 5—15.
[2] Matt. xv. 21—28; compare Keim, menschl. Entw., as before.   [3] Luke iv. 25.
[4] Matt. viii. 12; Luke xiii. 28, 29.   [5] Keim, Der gesch. Christus, p. 54.

from the theocracy, he was compelled, by the same course of development, to separate more and more from its representatives. Since the tax-gatherers were his followers, the Samaritans his favourites, the Gentiles the citizens of his kingdom, he had become to the Pharisaic party an apostate and seducer of the people, against whom a contest must be waged by every means in its power. It is only in accordance with the usual course of things that at first it was not the spiritual principles, but the outworks of the new kingdom, around which primarily the contest raged.

11. Moments in the Contest.

To write a history of Jesus' contest with the Pharisees is impossible, owing to the uncertainty about the chronology of the different controversies. The widely ramified party appears, moreover, in its several subdivisions, to have assumed a very varied position with regard to the preaching of the kingdom. Whilst some warned him about Antipas, for example, others had already shown signs of delivering him into the hands of the Herodians; and immediately before the party as a whole plotted his destruction, others offered themselves as his followers. Owing to the fundamental contradiction in principle, the contest was not so much a question of development in the opposition between him and the Pharisees, as of a more exact acquaintance on their part with the new doctrine. It was Jesus' attitude towards the most external of the precepts of the law which at first startled the men of the synagogue. The exaggerations of conformity to the law had already found opposition, it is true, elsewhere. At the unwearied purifications of the Pharisees we occasionally hear the Sadducees sneering: "The Pharisees will at last cleanse the sun for us!" whilst the anxiety about personal purity of the Saducean priesthood, willing to declare Jerusalem unclean because a bone had been found in the temple, is derided by the

Pharisaic Rabbi: "Where did the dead bodies remain after the flood, and where were the dead bodies buried after the Chaldean wars?"[1] But beyond a criticism of the exaggerations on either side, this disagreement had not ventured to go.

According to Jesus' view of things, on the other hand, the ritualistic precepts of Judaism were altogether doomed. If the kingdom of heaven is a matter of disposition, of the loving relation of the child to the Heavenly Father, all external practices have a meaning only so far as they are an expression of this relation. Whilst the Pharisee made the law more special, deducted the consequences from it in individual cases, balanced the commandments one against the other with subtle casuistry and heightened its claims, Jesus went in the very opposite direction. From the outward special precept, he goes back to its universal moral and religious purport, and allows these special claims of the law to be unhesitatingly neglected, provided only its spirit is regarded. The precepts of the Rabbis on the manner of sacrificing could scarcely be learned in a lifetime; Jesus says briefly, "Obedience is better than sacrifice." To the division of animals into clean and unclean, the school had added an infinite number of distinctions between the various parts of the carcase and their method of preparation; so much the simpler is Jesus' canon, "Not that which goeth into the mouth defileth a man, but that which cometh out of the heart." The teachers disputed after which use the vessels must be cleansed in river-water, after which use in well-water, and how earthen and copper vessels are thereby to be distinguished; Jesus says, "Cleanse first that which is within, that the outside may be clean also." Even the law regarding the Sabbath, with its hundred commandments, is regarded from the same point of view: "It is lawful to do well on the Sabbath-day;" for "the Sabbath was made for man, and not man for the Sabbath." Such a practice, however, was unheard of in Israel. The Pharisees who had come down from Jerusalem doubtless desired to ascertain whether Jesus immersed his hands,

---

[1] Derenbourg, Histoire de la Palestine, d'après les Talmuds, p. 196.

according to precept, before eating; whether he in so doing held them upwards or downwards; whether he moistened them as far as the elbow or the knuckles, or the tips of the fingers only, as the doctrine of the Rabbi Shammai prescribed in every case; and to their horror they found that he did not wash his hands at all, neither did his disciples.[1] On the Sabbath, when the pious Israelite avoided every useless step, he was seen walking for pleasure's sake through the fields, and his disciples rubbing the ears of corn with their hands, as though they knew not that he who thus plucks the ears of corn is as one who threshes corn, but he who threshes corn upon the Sabbath-day breaks the Sabbath and is guilty of death. Against such liberties the Pharisees had protested from the first, and even the cures Jesus performed, which otherwise would have seemed to the Rabbi proper enough, they would not consent should be done upon the Sabbath. On one occasion when he laid his hands upon a demoniac in the synagogue, the *archisynogogos* was in the highest degree indignant, and exclaimed to the congregation, "There are six days in which men ought to work; in them therefore come and be healed, and not on the Sabbath-day." Jesus, however, said to the rulers of the synagogue, "Ye hypocrites! doth not each one of you on the Sabbath loose his ox or his ass from the stall, and lead him away to water him? And ought not this woman, being a daughter of Abraham, whom Satan hath bound, lo, these eighteen years, to be loosed from this bond on the Sabbath-day?"[2] On another occasion he demanded, "Is it lawful on the Sabbath-days to do good, or to do evil?"[3] and adds also this question of conscience: "What man is there among you who, if his sheep fall into a pit on the Sabbath-day, will not lay hold on it and lift it out? How much, then, is a man better than a sheep?"[4] Such a justification was certainly almost more dangerous than the deed itself; Jesus, however, comes forward on this very point, conscious of his com-

---

[1] Mark vii. On the twenty-six precepts on washing the hands of Schylchan Aruch, compare Sepp, Thaten und Leben Jesu, 1864, p. 168.

[2] Luke xiii. 14—16.   [3] Luke vi. 10.   [4] Matt. xii. 11.

mission and vocation to destroy the curse of this servitude to the law. In full consciousness of being sent, he terms himself a Lord of the Sabbath, and demands of the teachers, "Did ye never read what David did, when he had need and was hungry, he and they that were with him? How he entered into the house of God in the days of Abiathar, the high-priest, and did eat the shewbread, which is not lawful to eat but for the priests, and gave also to them which were with him?" "Or did ye never read in the law how that on the Sabbath-day the priests in the temple profane the Sabbath, and are blameless? But I say unto you, that in this place is a greater thing than the temple."[1]

From the rapid extension which Jesus' ministry had gained in Capernaum, is it intelligible that from the very first the question was also raised in Jerusalem, the seat of the theocracy, whether earnest steps ought not to be taken against a prophetic work which was disturbing all the foundations of the state's existence as a theocracy. We know not by whom those Rabbis of Jerusalem had been commissioned when they came down to Capernaum and settled there,[2] but the summary proceedings which the Sanhedrin took against Jesus at the coming Passover, show that the high-priest Caiaphas and the mighty Annas were well informed as to the range of the movement begun by Jesus. That at an earlier date a desire had been manifested of inciting Antipas to take steps against Jesus, is a distinct remembrance of the primitive document;[3] but the purely spiritual doctrine of Jesus, which contemplated no external catastrophes of any kind, did not offer the least occasion for any political proceedings. If that interrogation as to the right of divorce, proposed on one occasion to Jesus by the Pharisees, were submitted in Galilee or Peræa,[4] then it would be possible to interpret it only as being an attempt to prepare the fate of John for Jesus through the agency of Antipas and his adulterous wife; but to the ideal height assumed by Jesus in his answer, the suspicions of an Herodian were not able

---

[1] Mark ii. 23—28; Matt. xii. 1—8; Luke vi. 1—5.
[2] Mark iii. 22. [3] Mark iii. 6. [4] Mark x. 1—12.

to follow. Whilst such a decisive failure was the result of the Pharisees' attempt against Jesus, the blows which his eloquence directed against their system cut, on the other hand, the deeper to the quick. In these assaults, too, he everywhere proceeds from the fundamental principle that with God nothing has value except the disposition; whilst the Pharisees, in their anxiety about the external, forgot the main thing. It was in this sense that he varied the saying: "Ye fools, did not he that made that which is without make that which is within also? But give alms of that which is within; and, behold, all things are clean unto you."[1] But to them, in truth, the tassels and knobs of the sanctuary were more important than the sanctuary itself, the gold on the temple more sacred than the temple, the sacrifice more sacred than the altar.[2] This forgetfulness of the moral foundations of the law for Rabbinical deductions from the law, is the theme peculiarly of Jesus' anti-pharisaic controversial discourses. "Woe unto you, Scribes and Pharisees, hypocrites!" he exclaims in one of the latter, "because ye tithe mint and anise and cummin, and have omitted the weightier matters of the law, judgment, mercy and faith." And in such diatribes it is not merely the rhetorical exaggerations of a popular address that we see. To what senselessness the endeavour to fulfil in actual reality every detail of the law to the utmost possible led, every page of the Talmud bears witness; and the moral blindness developed by this constant looking at the letter of the law can be proved even from Josephus himself. Are we not reminded of the words of Jesus, "Corban, it is a gift whatsoever thou mightest have been profited by me," when informed by the Pharisaic historian that, at the period of the famine in the year 45, when, according to his account, the assaron of wheat cost four drachmæ, according to the Apocalypse, the chœnix of wheat cost a denarius, and three chœnix of barley[3] as much, and when, owing to these exorbitant prices, hundreds of human beings literally perished for want of food, nevertheless in the temple, at the Passover, forty Attic

---

[1] Luke xi. 40.   [2] Matt. xxiii. 16.   [3] Rev. vi. 6.

bushels of corn were offered in sacrifice to fulfil the law? Nay, Josephus actually triumphs in the fact that not a crumb was lost to the temple, in spite of the crying hunger even of the sacrificing priests.[1] That not only this kind of unspiritual fulfilment, but also this too subtle refining of the law, leads to the destruction of its real essence, Jesus shows with especial distinctness in the case of the trifling with oaths by the Rabbis. Since gradations in oaths had been instituted, the belief had also sprung up that *one* oath was more binding than *another*, and even celebrated Rabbis taught forms of swearing which it was fearful to listen to, and yet were supposed to leave the heart unbound by the oath.[2] The commandment not to use the name of God had formed the starting-point of this mischievous trifling with oaths. Thus men swore "by heaven," "by earth," "by Jerusalem," "by my head,"[3] and so on. Worse forms, too, then came into use, and even Jesus the son of Sirach says, in this connection, "There is a word that is clothed about with death; let it not be found in Israel."[4] These very gradations show, however, that the obligatoriness of swearing was supposed to depend upon what was appealed to, and that oaths were distinguished as being sacred and common. "Woe unto you," does Jesus rebuke the Pharisees, "which say, Whosoever shall swear by the temple, it is nothing; but whosoever shall swear by the gold of the temple, he is bound. And whosoever shall swear by the altar, it is nothing; but whosoever sweareth by the gift that is upon it, he is bound."[5] In contradiction to this theory, he points out that

---

[1] Antiq. iii. 15, 3 .... καὶ λιμοῦ τὴν χώραν ἡμῶν καταλαβόντος, ὡς τεσσάρων δραχμῶν πωλεῖσθαι τὸν ἀσσαρῶνα, κομισθέντος ἀλεύρου κατὰ τὴν ἑορτὴν τῶν Ἀζύμων εἰς κόρους ἑβδομήκοντα, ... οὐδεὶς ἐτόλμησε τῶν ἱερέων κρίμνον ἓν φαγεῖν, τοσαύτης ἀπορίας τὴν γῆν κατεχούσης, δεδιὼς τὸν νόμον καὶ τὴν ὀργήν. According to Derenbourg and Geiger, this means that *after* the years of famine seventy cor of new fruit were stored up in the temple, which might not be eaten before the sacrificial gifts were presented! Compare Jüdische Zeitschrift v. Abr. Geiger, 1872, pp. 156 and 237.

[2] R. Akiba, Kalla, fol. 18, 2; R. Jochanan, Avoda sara, c. 2, 3, Sepp, 175; compare Matt. xxiii. 16—22, v. 33.

[3] Matt. v. 34—36. [4] Ecclesiasticus xxiii. 12. [5] Matt. xxiii. 16—19.

every oath is an appeal to God, and that therefore it is mischievous to devise more sacred and most sacred names for a vow. Not even by his head should a man swear, "because thou canst not make one hair white or black. But let your manner of speech be, Yea, yea; Nay, nay; for whatsoever is more than these cometh of evil." The same frivolous externality which was shown in the classification of oaths was also manifested in the divisions of the commandments of the law into higher and lower. Hillel, who had arranged the precepts of the Thorah—hitherto divided into 248 commandments, the number of the members of the human body, and 365 prohibitions, the number of days in the year—under 18 titles, had thereby raised the question in the schools, which of all the commandments was the highest, and thus given rise to a kind of classification of morality. The question, which was the great commandment in the law, already answered by Hillel in a manner worthy of Jesus,[1] was proposed to Jesus also by a scribe proud of his scholastic wisdom. Jesus, however, answers his interrogator with the שְׁמַע יִשְׂרָאֵל: "Hear, O Israel, the Lord our God is one God,"[2] taught to the lisping infant as his first prayer,[3] a reply that could not be in any way objected to from the standpoint of the school. Just as Jesus, on the one hand, contends against this specification of morality under separate commandments, so, on the other, does he draw with absolutely satirical features the piety that is exhausted in fulfilling such a register of duties, and in the endeavour to satisfy every single commandment beholds itself, finally, advanced to such a degree, that, like the Pharisee in the temple, it reckons up its own virtues by number and marks them off on a weekly calendar. The final result of the endeavour to fulfil the law to its minutest detail, and carry out each separate item with greater punctiliousness than any other fellow-disciple, was that the man, fully conscious of his virtue, recounted it to himself, to the world, and at last to God also. With a satire that is inexorable and will never become obsolete, does Jesus on this account chastise

---

[1] Grätz, iii. 226.   [2] Deut. vi. 4.   [3] Mark xii. 28—34.

these strutting popularity-seeking saints and pattern Israelites, who allow the light of their virtue to shine on every side; he chastises their practice of being surprised by the hour of prayer in the public streets, so that they may rehearse their prayers in public;[1] the wonderful accident that they always sit on the very first bench in the synagogue; their offended look if they are not greeted first in the street, and in conversation called Rabbi, Rabbi; their acrimonious, disfigured countenances, by which it can be seen that they are keeping an extra fast-day;[2] the ostentation of their almsgiving that is announced in the streets by the trumpet; their scrupulousness in paying tithes, which even tithes the few aniseed grains that come into their kitchens; and their intense anxiety about purity, which strains the wine before it is drunk to prevent any flies from being swallowed. Thus does he follow up all these absurdities of Pharisaism into all the petty, laughable varieties outwardly displayed, so that not even the elegance of a pious attire escapes his ridicule. When Judaism read in the law, "Thou shalt bind the words of the law for a sign upon thine hand, and they shall be as frontlets between thine eyes; and thou shalt write them upon the posts of thy house, and on thy gates,"[3] Jewish piety had taken this symbolical exhortation literally. From the thirteenth year, the one half of the above precept contained within two capsules was bound by leathern thongs on the forehead, whilst the other half written on parchment, in four parts, was put on the inner side of the left arm next the heart. Thus the law was literally ever before the eyes and upon the heart. The Sadducees had already made the comment upon this complete piece of externality, that the passage of Deuteronomy quoted was no more to be taken literally than Proverbs iii. 3: "Let not kindness and truth forsake thee; bind them around thy neck, write them upon the tablet of thy heart." But the Pharisees only cut their phylacteries so much the larger —true symbols of their conception of the external performance of the law. Thus they wore the tassels at the corners of their

[1] Matt. vi. 5.   [2] Matt. vi. 16.   [3] Deut. vi. 8, 9.

mantles that were to distinguish the Jewish garment, "that ye may look upon it, and remember all the commandments of Jehovah, and do them," as large as possible, in order that the extent of their piety might be inferred from the length of the Zizith.[1] Such little vanities also are not allowed them by Jesus. "All their works," he declares, "they do for to be seen of men; they make broad their phylacteries and enlarge the tassels on their garments: they desire to walk in long robes, and love greetings in the markets, and the highest seats in the synagogues, and the chief places at feasts; which devour widows' houses, and for show make long prayers."[2] "When ye pray," therefore is his instruction to his disciples, "ye shall not be as the hypocrites are; for they love to pray standing in the synagogues and in the corners of the streets, that they may appear unto men. And when thou doest alms, do not sound a trumpet before thee, as the hypocrites do in the synagogues and in the streets, that they may have glory from men."[3]

If, in a world in which, in addition to these errors of righteousness through the law, there were also so many other hindrances to the kingdom of God, we see Jesus coming forward thus emphatically and with such inexorable polemics against this tendency in particular, it is in consequence of the historical situation of the time. For the moment, he recognizes in the dominion of the Pharisees the chief hindrance of the kingdom of God. The people were too much in their hands for any results on a large scale to be hoped for, before they had been humiliated. They sit in Moses' seat, and hold the key of the kingdom of heaven. They shut the door of the kingdom against the people, and yet do not go in themselves. They are blind leaders of the blind, who fall into the ditch together with those they have led astray. As rulers of the people, they are, however, at the same time, with their system of ordinances, a real burden to them. Jesus accuses them of binding heavy burdens and laying them on the shoulders

---

[1] Numb. xv. 38—41.
[2] Luke xx. 46, 47; Matt. xxiii. 6, 7; Mark xii. 38—40.   [3] Matt. vi. 5, 2.

of the people, and yet that they themselves will not move them with their finger in order to relieve the neighbour.[1] Their numberless commandments, which no one can even retain in his memory, and therefore transgresses every moment quite unknowingly, he compares to concealed graves upon which one steps unwittingly and defiles oneself without knowing it,[2]—like those which a short time previously Antipas had come across in building the neighbouring Tiberias.[3] In conscious opposition to this harshness, Jesus emphasizes the fact that his yoke is easy and his burden light, and that, instead of new anxieties, he gives rest to troubled souls.

Few indications have been preserved in detail of what was the result of this contest against Pharisaism; but the final course of Jesus' life clearly shows that on the whole the people still sided with the Pharisees. Especially in Jerusalem itself and in Judæa did the fanatical persecution of the pious find a favourable ground, for there the masses were little inclined to understand the meaning of a kingdom of God the piety of which did not consist in the fulfilment of the law. But in Galilee, also, this contest against such an active opposition scarcely permitted him any longer to find a place of rest. Jesus had reason for avoiding Capernaum, and, as we have seen, frequently changed his place of abode at other places also on the lake.[4]

12. Jesus and the Messianic Idea.

The last journey which Jesus undertook before the coming Passover, that is, towards the end of the winter, was confined within the limits of Philip's territory that had just been transferred to the Roman administration. Starting from Bethsaida, he directed his course northwards. On the road to Cæsarea Phi-

---

[1] Matt. xxiii. 4.
[2] Luke xi. 44.
[3] Antiq. xviii. 2, 3.
[4] Mark viii. 10, 13, 22.

lippi, where the snowy summits of Lebanon and Hermon gleam above the numerous gorges of the highlands, he travels with the twelve from village to village.[1] The higher the road ascends, the more splendid does the view of the snow-capped mountains become. To the north lies mighty Hermon, the snow-fields of which glitter in the sun; to the north-west stare the gloomy, gigantic masses of Lebanon.[2] Across the marshy table-land of the upper valley of the Jordan, the way ascends to the town of Cæsarea Philippi, the most lovely spot in the Holy Land, situated near the mysterious sources of the sacred stream. To the north-east, bordered by deep gorges, there towers, even at the present day, the castle of Paneas, "the tower of Lebanon which looketh toward Damascus," the appearance of which was celebrated by the singer of the Song of Solomon.[3] Beneath the tower roars the forest stream, into the eddies of which the composer of the forty-second Psalm—a sorrowful prisoner—had looked down some five hundred years before: "My soul is bowed down within me when I remember thee from the land of Jordan and the mountains of Hermon. Deep calleth unto deep at the sound of thy waterfalls; all thy waves and thy billows pass over me."[4] To the south-west of the town, the plateau gradually descends. Numerous niches still show the places where formerly the statues of nymphs of the stream and satyrs stood. Here had Herod built a temple of white marble to Augustus, and the lately deceased Philip had made it the favourite pursuit of his peaceful reign to adorn the town with altars, votive tablets and statues.[5] In the face of the precipice that rises above the sources of the Jordan, there yawns a gloomy cavern. It was said that if this cave were followed up into the interior of the mountain, a concealed lake was reached, the outflow of which was supposed to form the springs at the foot of the hill. Everything here was new and still mysterious, and the inhabitants of that period, who had dedicated the whole

---

[1] Mark viii. 27.   [2] Furrer, p. 359.   [3] Song of Sol. vii. 4.   [4] Ps. xlii. 7, 8.

[5] Antiq. xv. 10, 3; Bell. i. 21, 3, iii. 10, 7; Vita Jos. 13; Renan, Vie de Jésus, cap. viii.

district to great Pan, had clothed forest and plain with legends of Gentile mythology. We shall in the course of this history once more come in contact with Cæsarea Philippi. After the conquest of Galilee, Titus and his beloved Bernice, Agrippa II. and other notable deserters, here sought a summer retreat. Then the valley rang with boisterous shouts of victory, and through the still night the clinking of wine-cups was heard. In the spring of the year 35, it was a quiet resting-place, deserted in consequence of Philip's death, and, in Roman hands, forming a secure asylum for the fugitive Messiah. Far removed from the contests of home, it became Jesus' last resting-place, where, in its tranquillity, he hoped to attain a right understanding with his disciples.

It was in the district of Cæsarea Philippi that, for the first time,[1] Jesus spoke to his followers about his Messianic rank, at the same time, however, keeping the end of John the Baptist in view. Here, then, will be the proper place for examining Jesus' position with regard to the Messianic idea.

As it has ever and again happened in the history of nations that the ideas which have long agitated the many ripen finally into clearness in the consciousness of *one* person, into decision in the will of *one*, so in Jesus had the Messianic thought attained personal existence. The impulse to preach the kingdom had come to Jesus, as we have seen, from John. Jesus had, like John, proclaimed the kingdom, and had—what John had not been able to accomplish—founded it. This kingdom, however, as it had been described by the prophets and lived in the faith of Israel, had A PERSONAL CENTRE. The Messianic kingdom was the kingdom of Messiah. John had not claimed to form this centre; he knew that it needed other powers than his to give existence and being to that which he had begun in reliance upon the help of one stronger than himself. But just as positively was it a fact of Jesus' consciousness that he himself was bringing the kingdom of God, that he had liberated all those elements which

[1] Implied in Mark viii. 27—34.

form it, that there was no need of any one else to come in order to fulfil the promises of Israel. Just as such considerations, when viewed thus abstractedly, are self-evident to us, so with equal necessity was it self-evident within the concrete national life of Judaism that Jesus recognized that he was the promised Messiah. Endowed as he was by Providence, and judging by the vocation to which it had appointed him, he could only regard himself as God's answer to the prayers of Israel. The Messianic faith was a desire, a hope, a promise. As surely as Jesus was conscious that he himself fulfilled this desire, this promise to the utmost, so surely must he have recognized that he was himself the Messiah. Faith in the kingdom was faith also in himself. Thus his Messianic position was not an outward adaptation of a contemporary idea, but was the perfectly regular development of his own consciousness. If, negatively, it be self-evident that Jesus' mission would have assumed another character had he grown up under the oaks of Germany, instead of under the palms of Nazareth, that the subject of Arminius or Maroboduus would have been different from that of Antipas, that the opponent of the Druids would have differed from the opponent of the Rabbis, so, positively, is it indisputable that for Jesus himself the facts of his consciousness were given him under those forms of viewing things in which Jewish thought in general was cast. Only by a freak of the imagination can it be supposed that an historical personality becomes conscious of the facts of its own inner life by conceptions other than those in which the thought of the age in general finds expression.

But he who thus apprehends the Messianic position of Jesus as being neither an accommodation nor a practical expedient, but a fact of his own consciousness, cannot assume that Jesus first arrived at this knowledge in the course of his public ministry. The consciousness of being Messiah was the starting-point, and not the result, of Jesus' work. Since it had become clear to him what the kingdom of the prophets meant, it must also have been clear to him that the breast which at the time was still alone in comprehending this kingdom was that promised personal source from which God would pour forth His stream of mercy. Was he certain, when he began his mission, of bringing the promised kingdom, then he was also sure that he was himself the promised one. Even at the time when John began to actually prepare for this kingdom, it was to Jesus no longer doubtful that in this man of the wilderness of Judah, part of the prophecy of the fathers had obtained life and being. He saw in him the promised Elijah—*not him of old* who the schools in their externality thought would come again with bald head, just exactly as the sorcerer of Tirathaba went to search for the very golden dishes, flagons and bowls, from which Aaron had once presented the drink-offering before the ark of the covenant[1] —but the Elijah of the promise, that is, the mighty pioneer of the kingdom, who had made the breach through which the Messiah was to enter. "And if ye will receive it, this is Elijah, which is to come."[2] *The* prophet, consequently, Jesus deemed had already come when he began his work, with whom, since the time of Nehemiah, the imagination of the people had been more occupied than with Messiah himself, because in the history of the Tishbite a connecting-point was given for its exercise.[3] Of him had the son of Sirach declared, "He was ordained for reproof for future time, to pacify the wrath of the Lord's judgment, and to turn the heart of the father to the son, and to establish the tribes of Jacob. Blessed are they that see thee and are adorned with love; for we also shall surely live."[4] The belief in his return has found its most official expression in the installation proclamation of Simon the Maccabee, in which it is declared that Simon shall be governor and high-priest until the time of the prophet.[5] In the days of Jesus, therefore, it had become the accepted dogma even of the common people, that "Elijah must

---

[1] Exodus xxv. 29.   [2] Matt. xi. 14.
[3] Malachi iv. 5.   [4] Ecclesiasticus xlviii. 10, 11.
[5] 1 Maccabees xiv. 41: εἰς τὸν αἰῶνα ἕως τοῦ ἀναστῆναι προφήτην πιστόν.

first come and restore all things."¹ This restoration of all things to a condition befitting the Messianic time, had, however, been already advanced by Malachi into the *moral sphere* when he promised that Jehovah would send Elijah the prophet, who would "turn the heart of the fathers to the children, and the heart of the children to their fathers, lest I come and smite the land with a curse."² Out of the fathers, the son of Sirach had made the father of Israel, Jehovah himself,³ and thus all the more assigned to Elijah a religious task. Now Jesus saw in the great revival which John had effected, the fulfilment of the prophecy, and the ways of God lay clearly before him. The one element could support and bear the other in him—belief in the Baptist and belief in his own mission. Moreover, no greater expenditure of religious faith was needed in order to see that part of prophecy which treated of the Messiah fulfilled, than had been required in order to recognize that the prophet of Machærus was Elijah. On all these grounds we have to assign Jesus' consciousness of being Messiah to a time prior to the beginning of his ministry.

But in so doing, it is not in any way denied that this consciousness was developed by constant friction with the external world, and that in its final form it was just as much the result of experience as it was a fact of original genius. This consciousness of being Messiah could only attain actual clearness and determination, indeed, by proving itself in life and wrestling with the external world. Thus did it become strong, certain of itself and of its individual determinations. The Messiah in Jesus rejoiced when Israel believed; it consoled itself with the love of the lowly and humble when the multitude refused belief; it retired within itself doubly proud when met with scorn and mockery.⁴ Even from passages from the Scriptures, as well as from the destinies of the age, do we find this consciousness of

---

[1] Mark ix. 12; Matt. xvii. 11. Not less than the ἀποκατάστασις πάντων consequently is assigned him.

[2] Malachi iv. 6. [3] Exodus iv. 22; Hosea xi. 1; Psalm lxxx. 17.

[4] Compare Keim, Jesus of Nazara, Vol. iv. pp. 45—76.

being Messiah deriving sustenance. But, above all, was it the joyous feeling of having brought the kingdom which sustained Jesus' faith in himself. In his little community's life of love, in the eight beatitudes which he had poured out over them, in the intercourse with the Father, to mediate between whom the angels ascended and descended, was the kingdom come. But if the kingdom were there, then the Messiah was there also.

But yet this consciousness of being Messiah was so far from being exclusively the product of success and of the opinion of others, it was so much a fact of his own consciousness, that it still remained intact when all external success was again dissipated. When the most evident promises of Scripture remained unfulfilled, when all the oaths of men proved false to him, when the disciple of Rock denied him, when for one hour there was no one, not even one, who believed in him, when God, too, forsook him,—still, even then he believed in himself, and saved the future of his work in that *he* alone did not despair of himself. So much was this consciousness of being Messiah the beginning and end of what he did and suffered.

Nevertheless, we saw that it had not in any wise been his first care, when he began his mission, to proclaim himself as the Messiah; but Jesus had first of all, in obedience to that mission, to found the kingdom itself. Thus we see him, it is true, even from the very first days in Capernaum, acting "as one who had authority;"[1] but yet rather concealing the extent of this authority than appealing to it, because the name of the Messiah would have led the people into trains of thought which were far distant from Jesus' province. Just as he had converted the Messianic kingdom of the national theocracy into a purely internal world of moral being, so also had he divested the office of the Messiah of all its political attributes. The consciousness of his followers, however, could only be gradually and gently led to the same perception. If the composer of the Psalms of Solomon had expected a king in armour as an aid against the catapults and ballistæ of

---

[1] Mark i. 22: ὡς ἐξουσίαν ἔχων.

Pompeius,[1] if even the philosopher Philo had promised a ruler and commander who would overthrow the nations,[2] what must have been the demands which the brave Galileans would have immediately made on Jesus as soon as he came to them with the name of the Messiah? On these deeper grounds was it, without doubt, that we see Jesus, whilst avoiding this name in reference to himself, yet at the same time assuming a polemic attitude towards the presentation of the Messiah as the son of David. As long as the people thought of the Messiah as belonging to the line of David, so long would they also represent the kingdom as being a day of vengeance on the Gentile, an enlargement of their own borders, an enriching of Jerusalem, and the dominion over the circle of the earth. The purple robe and sceptre of David must also be first completely driven out of the thoughts of the disciples, before Jesus could avow a name which otherwise could only be an occasion of misunderstanding. Therefore was it that Jesus, in presence of the people and in the hearing of the Rabbis, opposed this expectation of the son of David, and did so even with the weapons of the schools and on the ground of Scripture.[3] But the name of Messiah itself was altogether exposed to great misinterpretation; for how completely it had become intertwined with all the material hopes of the Jewish nation, and how well founded was the precaution with which Jesus availed himself of it, is proved by that account in the primitive document which states that, immediately after Jesus had revealed himself to his disciples as the Messiah, Salome, the mother of the sons of Zebedee, desired for her sons seats on the right and on the left of the Messianic throne.[4]

With this rejection of the worldly elements in the Messianic conception, with the assurance also that without his co-operation the enlisted children of the kingdom would turn to him as its centre, he had not yet, however, finished. Had he limited him-

---

[1] Psalmi Salomonis, ii. 1.
[2] Philo, de præm. Frankfurt. Ausgabe, 925. Bohn's translation, Vol. iii. p. 477.
[3] Mark xii. 35. [4] Mark x. 35; Matt. xx. 20.

self, as John had done, to once more proclaiming the coming kingdom, then his people would have remained in the belief that some successor would first bring the fulfilment of the kingdom of which Jesus knew that he was in full possession, and that it could only become truth by belief in himself. The work would have remained incomplete, and the followers would have consoled themselves by the coming of a Messiah whom Jesus yet knew was no longer to be expected. To prevent the one as well as the other error, Jesus designated himself as being the centre of the kingdom; but of all the titles of the Messiah, he selected the humblest, one that proclaimed, indeed, that the kingdom found its head in him and that excluded search for another, yet one that, at the same time, put aside all those worldly expectations which were indissolubly connected with the name of the Messiah, or of the Son of David, or of the Son of God. He called himself the Son of man![1] Under the image of the SON OF MAN, who was to come on the clouds of heaven, the book of Daniel had allegorically designated the universal dominion of Israel, but the later writers, the Messiah himself. The eighth Psalm also speaks of a son of man who is only a little lower than God, crowned with glory and honour, lord of the earth, which lays its gifts at his feet. As in the former case, Israel, so in the latter, humanity, is meant; but here, too, it was easy to find the Messiah. The selection of *this* official name, however, at the same time permitted a retreat upon Ezekiel, who is addressed by Jehovah as son of man, and who, by this title, describes himself as earth and dust in contrast with the Most High.[2] It was *this meaning* exactly that Jesus put into the words which yet, at the same time, betokened the Messiah, when he said, The Son of man hath not where to lay his head;[3] even as the Son of man is come not to be ministered unto, but to minister, and to give his life a ransom for many;[4] the Son of

---

[1] Mark iii. 11; Matt. xxvi. 63; Matt. xvi. 16.
[2] Ez. ii. 1, 3, 6, 8, iii. 1, 3, &c. &c.   [3] Matt. viii. 20.
[4] Matt. xx. 28.

man is come to save that which is lost;[1] and the Son of man shall suffer many things.[2] Whilst Jesus thus used this designation, there was not necessarily a reference in it to his Messiahship, otherwise he would not for the first time in the latter part of his life, at Cæsarea Philippi, have asked his disciples, "But whom say ye that I am?" That this name, however, was to lead the disciples up to Jesus' special position in the kingdom, is pointed out with sufficient clearness in other passages. Thus he who sows the good seed of the kingdom is the Son of man;[3] so also the Son of man has power on earth to forgive sins;[4] nay, the Son of man is a lord also of the Sabbath.[5]

More and more does he cast aside the humble cloak of the teacher, until at last at Cæsarea Philippi he stands before his disciples in the radiant adornment of the promised One of God. As the name of the Son of man becomes ever richer in allusions, the splendour of the Messiahship shines through here and there also in new sayings. Kings and prophets have desired to behold what the disciples behold, for he is more than Jonah and Solomon, and a greater thing than the temple. He it is of whom Isaiah prophesied, and Daniel and the Baptist; he is the bridegroom of Israel, who yet will be Israel's judge. But, above all, the name Son of man finds its counterpoise in the name Son of God. His Father is God, and it is before this Father that he will reveal himself to his own. "All things," he declares to his disciples, "are delivered to me by my Father; and none knoweth who the Father is but the Son, and he to whom the Son wills to reveal Him."[6] It is not, therefore, because he is to dash the Gentile into pieces like potsherds and burn up the transgressors with a devouring fire, that he is the Messiah, but because no one knows the Father as he does, because also no one is known by the Father as he is, and because it is he who has vouchsafed the world an insight into these mysteries of the Godhead, into the character of the love from above, into the communion between

---

[1] Matt. xviii. 11.   [2] Matt. xvii. 12.   [3] Matt. xiii. 37.
[4] Mark ii. 10.   [5] Mark ii. 28.   [6] Luke x. 22.

the Creator and creature. It is in this connection that Jesus declares the eyes of the disciples blessed on account of what they behold, and, in real consciousness of being a Saviour, utters the cry, " Come unto me, all ye that are weary and heavy-laden, and I will give you rest. Take my yoke upon you, and learn from me; for I am meek and lowly in heart; and ye shall find rest unto your souls. For my yoke is easy and my burden is light."[1] He hears fountains of living water gushing up within his own breast, and therefore calls unto himself all who are athirst, weary, sick and faint, in order that they may become whole. After all this, it was no longer possible for there to be any misunderstanding between Jesus and his disciples as to the fact that he was the Messiah, and in what sense he was so. Gradually had he allowed this conviction to ripen within them. The name only of the Christ, the title, remained unproclaimed. It was a sacred secret between him and them, not meddled with, reverently guarded and yet blissfully enjoyed in silent giving and taking. Now first at Cæsarea Philippi does Jesus cast aside the covering, and asks aloud about that which hitherto no one had dared to pronounce. A sign that now the time for speaking has come. No longer dare Jesus delay making it clear to the nation itself that the promised Messiah has appeared, and that it is not to await any other. But this could only take place at Jerusalem, where the nation, collected as such, was to be met. Just as previously Judas the Galilean had led his troops from Gamala southwards, as the Egyptian of the year 59 had occupied the Mount of Olives, as all the later Messiahs had stretched forth their hands towards the temple on which the guidance of the people depended, so now we behold Jesus starting forth for Jerusalem. That it was a journey of life or death, he could not conceal from himself. As certainly as hitherto he had prudently avoided the plots of the Pharisees and Antipas to quietly destroy him, so now with equal certainty did he go up to the feast in the full consciousness of going to meet his death. In the same

---

[1] Matt. xi. 28—30; compare Keim, Geschichte Jesu, 1873, p. 212.

hour in which he openly and unequivocally revealed himself to
the disciples as the Messiah, "he began to teach his disciples
that the Son of man must suffer many things, and be rejected
by the elders and the chief priests and the scribes, and be killed;"[1]
from which declaration the Collection of Sayings has without
doubt derived the words, " I have a baptism to be baptized with;
and how am I straitened till it be accomplished!"[2] John's
bleeding head had already foretold what his own end must be.
"They knew him not," did he declare of the Baptist, "but did
unto him whatsoever they listed. Thus shall also the Son of
man suffer at their hands."[3] Yet hardly did it any longer need
a spirit to rise from the grave in order to say this. He that,
already rejected by the people, stretches forth his hand to the
crown of the Messiah, cannot deceive himself as to the significance of this action, least of all if he be going up for this purpose
to Jerusalem, which not to-day for the first time is termed by
him "the grave of the prophets."[4] If Bethsaida, Chorazin and
Capernaum have rejected him, what can he expect in that city
which kills the prophets and stones them that are sent unto her?
Can one who has been outlawed in Galilee present himself to
the people in the temple as the Messiah with any other expectation than that expressed by Jesus in his last discourse, that the
people will snatch up stones and kill him, even as their fathers
slew Zechariah the son of Jehoiada in the temple fore-court?[5]
It was not the Roman cross—which probably first threw its
shadow backwards when Golgotha lay behind the disciples—
that stood before his spirit's eye; it was not the death of the
Baptist—from whose murderers he seemed secure in the land of
their enemy Pilate; but an end *at the hands of the people*, an end
to which that of the popularly beloved John presented rather
a contrast than the prophetic prototype. It was first from the
certainty of his own death that Jesus could compare his own

---

[1] Mark viii. 31.   [2] Luke xii. 50.   [3] Matt. xvii. 12.   [4] Luke xiii. 33.

[5] Matt. xxiii. 35, 37, significantly emphasizes the stoning twice, the legal punishment of those who have infringed the honour of Jehovah, and his own situation reminds
him of 2 Chron. xxiv. 20—22.

fate with that of the Baptist, and that of his disciples with that of the school of John;[1] for as regards the course of their development, the destinies of the two had nothing in common. In this connection is it, therefore, that Jesus seeks to disclose a glance into the times when the bridegroom will be taken away from them, and the days of mourning will come upon them, when it will be needful to stand firm.[2] Wholly in the watchwords of another man of Galilee of this period, Judas the Galilean, does Jesus call upon his disciples to follow him, for whosoever shall seek to save his life shall lose it, but whosoever shall lose his life shall save it. This had been the exact purport of the exhortations of the brave scribe of Gamala to his disciples, to serve God alone as Lord, and to despise death if only they could remain true to Jehovah,[3] surrendering the temporal to gain the eternal,[4]—watchwords with which the high-minded sons of the patriot who had fallen a generation before were able even now to inspire Galilee.[5]

But here the farther question at once presented itself to Jesus, How could the development of the kingdom of God continue to advance, if its Messiah fell at the very moment when he came forward as Messiah; and how was the contradiction of such an end with his position as Messiah to be reconciled by Jesus himself? Certainly he had given to the question why he must needs lose his life in Jerusalem, yet another answer than that of Jewish fanaticism, or the cruelty of Antipas and the want of conscience of the procurator; and he declares this answer in the well-attested words, that he is come to give his life a ransom for many. Should he shun the death apportioned by God, then the kingdom will fall into ruins even before it has become really visibly elevated above the earth; should he submit to the baptism which he dreads, then his blood will cement the new covenant. In this sense was it that he sealed his work with the blessing, "Take ye of it. This is my blood of the new cove-

---

[1] Matt. xvii. 12.   [2] Matt. xvi. 24—28; Mark viii. 34—38.
[3] Antiq. xviii. 1, 6.   [4] Antiq. xviii. 1, 1.   [5] Antiq. xviii. 1, 1.

nant which is shed for many."[1] It was the idea of sacrifice, therefore, so frequent in the Old Testament, which here furnished the answer.

With his death, however, Jesus' mission is not finished. Behind the shadow of death lies the future of the kingdom, bright and clear, a future that could not be contemplated apart from the permanent activity of its founder, centre and lord. Not only was Jesus most intensely conscious that those who stoned the body could not hurt the soul,[2] but he had also the certain presentiment of genius—AN EXTENSION OF HIS PERSONAL ACTION BEYOND THE LIMITS OF HIS TEMPORAL EXISTENCE.[3] Such presentiments of the soul, however, which cannot be brought, after the analogy of past and experienced circumstances, to individual expression, because lying beyond the domain of personal experience, are everywhere wont to be clothed in the imagery belonging to the circle of traditional religious conceptions. So at the present day also do the dying present their future existence in the imagery of their youth and of their church, though ever with the additional consciousness that the traditional, sacred hieroglyphics do not completely describe what the sacred voice itself within them declares. The traditional representation of the activity of the Messiah was for Jesus that given by the book of Daniel of the Son of man coming upon the clouds of heaven, and through this prophetically given representation Jesus arrived at the description of his future activity in the form of a regeneration to the judgment upon the clouds of heaven. Still we must not overlook the connecting terms. The first question to Jesus was not as to *his own* future, but as to the future of the kingdom, and this he neither could nor dared give up. Because he believed in the immediate coming of this kingdom, he believed also in his own return in this kingdom and with this kingdom. In heaven, whither he was going, was the kingdom of heaven, with which he now dared to hope that he should himself come,

---

[1] Mark xiv. 24.   [2] Matt. x. 28, xvi. 25.
[3] Holtzmann, Synoptische Evangelien, p. 493.

provided that God would bestow this kingdom on the earth, a thing which no one disputed. As certainly as he thought of ascending there where the angels behold the face of the Father, and as certainly as he knew that the kingdom of heaven was realized above, so surely must he now suppose also that he should return thence on the day of Jehovah; and this was the path of the Messiah which had been foretold by the very prophet from whom not only had his contemporaries generally derived their concrete conceptions of the constitution of the kingdom, but in whose intimate acquaintance the Messianic consciousness of Jesus itself had ripened.[1] In Daniel's expression of the Son of man, he had found the proper formula for his own personal position as the Messiah; in Daniel's image of the stone by which the kingdoms of the world are shattered, he saw a symbol of his position in regard to the opposition of the powers of this world, which would be ground to powder by the stone, "not by the hand of man," which Jehovah has chosen to be the head of the corner.[2] Thus does he also behold his own future kingdom described by the imagery of the same prophet: "Behold, one like a son of man came with the clouds of heaven, and came to the Ancient of Days, and they brought him near before him. And there was given him dominion, and glory, and a kingdom, that all people, nations and languages should serve him."[3] He alone who had Jesus' consciousness and occupied the standpoint of the Christ, who looked onwards through thousands of years, and bore within himself the presentiment of an action upon the world which should revolutionize it, could decide how far a true expression for this actual consciousness was here found. This, however, is indisputable, that the contemporaries whom Jesus gathered together into the first Messianic community would have been very speedily scattered had he expressed his sense of his own importance as enduring through all ages in a manner less

---

[1] Antiq. x. 10, 4; Bell. vi. 5, 4.
[2] Compare Matt. xxi. 44 and Luke xx. 17, 18, with Daniel ii. 34, 44, 45.
[3] Daniel vii. 13, 14.

sensibly comprehensible and less familiar to the children of his
own age. All his discourses end, therefore, after he had firmly
resolved to go up to Jerusalem, with this perspective. The
generation then living should not taste of death until it had
seen the Son of man coming in his kingdom;[1] the disciples
should not have finished the cities of Israel, till the Son of man
be come;[2] as by the putting forth of the buds in spring, so by
the increasing distress, shall they infer the nearness of his return.[3]
Most descriptively does Jesus, in the parable of Archelaus, compare himself to the prince who goes into a foreign country in
order to receive a kingdom. Until his return, he bids his disciples make the most of the pounds he has entrusted to them.
His people, however, act as at the time when an embassy was sent
to Rome after Archelaus; they declare to the lord who bestows
the kingdom, "We will not have this man to reign over us."
But it will happen to them before the throne of God as it did
before that of Augustus. The rejected man will nevertheless
return as their king, and will settle accounts with his people.
The industrious ones who have made the most of their pound,
he will place over ten or over five cities; from the slothful he
will take even what he had entrusted them with before his
departure. But those his enemies which would not that he
should reign over them, he will have brought and slain before
him.[4] Nor do the parables of the good and bad fish, of the tares,
of the ten virgins, all of whom have lamps but not all of them
oil, and of the righteous who in giving food and drink to the
least of their brethren have given unto Jesus himself, in any less
degree announce the return of Jesus as the judge of Israel. The
thought of the judgment, after all the offences and persecutions
which the kingdom has had to endure, comes forward altogether
more prominently than before. The vengeance of Jehovah was,
indeed, the essential feature in the Old-Testament descriptions
of the Great Day. Yet it is not, as in the prophets, Jehovah

---

[1] Matt. xvi. 28.   [2] Matt. x. 23.   [3] Matt. xxiv. 32.
[4] Luke xix. 12—27; Matt. xxv. 14—30.

who is the Judge, rather does Jesus claim the judgment-seat for himself.[1] He sits as Messiah upon the throne which Daniel had assigned to the Ancient of Days, and beside him are the twelve apostles as judges of the tribes of Israel. Those judged are his contemporaries, the people of Israel, especially the inhabitants of Capernaum, Chorazin and Bethsaida, to whom salvation had been first of all offered.[2] The attitude which men have taken towards him and his kingdom is the decisive point in this judgment. The kingdom itself, which now begins, is described quite generally as being the promised kingdom, prepared for the righteous by the Father from the beginning of the world. Abraham and the patriarchs will have a share in it, and the righteous shall, in the words of Daniel, shine forth as the sun.[3] The parable promises one ten, another five cities; houses and lands are also mentioned in the Jewish-Christian tradition as being restored an hundred-fold to those to whom they are due; certain is it, however, that, according to Jesus, the children of the kingdom possess the earth, whilst the unrighteous descend to everlasting torment.

How much of this imagery of the advent is due to the constructive tradition of a later age can hardly now be determined, inasmuch as it is exactly here that imagination was most prompted to create. As surely as Daniel's prophecy of the advent of the Son of man and the kingdom of God was Jesus' own belief—as certainly as some of the most essential parables of the Collection of Sayings would lose their point, and one section of the oldest tradition that has become common to the Synoptical Gospels out of the historical source would remain quite inexplicable on the supposition of a later origin of this belief—so certainly, on the other hand, have these discourses relating to the second coming of Jesus been enriched from a double source by our earliest informants. The accounts of the foretokens of the second coming are derived in part, it is manifest, from the experiences of the earliest community, and owe their origin wholly to the

---

[1] Matt. vii. 22, 23, xvi. 27, xxiv. 30, 31, xxv. 19, 31—46.
[2] Matt. xi. 20—24.   [3] Matt. xiii. 43.

yearning for the second coming of Jesus. The picture of the Christophany itself, however, is taken from pictures of the last things given by Daniel and Enoch, as drawing and colouring alike prove.

We shall not err, especially, if we accept those terms which *postpone* the second coming as the necessary extensions of a later period. For all the indications point to the fact that Jesus, on the contrary, placed his second coming and the advent of the kingdom immediately after the completion of his sacrificial death; just as in the parable the king undertakes only a short journey during which he leaves his servants behind in order that they may trade with their pounds until he come. If the disciples go up to Jerusalem with him in a firm expectation of the kingdom being revealed, then it is quite possible also that Jesus left it an open question whether God might not perhaps let the cup pass away from him, and, contrary to his expectation, bring the kingdom without demanding the sacrifice of the Messiah. But in any case his death was so much only a moment of transition to the glory that would then at once manifest itself, that the disciples dreamed of the latter alone, and put the transient troubles entirely out of their minds.

That Jesus, too, had not at all definitively negatived the question, whether his people might not still decide for him, is proved by the fact that he begins the discussion with the disciples at Cæsarea Philippi on this most important subject with the words, "Who do men say that I am?" The question as to the opinion of the people seems to be little in harmony with the proud self-confidence of the Messiah. But it was simply indispensable for the decisive attempt in Jerusalem to learn the temper of the people and their disposition. The disciples inform him that some—as the tetrarch Antipas—believe that he is John the Baptist risen from the dead. Others hold that he is the great prophet who is to precede the advent of the kingdom, whether, with 2 Maccabees ii. 1, they expect that this prophet will be Jeremiah, or, with Malachi iii. 1, Elijah. But Messiah, only the diseased and the beggars term him: by the people, as a whole, the disciples cannot testify that this wished-for name is given. Not content with such designations, Jesus now asks the disciples themselves, "But who do ye say that I am?" whereupon Peter, with his usual impetuosity, replies, "Thou art the Christ." Neither several failures, nor the banishment and flight of the last period, nor the thoroughly menial form of the Son of man, could disturb the view, in these simple minds, of the spiritual height and moral majesty of their Master. Whatever flesh and blood might say to the contrary, to them he remains the Christ. But undoubtedly he ought, they thought, to be so in a much higher degree than had yet been displayed; and they expected that he would succeed in becoming, externally and publicly, what he had long been to them in secret. Solemnly does Jesus address his favourite disciple with the words, "Blessed art thou, Simon, son of Jona, for flesh and blood hath not revealed it unto thee, but my Father in heaven." Compensated for all the unbelief of the nation by this confession of the leader of his little flock, he declares, "Thou art the rock, and upon this rock I will build my church; and the gates of hell shall not prevail against it."[1] But the faith of the disciples, ready to submit for the present, had not yet ceased taking counsel with flesh and blood with regard to the future. When Jesus proceeded to show them that the Son of Man, according to the Scripture, must suffer many things, that he would be rejected by the elders and chief priests and scribes, and that only through the gates of death could he enter into glory, in order after three days—perhaps the definitely or indefinitely remembered two times, time and half a time of Daniel—to return again in glory, then a panic seized upon the little community, and again Peter was the first to find utterance: "God forbid it thee, Lord: this shall never be unto thee!" Although Peter's confession had been to Jesus previously a sign from God, yet now he heard in this warning the devil speak. "Get thee behind

[1] Matt. xvi. 18.

me, Satan!" he exclaims; "for thou savourest not the things that be of God, but those that be of men."

So they proceeded, and when the people collected around the Master, who was known here, too, Jesus again took up the thread of his discourse—only too intelligible for the disciples—by directing the solemn words to the crowd that was offering itself to him: "If any man desire to come after me, let him deny himself, and take up his cross, and follow me. For whosoever desireth to save his life shall lose it; and whosoever shall lose his life for my sake, shall find it. For what is a man profited, if he gain the whole world, but lose his life? or what shall a man give in exchange for his life? For whosoever shall be ashamed of me and of my words, of him shall the Son of man be ashamed when he shall come in his glory, and in the glory of his Father, and in the glory of the holy angels."[1] Second coming, angels and the kingdom of heaven, are nevertheless always the end of this announcement of his sufferings; and thus it is perfectly intelligible that the disciples seem far more intoxicated by dreams of glory than depressed by thoughts of death. Nay, they immediately raise the question,[2] how comes it that Elijah has not appeared, who, according to the opinion of the teachers, ought to precede the coming of the Messiah: "Why say the scribes that Elijah must first come?" It yet needed the special assurance of Jesus that Elijah had come before they thought of the Baptist, who had appeared to the people in Elijah's mantle. Tradition was not satisfied with this spiritual return of the Tishbite, and was afterwards able to tell how at that very time Moses and Elijah had descended from heaven in order to greet the Messiah on the Mount of Transfiguration. Under the impression of this great disclosure did Jesus retrace his steps towards Capernaum, and it is significant that the conversation of the disciples turned upon their position in the coming kingdom, whilst Jesus himself earnestly and silently preceded them.

[1] Matt. xvi. 24—27; Luke ix. 23—26.   [2] Mark ix. 11; Matt. xvii. 10.

13. THE PASSOVER OF DEATH.

One of the parables of the *Parousia* is taken from the fig-tree, which tells of the coming spring by its branches being full of sap and putting forth buds; thus it was the first harbingers of spring which had called to mind that the time of the Passover was nigh, when Jesus intended to begin his journey to Jerusalem.[1] According to a remembrance of the first Gospel, his arrival in Capernaum happened just at the time when the temple-tax was collected, i.e. between the 15th and 25th of Adar,[2] thus giving Jesus a fresh opportunity for describing himself as the King of Israel, and his followers as the King's children who ought legally to be exempted from the tribute.[3]

What was the present position of affairs in Galilee, however, can be clearly seen from the fact that Jesus was seeking so to arrange his journey that no one in the country of Antipas should be aware of his presence. So he journeyed by little frequented paths through the apostate land of his home. The narrative of the Synoptics manifestly distinguishes between *his* interpretation of this last journey and the expectations of the twelve. Jesus himself is occupied with thoughts of death; the disciples, who follow behind him, are rejoicing, on the other hand, at the decision, and debate who shall probably be the first in the new kingdom. So they arrived quietly in Capernaum. In the house of Peter, Jesus asked them, "What disputed ye by the way?" But they held their peace, for by the way they had disputed among themselves who should be greatest. And he sat down and saith unto them, "If any man desireth to be first, he shall be last of all and minister of all." And he took one of the little children "who believed on him,"[4] embraced it, and set it in the midst of them, with the words, "Except ye become as little children, ye shall not enter into the kingdom of heaven."[5] "Take heed that ye despise not

---

[1] Matt. xxiv. 32.
[2] Compare Keim, Jesus of Nazara, Vol. iv. p. 304.
[3] Matt. xvii. 24—26.
[4] Mark ix. 42.
[5] Matt. xviii. 1—5.

one of these little ones; for in heaven their angels do always behold the face of the Father which is in heaven."[1] Thus once more does the loving warmth of a family circle with which he is acquainted even to the children surround him, before he advances to the crisis. We see him again in the country beyond the Jordan in intercourse with the people before the time of the Passover has arrived.

The news that the Prophet of Galilee intended going up to the feast at Jerusalem must have sounded in the ears of his followers like a mighty call to arms, for it was known what such prophetic expeditions to the holy city betoken. Thus we see a troop of believers—among them numerous women—entrust themselves to his guidance. When the signal-lights in the night of the first of Nisan had announced the new moon, the faithful were found collected together, and on the third the procession to the feast set forth. Whilst the great column of Galileans going to the feast chose the nearer way up the mountains through Samaria, Jesus proceeded with his flock through the territory beyond the Jordan to Jericho.

Passing the ever-green forests of the mountains of Gilead,[2] passing the roaring waters and tributary streams of the Jabbok, Jesus reached the theatre of John's baptism, from which he had formerly started. The distant mountains of Machærus cast their shadows across his path, and everywhere did he here wander through reminiscences of the man who had first begun preaching the kingdom of God. Mount Nebo, where is Moses' grave, and Mount Attarus, on which John had been lowered into his sepulchre, shut in the view. A grave and earnest frame of mind settled upon the wanderers. "And Jesus went before them; and they were amazed; and as they followed, they were afraid."[3]

It was probably the evening of the third day when, crossing the Jordan, they reached the first villages in Judæa. The Prophet from Nazareth was here greeted with joy, and the mothers brought

---

[1] Matt. xviii. 10. [2] See Robinson, Physical Geography of the Holy Land.
[3] Mark x. 32.

their darlings to him in order that he might bless them. With the grand plans of the disciples this idyllic beginning harmonized but badly, and they rebuked the women and their children, so that Jesus had to remind them that it was to the child-like heart that he had promised the kingdom. "And he took them up in his arms and blessed them, putting his hands upon them."[1] Behind the women came soon enough the men also; the crowds increase, and the procession of the Galilean Prophet to the feast more and more assumes the appearance of the march of the Messiah to the city of David. In vain do the Pharisees here again, too, cross his path; their speedy discomfiture only increases the number of his adherents. The multitude were, as a matter of fact, desirous of making a movement of a religious tendency at every feast, and thus the Prophet of Nazareth afforded them a convenient opportunity on this occasion of attaching the national demonstration to him. The disciples rejoiced, "for they thought that the kingdom of God would immediately appear."[2] As their goal drew nigh, their covetousness increased; and Peter here, too, was the first to venture to ask the question, "Behold, we have forsaken all and followed thee: what shall we have therefore?" Under present circumstances, Jesus will only adjust the form and not the contents of this petition. He promises the disciples at the renewal of all things twelve thrones for judging the twelve tribes, and rich recompence for their sacrifices; but adds this warning also, "the first will be last, and the last first." And since there is a personal contest once more, whether those who followed the preaching of the kingdom in the very first hour must not also receive the greater recompence, Jesus casts a glance backwards upon the day's work that he has accomplished, and upon the labourers of the first, third, sixth and ninth hour, and foretells that the householder will make no distinction, but say to his steward, "Give every man his penny."[3]

But the promise of the twelve thrones nevertheless acted upon their minds, and Salome especially, the mother of the sons of

[1] Mark x. 16. [2] Luke xix. 11. [3] Matt. xx. 1—16.

Zebedee, indulged in the thought that two brothers—her sons naturally—ought to sit on the right hand and on the left of the Messiah.[1] She therefore approached Jesus with this petition, and in regard to her, too, Jesus by no means assumes a merely repellent attitude. From the answer to this very petition does it become clear, on the contrary, how Jesus himself regarded the coming hour of suffering as being merely the transition to the Messianic glory which would then be immediately revealed. "Are ye able," does Jesus inquire directly of the sons of Zebedee, "to drink the cup that I drink? or be baptized with the baptism that I am baptized with?" "We are able," was the resolute answer of the sons of thunder. But Jesus replied: "The cup that I drink of ye shall indeed drink ... but to sit on my right hand or on my left hand is not mine to give: but it shall be given to them for whom *it is prepared*."[2] The ambition of the house of Zebedee, however, had brought discord into the day's tone, and it became necessary for Jesus to refer to *his own* example. "Ye know that the princes of the Gentiles exercise lordship over them, and they that are great exercise authority over them. It shall not be so among you: but whosoever will become great among you, let him be your minister; and whosoever will be first among you, let him be your servant: even as the Son of man is come not to be ministered unto, but to minister, and to give his life a ransom for many."[3] Thus Jericho was reached. Here, too, did the favourable disposition of the inhabitants and of the processions to the feast, now crowding together, continue. With shouts of joy is Jesus greeted; the people even climb into the trees in order to see the Prophet. Certainly this excitement of the masses was of a dubious character. For just as formerly, in the days of Herod, the Roman Agrippa had been made, in a similarly boisterous manner, the centre of the festal tumult, so, too, at a later period there was never wanting at every feast some Prophet, Rabbi or Messiah whom, in defiance of the Romans,

---

[1] Compare Keim, Geschichte Jesu, 1873, p. 269.
[2] Matt. xx. 20—23; Mark x. 35—40. [3] Matt. xx. 25—28.

they could elevate into prominence. Jesus did not decline the
acclamations which now he needed, but he gave the people a
token of how he understood his Messiahship. Out of all who
now pressed around him, he chose the hated chief among the
tax-gatherers in order to abide at his house; and when the
multitude began to murmur, he declared, "This day is salvation
come to this house, forsomuch as he also is a son of Abraham.
For the Son of man came to seek and to save that which was
lost."[1] The excitement due to the feast proved to be stronger
than their political disappointment, and the departure from
Jericho was even accompanied by a miracle of healing, which
calls to mind the stormy days of the Galilean enthusiasm.

A great body of followers attached itself to him, and we have
to think of Jesus as being at the head of an imposing procession
when he advanced from the City of Palms upwards through the
rose-gardens and date-groves towards the barren rocky mountains
over which the way to Jerusalem leads. Through a steep and
narrow path hewn out of the rock, the bridle path ascends up the
mountain-side. This was the spot where the good Samaritan
found the man who had fallen among thieves. Half-way there
was an inn.[2] The road beyond runs through a lonely valley.
Thorn-bushes and fragments of rock cover the slopes.[3] On
an eastern spur of the Mount of Olives, Bethany and Beth-
phage then first emerge, half hidden between hills and trees.
Here Jesus had friends. He sent forward his disciples: they
were to bring him an ass's foal. For according to the prophecy
in Zechariah ix. 9, did he intend entering into Jerusalem:
"Behold, thy king cometh unto thee: he is righteous and victorious; lowly, and riding upon an ass, the foal of a she-ass,"
symbolically pointing out the character of the Messiahship which
he has to bring. A charming vale adorned with figs,[4] almonds,
olives[5] and palms,[6] leads to the saddle between the Mount of

---

[1] Luke xix. 9, 10. [2] Luke x. 34. [3] Furrer, Wanderg. pp. 65 and 145—187.
[4] Mark xi. 13, xiii. 28. [5] Matt. xxi. 8.
[6] Matt. xxi. 8; compare Furrer, Wanderung, p. 64.

Olives and the Hill of Offence. There lay Jerusalem, extended to the west, in front Mount Moriah with its glittering roofs. Quickly does the way descend towards the city; but it led even then past Gethsemane. The view of Zion's city, and the knowledge that they were led by "the righteous and victorious one," kindled a violent enthusiasm in the Galileans. In full consciousness of the importance of the moment, they broke out into cries of joy: from palms, myrtles and other shrubs they tore off boughs, they waved branches, strewed the path with green leaves; they even spread their garments in the way, in order that Jesus as he advanced might ride over them. All this called to mind the joyous Feast of Tabernacles, when they sang, "Hosanna! save now, O Lord; send now prosperity," and the praises of him that cometh in the name of the Lord, in the one hundredth and eighteenth Psalm, which the pilgrims to the feast usually sang as they entered Jerusalem. So the cry arose, "Hosanna to the Son of David! Blessed is he that cometh in the name of the Lord. Hosanna in the highest!" Thus those "that went before and that followed after," cried, and the hopes of the disciples seemed to be fulfilled. The city of David also was moved. The peaceful picture of the Messiah here unfolded as a reminiscence out of Zechariah excited wonder, and satisfied with such a beginning of the feast, they said one to another that the Prophet of Galilee had on this occasion appeared. The children joined in the cry of the Galilean visitors, and the propitious entry gave hopes of a favourable advance.

This solemn entry at the head of the Galilean bands in itself shows that Jesus intended acting here otherwise than in Galilee. The path of instruction could not here lead to the goal; for it, the feast was too short, the authorities too hardened. It was upon the path of action that he must establish his Messiahship. Only by making speedy use of the favourable disposition of the people could he become their recognized Leader, Prophet and Lawgiver, that is, their Messiah. If he did not wish to be crushed by the priests and those in power, then he must take them by surprise by suddenly unfurling the Messianic banner, and overwhelming the murmurs of opposition by the rejoicing shouts of the people. This plan was not too Utopian among a nation that from the days of the patriarchs had entrusted the fulness of power to the wisest, to a Moses, a Joshua, and other judges and prophets, kings and Maccabees, and that, unlike any other nation, was accustomed to elect spiritual monarchs— JUDGES. Should he, however, succumb, as he himself expected, then there was God who would interfere for the kingdom, and the definite assent of his own internal consciousness that then he would become, not merely a judge in Israel, but Judge of the world, Saviour of all peoples. For the first day, the greetings of those who had gone out to meet him could suffice; and Jesus confined himself for the present to walking round in the temple, which was directly accessible from the valley of the Kidron. Through the eastern gate of the temple, to which the temple synagogue was immediately adjacent, they entered into the porch of the outer fore-court. As the Passover was close at hand, and the first visitors to the feast had already entered the city, a brisk life prevailed here. Women, convalescent after child-bed, were bargaining at the dove-stalls in the outer porch for the usual sacrificial offering; strangers were purchasing Jewish money for their Gentile coins;[1] cattle, ready bound, were bellowing and occasioning confusion and uproar;[2] into the thirteen treasury-chests the passers-by cast their offerings from the money just exchanged.[3] The whole made a painful impression upon Jesus. The same evening he returned to Bethany, in order to seek accommodation, as was usual among the less wealthy, in one of the surrounding villages. The friendly house of Simon the leper offered him on this occasion its hospitable shelter.[4]

Only from Jesus' intention of bringing the people collected at the feast to an immediate decision, does it become intelligible why he now exchanges the gentle forms of the Galilean dis-

[1] Mark xi. 15.   [2] John ii. 14.   [3] Mark xii. 41.   [4] Mark xiv. 3.

courses for a vehemently offensive attitude towards the priests and teachers of the people, by which the Messiah of Galilee recalls rather the lion of Judah than the lamb of the second Isaiah that is led to the slaughter. So on the following day he began his mission in Jerusalem with one of those symbolical actions with which the ancient prophets at times confronted erring Israel, and indeed with an action such as pious expectation had reserved for the Messiah—the renovation or purification of the temple. When he came again into the temple, and saw in the porch the chafferers at the dove-stalls and the money-changers' tables, he made use of his Messianic rights, overturned the tables of the dealers, and exclaimed to the people: "It is written, My house shall be called the house of prayer; but ye are making it a den of thieves."[1] It is in this connection probably that he spoke of a destruction and restoration of the temple. The multitude flocked around him, and so the temple authorities did not venture to apprehend him. But when the children, remembering the greeting of yesterday, began once more to exclaim, "Hosanna to the Son of David!" the Rabbis and priests addressed themselves to him, and demanded that he should himself check this sacrilege. He, however, said, "Have ye never read, Out of the mouths of babes and sucklings thou hast perfected praise?"[2] On the next morning, also, Jesus returned to the temple in order to address the people. The priests meanwhile had remembered their official authority, and now met him with the question, "By what authority doest thou these things?" Jesus replied, before the assembled people, "I also will ask you one question, which, if ye tell me, I also will tell you by what authority I do these things. The baptism of John, was it from heaven or from men? Answer me." The answer was difficult. If the priests recognized John's mission, why had they then not believed in him in his day, and what had they now to remember against Jesus' prophetic action? Did they disown his mission, then they had to fear the people, who, as

[1] Matt. xxi. 13.   [2] Matt. xxi. 16.

Josephus also informs us, would not allow the prophet to be defamed with impunity; so they preferred leaving the question unanswered, and had to allow Jesus also to turn his back upon them without answering them farther. It is a picture with genuine Oriental local colouring that the Gospel narrative unfolds of the succeeding days. We see Jesus sitting, now in Solomon's porch and now in the treasury, without uttering a word, surrounded by a multitude awed into silence. They are all devoutly meditating on the great Messianic question. From time to time an emissary from his opponents steps up to him, with Eastern solemnity and ceremoniousness, to propose some well-considered question. Anxiously do the multitude listen for Jesus' answer; then again follows a meditative silence as before, until at last Jesus himself delivers a connected discourse. The discourse, which Jesus delivers on the third day, follows in the lines of Isaiah v. 1, &c., and states to the people the fate of the prophets, of which that of the Messiah will not fall short. Israel is the vineyard, the husbandmen of which refuse to pay the fruits due to their lord; they kill his servants, and will finally kill the son of their lord also; but these wicked men will not escape punishment. For the one to whom God will give his estate for an inheritance does not depend upon his being acknowledged by its present occupiers. "Did ye never read in the Scriptures," Jesus asks them, "The stone which the builders refused is become the head of the corner: this is the Lord's doing: it is marvellous in our eyes?"[1]

After this discourse, it was no longer possible for the members of the hierarchy to conceal from themselves that *they* were the object of attack. Their sins are his theme; from their guardianship will he withdraw the people, and re-mould the statutes of the people and temple. They now, in fact, did make a feeble attempt to seize him,[2] but in face of the attitude of the people they were compelled to yield. Then they matured the diabolical scheme of removing him by means of the Romans, and so keeping

---

[1] Psalm cxviii. 22, 23. [2] Mark xii. 12.

their own hands unstained by prophet-murder. Whilst they withdrew the organs of the temple supervision, they put forward certain Pharisees and known members of the Herodian faction as witnesses for the procurator, who should compel Jesus to speak out about the position of his Messiahship to the Roman sovereignty. In the hearing of the multitude, they solemnly propounded a question, the answer to which must irreconcilably envenom his relations with the patriotic people, or, what was more probable and desirable, deliver him over to a Roman prison. "Master," the emissaries began, "We know that thou art true, and teachest the way of God in truth, neither carest thou for any man, for thou regardest not the person of men. Tell us, therefore, what thinkest thou? Is it lawful to give tribute unto Cæsar or not?" Had he, yesterday, laid a snare for them when he asked concerning the mission of the Baptist, they now in return had placed a double pitfall before him. On the right hand and the left yawned destruction. Here the glaring eyes of the multitude; there, Herod's officer; here, the cry, "taxgatherer," "sinner;" there, the cell of Barabbas. And *he* could not do, as they had done, withdraw with a mere, "we know not." The ideas of the Gaulonite were mighty amongst this densely thronged multitude: and it was for the very purpose of giving an answer to the great questions of the time that he was a prophet. Here probably there was not a single Galilean that did not expect a decisive No from him. For the payment of taxes to an idolatrous state was forbidden and desecrated the land; thus had Judas the Gaulonite taught the youth of the country, and many had already shed their blood or were living as fugitives in caves on account of this doctrine. The Herodians probably were already preparing to seize him on account of this No when Jesus spoke, pointing out to the people with a loud voice what was the real subject of controversy. "Why *tempt* ye me, ye hypocrites? Bring me a denarius that I may see it. Whose is this image and superscription?" "Cæsar's," unwillingly replied the hunters, seeing how their noble prey was escaping them. "Then render unto Cæsar the things that are Cæsar's, and to God the things that are God's," was his answer, at which no pious patriot could take offence, and no denouncer could find grounds for an accusation. Rome might rest in peace, and yet the words, "Render to God the things that are God's," sounded in the ears of the people as a watchword for better days. The attack had recoiled upon themselves; the assaulters were ridiculously prostrated. The Sadducean temple nobility could be little edified by the transactions of their Pharisaic allies, and determined to see what they could do themselves. As the Sadducees had long ago given up the people, and Jesus, consequently, threatened their authority far less than that of the Pharisees, they did not much trouble themselves. They were satisfied for the time with a rub at the hated preaching of the coming kingdom, and with turning all these dreams about the future into ridicule. The Prophet was still remaining in his place, surrounded by the multitude, which was absorbed Oriental-like in meditation, when the Sadducees approached with one of those controversial points which they were accustomed to propound for decision to subtle-minded teachers. According to the leviratical institution, a man was obliged to marry the widow of his brother if the latter had died without children. So they described the marriage of a childless woman with seven brethren, all of whom she survived. "Whose wife will she be at the resurrection of the dead?" The question was well adapted for raising laughter upon their side, but no frivolous tones were heard in the neighbourhood of this mysterious man. "Ye do err," replied the Prophet, "not knowing the Scriptures, nor the power of God. For in the resurrection they neither marry nor are given in marriage, but are as angels in heaven. But as touching the resurrection of the dead, did ye never read that which was spoken unto you by God, saying, I am the God of Abraham, and the God of Isaac, and the God of Jacob? God is not God of dead men, but of living!"[1] An unsuccessful attempt to provoke hilarity is, especially before a large assembly, painful to those who have made it, and so the

[1] Matt. xxii. 23—32; Mark xii. 18—27; Luke xx. 27—38.

Sadducees willingly excused themselves from another trial. The skirmishing was continued for some time. The Pharisees once more approached with a question as to the greatest commandment in the law, in order to be silenced with the current answer of children; finally, Jesus energetically put an end to this contention about words. Referring to their worldly Messianic hopes, he proposed a problem to them, too, which they should solve for him, or else spare him any more questions. In so doing, he took just one of the very points in their worldly conceptions where he personally was beyond reproach, the descent from David, in order to show how little these carnal things had to do with the true dignity of the Messiah. Here his opponents could not scoff; the grapes are sour; for whilst his brothers were yet alive, Paul notified that Jesus was of Davidic descent. The greater must the impression have been when he himself declared, "*It is not on this account* that I am the Messiah; my kingship is due to another Father." So he asks the people, Pharisees, the hierarchy, whoever will hearken to him, "What think ye of the Christ? whose son is he?" They said, "David's." Then he replied, "How, then, doth David in spirit call him Lord, saying, the Lord said unto my Lord, Sit thou on my right hand, till I put thine enemies under thy feet? If David then calleth him Lord, how is he his son?" "And no man was able to answer him a word, neither durst any man from that day forth question him any more."[1] Jesus, on the other hand, himself now directs the whole force of his eloquence against his opponents, and here it was that he delivered those keenest of his discourses against the Pharisees, which cut the Rabbis to the heart like daggers. As they stand before him, they become the objects of his satire and of the laughter of the multitude. They had come in the most pious of their robes to the temple, and now he mockingly speaks of their tassels and phylacteries. The proselytes whom they have converted abroad they seek to lead paradingly to the feast, and he calls the sons of their faith two-fold more the

---

[1] Matt. xxii. 46.

children of hell than themselves.¹ Their silver falls with loud jingling into the treasury of God, and he points out the widow who casts in two mites. Here in the temple is it that he proclaims, "Woe unto you, blind guides, which say, Whosoever shall swear by the temple, it is nothing; but whosoever shall swear by the gold of the temple, he is a debtor. Ye fools and blind; for which is the greater, the gold, or the temple that hath sanctified the gold?" Thus they appeared as scorners of their temple, the renown of which they nevertheless everywhere proclaimed, rebuked by him who was called a blasphemer of their temple. On the 15th of Adar, at the conclusion of the rainy season, they had newly whitened the grave-stones around Jerusalem, in order that no one might be unwittingly defiled by them. To these fair-seeming sepulchres, which the pilgrims had passed on their way to the feast, does the Galilean compare the pure of Jerusalem: "Outwardly they appear beautiful, but are within full of dead bones and all uncleanness."²

It was probably the physiognomy of the multitude, yet clinging faithfully to their teachers, which reminded Jesus in the course of his speech of the fate of that prophet Zechariah, the son of Jehoiada, who had also hurled denunciations at the leaders and elders of the people in the forecourt of the temple. "Why transgress ye the commandments of Jehovah that ye cannot prosper? Because ye have forsaken Jehovah, He hath also forsaken you," had he declared. The people had on that occasion, however, seized stones, and stoned the rebuking prophet to death in the court of the house of Jehovah.³ Opposite the eastern porch, in which Jesus was then speaking, and out of which one looked down into the valley of the Kidron, there lay on the slope of the Mount of Olives the artificial tombs of the prophets, the most southerly of which is at the present day called the tomb of Zechariah.⁴ With these

---

[1] Matt. xxiii. 15. Tacitus, Hist. v. 5, expresses a similar opinion.
[2] Shekal, c. i. h 1, in Keim's Jesus of Nazara, Vol. v. [iii. 180, in German ed.].
[3] 2 Chron. xxiv. 20, 21.   [4] Furrer, in Schenkel's Bibel-Lexicon, iii. 527.

tombs in view, passing from sepulchre to sepulchre, Jesus exclaimed, in full consciousness of the historical importance of the moment, "Woe unto you, Scribes and Pharisees, hypocrites, because ye build the tombs of the prophets, and garnish the sepulchres of the righteous .... so then ye are witnesses unto yourselves that ye are the sons of them which killed the prophets .... that upon you may come all the righteous blood shed upon the earth, from the blood of righteous Abel unto the blood of Zechariah, whom ye slew between the temple and the altar." But even this authoritative speech no longer awakened any echo. His opponents threatened, and the people did not stir. The hosannas had died away, and it remains as a remarkable proof of their lukewarm disposition that, during the whole period of the feast, no miracle of any kind was wrought. Then Jesus appealed to the future and its coming judgment, while he attributes his woes to the leaders of the people, and concludes his address with the same menacing words with which, two years before, the Baptist had begun. It was the third day before the Passover[1] when he delivered this his last speech. With the words, "For I say unto you, Ye shall not see me henceforth till ye shall say, Blessed is he that cometh in the name of the Lord," had he departed from the temple. As he descended the eastern temple-steps to the valley of the Kidron with his disciples, the colossal blocks of the basement, twenty feet long and four feet broad, fitted one into the other, which Herod had here piled up, and which at the present day are the wonder of the traveller to Jerusalem,[2] were pointed out by one of the disciples, who said, "Master, what buildings are here?" Jesus, however, replied, "Seest thou these great buildings? there shall not be left one stone upon another that shall not be thrown down."[3] Sitting on the summit of the Mount of Olives, he discoursed this evening, according to our historical source, circumstantially of the future of the people whose capital lay opposite him in its full splendour. When Jerusalem lay in ruins, Josephus still remembered with enthusiasm the glory of the view which the city presented at this

---

[1] Matt. xxvi. 2.   [2] Furrer, Wanderung in Pal. p. 34.   [3] Mark xiii. 1, 2.

point. The marble-crowned Hill of Moriah appeared like a snow-covered rock: at sun-rise the gilded spikes of the roof gleamed, and the fiery splendour dazzled the eyes like the sun itself.[1] Nevertheless it was only earnest and mournful words as to the future of the city which Jesus here addressed to his disciples. The lamentation over Jerusalem with which he had just separated from the people was still re-echoing in his soul. Not less gloomy than his own fate does he behold that of Jerusalem hastening on. He recognizes the necessary development of the courses which his people, led by the blind, have chosen, and his sharp ear already hears in the distance the roaring of the cataracts towards which the bark of the Jewish state is irretrievably drifting. The people who scorn the mild hand of God will find His angry one in their path; the temple will be destroyed, so that not one stone shall be left upon another.[2] Before his mind's eye there lay the Jerusalem which the grandchildren beheld when, above the ashes of the overthrown city, the towers of Phasael and Mariamne and the mighty Hippicus were alone left gloomy ruins keeping watch upon the land.[3] This, however, was also to be the time—so at least the disciples afterwards believed they heard him declare—when the promise of the Messianic kingdom would be also externally fulfilled. As *he* was now founding it in stillness and obscurity, so, too, on that day of the catastrophe which all the prophets had foretold, it would be vouchsafed *to him* to herald in this external manifestation.[4]

And now the Passover was come. From Tiberias the tetrarch

---

[1] Bell. v. 6, 6.

[2] For a genuine basis of the prophecy, Matt. xxiv. 2. Keim, in his Jesus of Nazara, Vol. v. [Vol. iii. p. 190, German edition], has rightly maintained that Jesus foretold another kind of destruction from that which afterwards occurred (demolition, and not deflagration); see the declarations of his opponents before the Sanhedrin, the accusation of Stephen for repeating this prophecy, Acts vi. 14, and also numerous parallels in Josephus, Bell. ii. 12, 5; 15, 4; 16, 4; 17, 10; 19, 5, &c. &c. Matt. xxiv. is to be accepted as a fugitive piece, which had its origin in the year 68.

[3] Bell. vi. 9, 1; Luke xix. 44.

[4] That Jesus himself at this time put this terminus to his second coming is probable from the reason that a period of alarm as antecedent to the catastrophe was an integral portion of every expectation of the kingdom. Das Buch Henoch, 99, 100, 102, 103. Oracula. Sibyll. iii. 334, 633, iv. 168, v. 511. Daniel vii. 25, viii. 23, ix. 26, xii. 1.

Antipas came up, in order to show himself during the feast at the centre of the theocracy. The ancient castle of the Asmoneans on the Xystus had remained in the hands of Herod's family.[1] Here, just opposite to the temple, did he take up his abode. Pilate, who was accustomed to keep watch upon public order in person during these dangerous feast-days, appeared from Cæsarea. He occupied the castle on Zion which Herod had built and richly adorned with gardens, marble courts and gorgeous furniture. This new royal residence was the pride of Jerusalem. "Innumerable was the variety of stone of which it was built. Whatever rarities the country produced were to be found here in abundance. The roofs were worth seeing on account of the length of their beams and their splendid adornments. There were apartments without number, with a thousand variations in form; rich in different gorgeous vessels, chiefly of gold and silver. The corridors crossed each other many times, each with a different arrangement of pillars. The open spaces around the palace were everywhere planted with long avenues of trees of various species; beside them were broad canals and basins rich in all sorts of works of art, through which water poured forth."[2] This was the residence in which the tragedies of Herod's family had been enacted, where Archelaus had played the tyrant, and where Glaphyra had died. According to right of conquest, the Romans had reserved this, the chief palace of the city, for the procurator, and to it transferred the prætorium. Whilst the strengthened garrison occupied the castle of Antonia, the procurator and his retinue took up their quarters here. This was the last Passover during which Pilate inhabited the palace, where he had never yet set foot without experiencing some most disagreeable conflict with the population.[3]

The high-priest at the time of this passover was Joseph, who had the surname Caiaphas. He had been installed by Valerius

---

[1] Compare Antiq. xx. 8, 11.   [2] Bell. v. 4, 4.
[3] Philo, Leg. ad Caium; Frankf. Ausgabe, 1033; Bohn's translation, Vol. iv. page 164; Antiq. xviii. 3, 2; Bell. ii. 9, 4; Luke xiii. 1; Matt. xxvii. 24.

Gratus, and, whether it were owing to his nullity or to his discreet management, contrived to retain office for an unheard-of number of years. The fourth Gospel has nevertheless made, not him, but Annas—the father of the most eminent of the Sadducean families—the chief person in Jesus' trial, after the third Evangelist, who was acquainted with the histories of Josephus, had elevated the there celebrated theocrat to a spiritual co-regency with Caiaphas.[1] All that can be proved historically is, that Annas' house was at this time the most powerful in Jerusalem, that without his co-operation scarcely anything was done in the affairs of the theocracy, that it was notorious on account of its sentences of death, and that even years afterwards it encountered the brother of Jesus, James, with deadly hatred.[2] The head of the house had been made high-priest by Quirinius in the year 7 of our era, and was deprived of this dignity in the autumn of the year 14 by Valerius Gratus. But he saw his five sons in succession raised to the same office—to one of them indeed it was offered twice—and was on this account called by the people the most fortunate of the human race. The family of Annas belonged, as did the whole of the temple aristocracy, to the Sadducees, and shared their reputation for harshness and violence.[3] To them pre-eminently does that lamentation of one of the inhabitants of Jerusalem during its last days seem to refer, who sums up his lamentations over the race in these words: "They are high-priests, their sons are keepers of the treasury, and their servants beat the people with staves!"[4] In fact, it is not an unjust characteristic if we read in the same place: "Woe is me on account of the race of Annas, woe is me on account of their serpent's hiss." Intrigue, and unwearied conspiracy that never failed in its purpose, was the life proper to this house. Thus was this contemporary already struck by the gentle yet firm, serpent-like gripe with which this race was accustomed to seize its prey. When Quirinius, after the census, sacrificed his high-priest

---

[1] Luke iii. 2; Acts iv. 6. Relying upon this, John xviii. 13.
[2] Antiq. xx. 9, 1.   [3] Acts v. 17; Antiq. xx. 9, 1.   [4] Comp. Vol. i. p. 79.

Joazar because, in consequence of his complacency towards
Rome, he had drawn universal hatred upon himself, there was
one member of the temple aristocracy who appeared equally
acceptable to the Romans *and* the population—the first Annas.[1]
Under three procurators had he known how to retain his office,
at times in situations that had not been wholly easy. When,
under Coponius, the Samaritans had desecrated the temple at
night, Annas heightened the impression this sacrilege produced
by sending away the multitudes that had flocked together from
most distant parts to the feast, at the closed doors of the outraged
sanctuary, in order that they might not themselves be defiled,
and thus exaggerated the boyish trick of a few Samaritans into
an event which exasperated the Jews throughout the whole
empire.[2] Under Valerius Gratus, Annas had been compelled to
give place to Ismael ben Phabi, who, however, after a very short
term of office was in turn supplanted by Annas' son Eleazar.[3]
The reasons why Annas did not install himself once more in
Ismael's place are probably the same as those which afterwards
one of his sons, Jonathan, raised in objection to king Herod
Agrippa, when the latter wished to make him high-priest for
the second time. The family, which was little concerned as to
all other precepts of morality, yet strongly respected the basis of
the hierarchical ordinances. No one might assume the sacred
robe a second time who had once laid it aside and released himself from the obligations which were entailed upon its wearer.[4]
These principles claimed the respect of Annas also, because
they appeared to him to constitute the basis of the theocratic
ordinances on the strength of which his house stood at the
head of Israel. So he preferred guiding the reins from a secure
obscurity, but with a firm hand. His sons Eleazar, Jonathan,
Theophilus, Matthias and Annas in succession assumed the
sacred robe, stood, as long as their father lived, firm in conflict
with Caligula's sacrilegious assaults upon the temple, and even
wore probably the chains of Rome as prisoners;[5] but when their

---

[1] Antiq. xviii. 2, 1.   [2] Antiq. xviii. 2, 2.   [3] Antiq. xviii. 2, 2.
[4] Antiq. xix. 6, 4.   [5] Antiq. xx. 6, 2.

father died, at an advanced age, and, with the surname of "the Fortunate," had been laid in a pompous grave, and thus the controlling spirit had been removed, then the Sadducean brutality of the sons of Annas came the more glaringly to the front, and speedily caused the overthrow of the house.[1] Among the high-priests who interrupted the succession of this family, the one who kept his position for the longest period was the Caiaphas who was now in office, and whom the fourth Gospel, moreover, represents as being the son-in-law of the old Annas. He had maintained his position for now seventeen years, and in spite of the mighty conflicts about the eagle, the shields and aqueduct of Pilate, had given the latter no ground for deposing him.[2] Moreover, in the year 36, he lived to see the great day of the high-priesthood, when the sacred robe was entrusted to the Jews for their own guardianship by Vitellius. This robe had been hitherto kept by the Gentiles in the Antonia, and previous to its use had on each occasion to be subjected to every kind of purification, lustration and consecration, before it was once more considered fit to be transferred from the Gentile prison to the Holy of Holies of Jehovah. How little the person of Caiaphas, however, was connected with this important result, is proved by the fact that almost simultaneously he was deposed by Vitellius, and Annas' son Jonathan was installed in his place to wear the unprofaned robe.[3] Thus we find ourselves at a time when the actual high-priest was of no importance whatever, while one house was all-important. Annas, especially, had a position for which the other members of the aristocrary not a little envied him. "Annas the elder," does Josephus declare of the murderer of Jesus, "is deemed the most fortunate of men, because he experienced in his sons what has happened to no other high-priest amongst us."[4]

Although the personal pre-eminence of Annas, of which the latter accounts are the first to have any knowledge, may be simply a composition suggested by the perusal of Josephus, yet

---

[1] Antiq. xx. 9, 1. [2] Antiq. xviii. 2, 2.
[3] Antiq. xviii. 4, 3. [4] Antiq. xx. 9, 1.

in any case this composition has rightly indicated the circle that was now considering how Jesus' intention of inducing a public decision might speedily be baffled.[1] The advice of the sons of Annas calls to mind, certainly, that serpent's hiss at which the Jerusalemite shuddered. It was thought safer not to wait for the decision of the people at the appeal which Jesus would certainly make, but to quietly remove him beforehand. This quiet method was recommended, not only by the traditions of this mighty house, but also by the circumstance that the multitude was not to be depended upon, and had already shown at Jesus' entry how easily it followed any momentary impulse.[2] This purpose of preventing Jesus appearing before the people on the chief day of the feast, the 15th of Nisan, now met with unexpected aid from one of the twelve disciples of Jesus. He offered, or allowed himself to be prevailed upon, to point out the place where his teacher intended passing the night before the feast. This traitor, Judas of Karioth, was the only Judæan in this circle of Galileans. In order to discover the motives for his apostacy, we must know more about the man than the Gospels tell us. His surname, "the man from Karioth," by which he was distinguished from Judas Lebbæus, "the man of heart," seems to indicate that the other disciples were not very intimate with him. Of his farther fate, legend first concerned itself. Thus he seems to have been, even to his contemporaries, pretty well impenetrable; at least, the motive of avarice, attributed to him by the Gospels, hardly seems sufficient to explain his action. It is possible that Judas, disappointed about the development of the expected kingdom, wished to make his peace with the authorities betimes, and have his revenge upon an undertaking which had so thoroughly deceived his hopes.

According to the synoptical Gospels, Jesus had taken the Paschal-meal with his disciples in Jerusalem on the 14th of

---

[1] Matt. xxvi. 3; Mark xiv. 1.
[2] Matt. xxvi. 5, ἵνα μὴ θόρυβος γένηται. They were afraid of the Galileans, "οἷς ἔθος ἦν θορυβεῖν." Bell. i. 16, 5.

Nisan, as being the legal day.[1] A spacious chamber, which the owner had furnished for this purpose with table and couches, was chosen for the celebration. One of the disciples undertook the task of killing the lamb, which, according to the obtaining ritual, had to be slaughtered by the head of the family in the forecourt of the sanctuary.[2] In the evening, Jesus repaired with the others to the upper chamber that had been prepared in order to partake of the meal. The formalities to be observed at it were prescribed with the utmost stringency. It began, like every other meal, with washing the hands and prayer. After they had taken their places, a cup was passed round, which the head of the family blessed with the words, "Blessed be Thou, O Lord our God, Thou King of the world, who hast created the fruit of the vine." Then bitter herbs, consisting of endive, lettuce, &c., were distributed among those present, often in such a manner that they were dipped into a compôte, the so-called Charoseth, prepared from almonds, nuts, figs, and similar fruits. This compôte was to remind them by its colour of the bricks of Egypt, under the burden of which their fathers had groaned. With this bitter dish unleavened bread had to be eaten, "the bread of misery," the Mazzoth, as a reminder of the hasty flight out of Egypt. The head of the family took several such cakes of bread, broke one of them, pronounced the blessing, Blessed be He who has brought forth bread out of the earth," and then distributed it to those present. Once more was the unleavened bread eaten in conjunction with the bitter herbs, and then followed the chief point of the whole solemnity, the eating of the Easter lamb, when the cup was passed round the second time. With the third cup, "the cup of blessing," the meal was concluded. While partaking of the fourth cup, the so-called Hallel was sung (Psalms cxv.—cxviii.), as the conclusion of the

[1] Mark xiv. 12.
[2] The rites at the time of Jesus are to be gathered from Bell. vi. 9, 3; Jubil. 49 (Göttg. Jahrb. 1851, p. 68); also from Philo, Vita Mos. iii.; Mang. 169; Bohn, Vol. iii. p. 121; especially, however, in Mishna Pesachim. Further details in Keim, Jesus of Nazara, Vol. v. [iii. 255 of German edition]; Langen, die letzten Tage Jesu, p. 147, f.

whole solemnity. Although these four cups, like everything else which took place until then, were stringently prescribed to the members of the Passover, it was now left to the free-will of every individual to partake of a fifth cup, with which then the great Hallel (Psalm cxxxvi.) was sung. Every cup was blessed as the head of the family raised it, gazed upon it, and then pronounced the specified formula over it. The bread was usually distributed with the formula, "This is the bread of suffering;" the lamb with the words, "This is the body of the paschal-meal."[1] When the paschal-meal was already at an end,[2] Jesus took a piece of bread, pronounced the blessing, broke it, and distributed it to the disciples, saying, "Take, eat; this is my body which is given for you: this do in remembrance of me." Then in like manner he took the cup, blessed it, and gave it also with the words, "Drink ye all of it, for this is my blood of the covenant which is shed for you; this do, as oft as ye drink it, in remembrance of me." For himself, however, he declined the cup. "Verily I say unto you, I will never drink more of the fruit of the vine until that day when I drink it new in the kingdom of God."[3] With the great Hallel (Psalm cxxxvi.) the evening was ended.[4] "O give thanks unto the Lord; for He is good: for His mercy endureth for ever"—those are the words of the Psalm with which this last communion of Jesus with his disciples was concluded. "And when they had sung the hymn, they went out into the Mount of Olives."[5]

When we ask, what was the meaning of the institution which Jesus founded on this last evening, he tells us when he designates the cup as a covenant-cup which should serve for his remembrance, under a reference to the power of his blood with which this new covenant is to be cemented. The thought of the necessity of his death had thoroughly permeated his mind, and as the blood of the Paschal lamb had redeemed the Israelites, so that the destroying angel passed over them, so also should his

---

[1] Mishna Pesachim, last chapter, § 3. [2] 1 Cor. xi. 25, μετὰ τὸ δειπνῆσαι.
[3] 1 Cor. xi. 24, 25; Mark xiv. 22—25.
[4] Delitzsch, Zeitschr. für luth. Theol. und Kirche, 1855, iv. 653. [5] Mark xiv. 26.

blood be a ransom for many. It is the sacrificial blood which seals the covenant, it is the covenant blood which unites his followers, it is the blood of a new Paschal lamb with which one marks oneself out, so that the destroying angel will pass over at the coming judgment. Thoughts of the Scripture, of his life and death, were thus combined under the one act. If, on the one hand, there were present in his mind thoughts of the Passover, and probably also the imagery of the prophet who compares the suffering servant of Jehovah to a lamb which is led to the slaughter, so, on the other, there was also dominant the custom of his people of celebrating religious communion in a common meal. As in the temple the people ate of the sacrifices and drank of the temple-wine, so were those to eat of the symbolical body and blood for whom that body and blood had been sacrificed. After doing nothing to unite the citizens of his kingdom externally, he had in the last hour given only this one commandment: "Do this, as often as ye drink, in memory of me." The remembrance of him, of his broken body, of his spilled blood, was to distinguish the assemblies of his people from those of the world. The communion of breaking bread with reference to him was the only outward custom which was to unite his followers until he himself came again, in order to drink with them the fruit of the vine new in the kingdom of the Father.[1] So much the more significant did this institution become to the circle of disciples, so much the more important did it become for the future.

When they were breaking up, Jesus asked his disciples about weapons, and said, "He that hath no sword, let him sell his garment and buy one." The disciples showed him two swords; he, however, said, "It is enough."[2] An attempt at assassination was accordingly to be met with resistance. Instead of in Bethany, it was determined to spend this last night before the great day of the feast upon the nearer side of the Mount of Olives. For this purpose a farmstead, the so-called "oil-press" (Gethsemane),

---

[1] Compare for the whole, Keim, Jesus of Nazara, Vol. v. [iii. 247, German edition].
[2] Luke xxii. 35, 36.

had been selected. Here it was where Jesus, after nightfall, was surprised by the emissaries of the Sanhedrin and a troop of armed temple servants. The terrified disciples dispersed, and Jesus was marched as a prisoner to the high-priest's palace, where the examination was at once begun. Of all his utterances which had been gathered in the temple, there were only two which could be interpreted as punishable: the one, that Jesus had promised to destroy the temple, and within three days to build it anew again;[1] the other, that he was the promised One of Israel. As far as regards the first charge, it could be qualified by the Gospels, in the form in which it was raised by the Sadducean priesthood, as a false one; but nevertheless it will have had some sort of a foundation. If the universal belief undoubtedly expected the destruction and restoration of the temple by the Messiah,[2] the question about it was probably put to Jesus also, and answered by him with a higher meaning. The testimony, apprehended externally and misinterpreted, yielded no results, certainly, but it led the high-priest on to the chief question, whether the prisoner was the Messiah, and to this question Jesus replied without any reservation, "I am;" nay, he even voluntarily added the more important confession, "I say unto you, From this time ye shall see the Son of Man sitting on the right hand of power, and coming upon the clouds of heaven."[3] Then the high-priest, appalled, rent his robe and cried, "He hath spoken blasphemy against God; why need we any further witnesses?" Jesus' fate was now determined. A second sitting of the Sanhedrin, held in the morning, could only confirm this result.

It would be too much opposed to every healthy sentiment were we to scrutinize the most sacred hours of human history, successively, for the interests of that period which are manifest in them. It will suffice to briefly point out those tendencies which conspired for the destruction of Jesus, and which, historically considered, led to it. In so doing, it can be specified as

---

[1] Mark xiv. 58.   [2] See p. 21.
[3] Matt. xxvi. 64; Mark xiv. 62; Luke xxii. 69.

one of the signs that the evangelical tradition, as regards the most decisive circumstances, rests throughout upon a firm historical basis, that it assigns to every party in this single case the very position which, according to other sources, is characteristic of it. It is the point of view of the SADDUCEES which is emphasized in the accusation of the high-priest and the members of the Sanhedrin, consequently of Caiaphas, of Annas and his house, of his sons Phabi, Kamith, Kanthera and so on. They interpret Jesus' appearance as the Messiah, in brief, as an attempt at revolution that must be anticipated in time. The Sadducean opposition to the expected kingdom in general and to the national tendencies, is pretty strongly expressed in the passionate cries of the accusers, "We found this man perverting our nation, and forbidding to give tribute to Cæsar;"[1] and, "He stirreth up the people, teaching throughout all Judæa, beginning from Galilee to this place."[2] The same watchwords that the priestly aristocracy had, since the revolt of Judas the Gaulonite, used in opposition to every Messianic movement, were thus pronounced here also; just as we see the highly-born Josephus developing a hatred that becomes incapable of judgment towards the prophetic enthusiasm of a later date. The accounts also perfectly agree in their statement that it was the chief priests who, by means of instigating the multitude and by the temple servants amongst them, brought about this unnatural tumult, in which the mutinous population of Jerusalem accused one of their own people with being a rebel before the hated Roman.[3] "And the voices of the chief priests prevailed,"[4] does Luke significantly declare. Such an attempt, however, would have been baffled, in spite of the people's inclination for tumults of every kind, by the influence of the Pharisees over them, and their sympathy with the preaching of the kingdom; and the cries of loyalty, so perfectly meaningless in the mouths of the inhabitants of Jerusalem, would have fallen resultless to the ground, had it not been for

---

[1] Luke xxiii. 2.
[2] Luke xxiii. 5.
[3] Mark xv. 11; Luke xxiii. 10, 23.
[4] Luke xxiii. 23.

the deadly hatred of the PHARISEES, which was of longer standing than the Sadducees' alarm about a Messianic revolution. Their accusation of the *false* Messiah, of the temple profaner, of the blasphemer of God, was repeated by the full chorus of the law-zealous multitude. "This man said, I am able to destroy the temple of God;"[1] "He hath spoken blasphemy;"[2] "Away with this man, and release unto us Barabbas!"[3] These are cries in which the fanatical multitude could join more heartily than in hypocritical warnings of a riot. PILATE, however, confronted this raging and boisterous crowd also with that inward want of firmness which was no longer a secret to any one in Israel. Five days long had he, in Cæsarea, allowed the Jews to clamour against the Roman standards, only to remove them on the sixth. Haughtily had he rejected those who were aggrieved at the votive tablets on the palace, only to grant a deputation afterwards to Tiberius. Meanwhile, the register of his misdeeds had only become the longer, Tiberius the more jealous, and the more dangerous for officials at the time of Sejanus' downfall. He, the procurator, could not allow a conflict to break out with the courage of a good conscience. His first thought is now, to spill no fresh blood without absolute necessity, to increase the long series of executions by no new one; and with this view he refers to the Roman laws which do not allow sentence of death; he will appeal to the mercy of the people by recommending the prisoner to the amnesty of the multitude; he throws doubt upon his competence to act by delivering the Galilean to the tetrarch. But ANTIPAS also acts in accordance with the character which he elsewhere reveals. He is not the man to charge himself with the blood of a second Prophet unnecessarily, in order to relieve the procurator, who disliked him, of a difficulty. The murder of John had borne too bitter fruit for him to venture on a deed of which the fickle Galileans might perhaps approve to-day, in order to-morrow to condemn, or even avenge it. It was to him remarkable that he should see the celebrated Prophet of his own

---

[1] Matt. xxvi. 61.   [2] Matt. xxvi. 65.   [3] Luke xxiii. 18.

home here in Jerusalem, and the moral coarseness of the Herod could not conceal its joy. Although he might not wish to shed this man's blood himself, yet still less did he intend saving Jesus. In a royal robe, thus corroborating the accusation that Jesus intended making himself king, does he send him back to the procurator. Never had the people seen such a competition between Antipas and Pilate in making advances towards each other, and the tradition arose that from that time they were friends.[1] In fact, Antipas had only increased the procurator's difficulty by sending back the prisoner to him in a manner which indirectly confirmed the accusation. His enemy Antipas, who kept up a correspondence with Tiberius, sends him one of those who have been charged with sedition in a purple robe. The Sadducean nobility, who were Roman in their tendencies, demand the death of this Galilean disturber. Should he, who soon afterwards fell, and now even was tottering, subject himself to the suspicion of favouring a revolt in this remote province, of setting free an insurgent? And if he ventured, should he allow the multitude, which more and more madly opposed him, to proceed to a riot, and occasion a fresh massacre, which would certainly be his last? As Pontius Pilate has been described to us by history, he could not act otherwise than he did act. Thus the death of Jesus followed as a necessary consequence of the given circumstances.

That nevertheless the final reasons for this course belong to another and higher order of things, does not need to be mentioned. Our faith gives to the question, "Why must Christ die upon the cross?" yet another answer than the historical, and one more exhaustive. For the history of the Ideal is never the history of the individual, and has a yet deeper signification than that contained within the efforts and currents of the passing day, an eternal signification and an absolute purport which belong not to the history of a period but to humanity, and in which every individual has to reverence a mystery of mercy he also shares.

[1] Luke xxiii. 12.

14, Henrietta Street, Covent Garden, London;
20, South Frederick Street, Edinburgh.

CATALOGUE

OF

WILLIAMS AND NORGATE'S PUBLICATIONS.

Æschylus. Agamemnon. Greek Text revised and translated by John F. Davies, B.A. 8vo, cloth. 3s.

Ali (Syed Ameer) Life of Mohammed. A Critical Examination of the Life and Teachings of Mohammed, from a Mohammedan Standpoint, including Chapters on Polygamy, Slavery, Moslem Rationalism, Moslem Mysticism, &c. Crown 8vo, cloth. 9s.

Attwell (Professor H.) Table of Aryan (Indo-European) Languages, showing their Classification and Affinities, with copious Notes; to which is added, Grimm's Law of the Interchange of Mute Consonants, with numerous Illustrations. A Wall Map for the use of Colleges and Lecture-rooms. 2nd Edition. Mounted with rollers. 10s.

—— Table of the Aryan Languages, with Notes and Illustrations. 4to, boards. 7s. 6d.

Agnostic's Progress, An, from the Known to the Unknown. 268 pp. Crown 8vo, cloth. 5s.

Bannister (Rev. Dr. J.) Glossary of Cornish Names, Ancient and Modern, Local, Family, Personal, 20,000 Celtic and other Names in use in Cornwall. 8vo, cloth. 12s.

Barnabas' Epistle, in Greek, from the Sinaitic Manuscript of the Bible, with a Translation by S. Sharpe. Crown 8vo, cloth. 2s. 6d.

Barratt (A.) Physical Metempiric. By the late Alfred Barratt. With a Portrait. 8vo, cloth. 10s. 6d.

Barratt (A.) Physical Ethics, or the Science of Action. 8vo, cloth. 12s.

Baur (F. C.) Church History of the First Three Centuries. Translated from the Third German Edition. Edited by Rev. Allan Menzies. 2 vols. 8vo, cloth. 21s.

—— Paul, the Apostle of Jesus Christ, his Life and Work, his Epistles and Doctrine. A Contribution to a Critical History of Primitive Christianity. Translated by Rev. A. Menzies. 2 vols. 8vo, cloth. 21s.

Bayldon (Rev. G.) Icelandic Grammar. An Elementary Grammar of the Old Norse or Icelandic Language. 8vo, cl. 7s. 6d.

Beard (Rev. C.) Lectures on the Reformation of the Sixteenth Century in its Relation to Modern Thought and Knowledge. (Hibbert Lectures, 1883.) 8vo, cloth. 10s. 6d.

—— Port Royal, a Contribution to the History of Religion and Literature in France. 2 vols. 8vo. 12s.

Bentham et Hooker Genera Plantarum, ad exemplaria inprimis in Herbariis Kewensibus servata definita; auctoribus G. Bentham et J. D. Hooker. Vol. I. 1, 16s., I. 2, 10s. 6d. Vol. II. 56s. Vol. III. 56s. Imp. 8vo, cloth. Vol. I. Part 3, is out of print.

Bernstein and Kirsch. Syriac Chrestomathy and Lexicon. Chrestomathia Syriaca cum Lexico. 2 vols. in 1. 8vo, cloth. 7s. 6d.

Bible, translated by Samuel Sharpe, being a Revision of the Authorized English Version. 5th Edition of the Old Testament, 9th Edition of the New Testament. 8vo, roan. 4s. 6d.

—— vide also Testament.

Bible for Young People. A Critical, Historical, and Moral Handbook to the Old and New Testaments. By Dr. H. Oort and Dr. J. Hooykaas, with the assistance of Dr. Kuenen. Translated from the Dutch by the Rev P. H. Wicksteed. 6 vols. Crown 8vo. 20s.

Bisset (A.) Short History of the English Parliament. 2 vols. Crown 8vo. 7s.

—— Notes on the Anti-Corn-Law Struggle. 8vo, cloth. 9s.

Bleek (F.) Lectures on the Apocalypse. Edited by Dr. S. Davidson. 8vo, cloth. 10s. 6d.

Cobbe (Miss F. Power) The Peak in Darien, and other Inquiries touching Concerns of the Soul and the Body. Crown 8vo, cloth. 7s. 6d.

—— A Faithless World. With Additions and a Preface. 8vo, cloth. 2s. 6d.

—— The Duties of Women. A Course of Lectures delivered in London and Clifton. 2nd Edition. Crown 8vo, cloth. 5s.

—— The Hopes of the Human Race, Hereafter and Here. Essays on the Life after Death. With a Preface having special reference to Mr. Mill's Essay on Religion. 2nd Edition. Cr. 8vo. 5s.

—— Alone to the Alone. Prayers for Theists, by several Contributors. 3rd Edition. Crown 8vo, cloth. 5s.

—— Broken Lights. An Inquiry into the Present Condition and Future Prospects of Religious Faith. 3rd Edition. 5s.

—— Dawning Lights. An Inquiry concerning the Secular Results of the New Reformation. 8vo, cloth. 5s.

Cobbe (Miss F. Power) Darwinism in Morals, and (13) other Essays (Religion in Childhood, Unconscious Cerebration, Dreams, the Devil, Auricular Confession, &c. &c.). 8vo, cloth. 5s.

Crawford (Rev. Dr.) Horæ Hebraicæ. Cr. 8vo, cloth. 4s. 6d.

Crowfoot (J. R.) Fragmenta Evangelica quæ ex antiqua recens. vers. Syriac. Nov. Test. a Curetono vulg. Græce reddita, &c. 2 Parts; and Observations, 1 Part. 4to. 20s.

Cureton (Dr. W.) History of the Martyrs in Palestine, by Eusebius, in Syriac. Edited and translated. Royal 8vo, cloth. 10s. 6d.

Dante's Inferno and Purgatorio. Translated into Greek verse by Mussurus Pasha, D.C.L. 2 vols. 8vo, cloth. each 12s.

Davids (T. W. Rhys) Lectures on the Origin and Growth of Religion, as illustrated by some Points in the History of Indian Buddhism. (Hibbert Lectures, 1881.) 8vo, cloth. 10s. 6d.

Day (Dr. F.) The Fishes of Great Britain and Ireland; being a Natural History of such as are known to inhabit the Seas and Fresh Waters of the British Isles, including Remarks on their Economic Uses and Various Modes of Capture. 179 Plates. 2 vols. imp. 8vo, cloth. £5. 15s. 6d.

Delitzsch (Dr. F.) The Hebrew Language viewed in the Light of Assyrian Research. By Dr. Fred. Delitzsch, Professor of Assyriology at the University of Leipzig. Crown 8vo. 4s.

Dipavamsa, the : a Buddhist Historical Record in the Pali Language. Edited, with an English Translation, by Dr. H. Oldenberg. 8vo, cloth. 21s.

Echoes of Holy Thoughts : arranged as Private Meditations before a First Communion. 2nd Edition, with a Preface by Rev. J. Hamilton Thom. Printed with red lines. Fcap. 8vo, cloth. 2s. 6d.

Engelhardt (C.) Denmark in the Early Iron Age. Illustrated by recent Discoveries in the Peat-Mosses of Slesvig. 33 Plates (giving representations of upwards of a thousand objects), Maps, and numerous other Illustrations on wood. 4to, cloth. 31s. 6d.

Ethica; or, the Ethics of Reason. By Scotus Novanticus. 8vo, cloth. 6s.

—— vide Metaphysica Nova et Vetusta.

Evans (George) An Essay on Assyriology. By George Evans, M.A., Hibbert Fellow. Published for the Hibbert Trustees. With 4to Tables of Assyrian Inscriptions. 8vo, cloth. 5s.

Evolution of Christianity, The. By Charles Gill. Second Edition, with Dissertations in answer to Criticism. 8vo, cloth. 12s.

Ewald's (Dr. H.) Commentary on the Prophets of the Old Testament. Translated by the Rev. J. F. Smith. Complete in 5 vols. Vol. I. General Introduction, Yoel, Amos, Hosea and Zakharya 9—11. Vol. II. Yesaya, Obadya and Mikha. Vol. III. Nahûm, Ssephanya, Habaqqûq, Zachârya, Yéremya. Vol. IV. Hezekiel, Yesaya xl.—lxvi. Vol. V. and last, Haggai, Zakharya, Malaki, Jona, Baruc, Daniel, Appendix and Index. 8vo, cloth. 5 vols. Each 10s. 6d.

—— **Commentary on the Psalms.** Translated by the Rev. E. Johnson, M.A. 2 vols. 8vo, cloth. Each 10s. 6d.

—— **Commentary on the Book of Job,** with Translation. Translated from the German by the Rev. J. Frederick Smith. 8vo, cloth. 10s. 6d.

Frankfurter (Dr. O.) Handbook of Pali; being an Elementary Grammar, a Chrestomathy, and a Glossary. 8vo, cloth. 16s.

Fuerst (Dr. Jul.) Hebrew and Chaldee Lexicon to the Old Testament. 4th Edition, improved and enlarged. Translated by Rev. Dr. Samuel Davidson. Royal 8vo, cloth. 21s.

—— Kept also half-bound morocco. 26s.

Goldschmidt (H. E.) German Poetry; with the English Versions of the best Translators. Poems of Goethe, Schiller, Freiligrath, Bürger, Heine, Uhland, Körner, &c. &c. Translated by Carlyle, Anster, Blackie, Sir Th. Martin, Shelley, Lord Ellesmere, Lord Lytton, Coleridge, Longfellow, Edgar Bowring, Garnett, &c. 8vo, cloth. 5s.

Gostwick (J.) and R. Harrison. Outlines of German Literature. Dedicated to Thos. Carlyle. New Edition. 8vo. 10s.

Gotch (Rev. Dr. J. W.) Codex Cottonianus. A Supplement to Tischendorf's Fragments in the Monumenta Sacra. Together with a Synopsis of the Codex. Facsimile. 4to, cloth. 7s. 6d.

Gould (Rev. S. Baring) Lost and Hostile Gospels. An Account of the Toledoth Jesher, two Hebrew Gospels circulating in the Middle Ages, and extant Fragments of the Gospels of the first Three Centuries of Petrine and Pauline Origin. Crown 8vo, cloth. 7s. 6d.

Hanson (Sir R. D.) The Apostle Paul and the Preaching of Christianity in the Primitive Church. By Sir R. D. Hanson, Chief Justice of South Australia, Author of "The Jesus of History," &c. 8vo, cloth. (Published at 12s.) 7s. 6d.

Hardy (R. Spence) Manual of Buddhism in its Modern Development. Translated from Cingalese MSS. 2nd Edition, with a complete Index and Glossary 8vo, cloth. 21s.

—— **Eastern [Buddhist] Monachism;** an Account of the Origin, Laws, Discipline, Sacred Writings, &c. &c. of the Order of Mendicants founded by Gotama Buddha. 8vo, cloth. 12s.

Hariri. The Assemblies of Al Hariri. Translated from the Arabic, with an Introduction and Notes. Vol. I. Introduction and the first Twenty-six Assemblies. By T. Chenery, Esq. 8vo, cloth. 10s.

Hausrath. History of the New Testament Times. The Time of Jesus. By Dr. A. Hausrath, Professor of Theology, Heidelberg. Translated by the Revds. C. T. Poynting and P. Quenzer. 2 vols. 8vo, cloth. 21s.

Hemans (Chas. I.) Historic and Monumental Rome. A Handbook for the Students of Classical and Christian Antiquities in the Italian Capital. Crown 8vo, cloth. 10s. 6d.

—— **History of Mediæval Christianity** and Sacred Art in Italy (A.D. 900—1500). 2 vols. Crown 8vo, cloth. 18s.

Herbert (Hon. Auberon) The Party of Individual Liberty. The Right and Wrong of Compulsion by the State. Crown 8vo, cloth. 1s. 6d.

Horne (W.) Religious Life and Thought. By William Horne, M.A., Dundee, Examiner in Philosophy in the University of St. Andrews; Author of "Reason and Revelation." Crown 8vo, cloth. 3s. 6d.

Keim's History of Jesus of Nazara. Considered in its connection with the National Life of Israel, and related in detail. Translated from the German by Arthur Ransom. Vol. I. 2nd Edition. Introduction, Survey of Sources, Sacred and Political Groundwork, Religious Groundwork. Vol. II. The Sacred Youth, Self-recognition, Decision. Vol. III. The First Preaching, the Works of Jesus, the Disciples, and Apostolic Mission. Vol. IV. Conflicts and Disillusions, Strengthened Self-confidence, Last Efforts in Galilee, Signs of the approaching Fall, Recognition of the Messiah. Vol. V. The Messianic Progress to Jerusalem, The Entry into Jerusalem, The Decisive Struggle, The Farewell, The Last Supper. Vol. VI. Arrest and Pseudo-Trial, The Death on the Cross, Burial and Resurrection, The Messiah's Place in History. 8vo, cloth. Each 10s. 6d.

Kuenen (Dr. A.) The the Fall of the Je lated by A. H.

—— **Lectures on N** Universal Religio tures, 1882.) 8v

Laing and Huxley. of Caithness. By with Notes on t by Th. H. Huxl gravings. 8vo, c

Lane (E. W.) Aral derived from the l Eastern Sources. be completed in

—— Vol. VIII. Fo

Latham (Dr. R. G.) the Hamlet of Sa of Shakespear.

Lepsius (C. R.) St reducing Unwrit Foreign Graphic Orthography in 2nd Edition. 8v

Letters to and from A.D. 61, 62, and C. V. S. (by Sir Crown 8vo, cloth

Lindsay (Dr. James, Interpretation of Government of M cloth.

Linguistic Notes on fixes in Greek ar Crown 8vo, cloth

Macan (R. W.) The Christ. An Essa Published for th 8vo, cloth.

Mackay (R. W.) Sk Progress of Chris (Published at 10.

Malan (Rev. Dr. S. C.) The Book of Adam and Eve, also called the Conflict of Adam and Eve with Satan. A Book of the early Eastern Church. Translated from the Ethiopic, with Notes from the Kufale, Talmud, Midrashim, and other Eastern works. 8vo, cloth. 7s. 6d.

Massey (Gerald) A Book of the Beginnings. Containing an Attempt to recover and reconstitute the lost Origines of the Myths and Mysteries, Types and Symbols, Religion and Language. 2 vols. Imperial 8vo, cloth. 30s.

—— The Natural Genesis. 2 vols. Imp. 8vo, cloth. 30s.

Metaphysica Nova et Vetusta: a Return to Dualism. By Scotus Novanticus. 200 pp. 8vo, cloth. 6s.

Milinda Panho, the. Being Dialogues between King Milinda and the Buddhist Sage Nāgasena. The Pali Text, edited by V. Trenckner. 8vo. 21s.

—— vide also Pali Miscellany.

Mind, a Quarterly Review of Psychology and Philosophy. Nos. 1—40. 1876-85. 8vo, each 3s. Annual Subscription, post free, 12s.

Müller (Professor Max) Lectures on the Origin and Growth of Religion, as illustrated by the Religions of India. (Hibbert Lectures, 1878.) 8vo, cloth. 10s. 6d.

Nibelungenlied. The Fall of the Nibelungers, otherwise the Book of Kriemhild. An English Translation by W. N. Lettsom. Crown 8vo, cloth. 7s. 6d.

Nicolson (Rev. W. M.) Classical Revision of the Greek New Testament. Tested and applied on uniform Principles, with suggested Alterations of the English Version. Crown 8vo, cloth. 3s. 6d.

Norris (E.) Assyrian Dictionary. Intended to further the Study of the Cuneiform Inscriptions of Assyria and Babylonia. Vols. I. to III. 4to, cloth. Each 28s.

O'Curry (Eug.) Lectures on the Social Life, Manners and Civilization of the People of Ancient Erinn. Edited, with an Introduction, by Dr. W. K. Sullivan. Numerous Wood Engravings of Arms, Ornaments, &c. 3 vols. 8vo. 42s.

Oldenberg (Prof. H.) Buddha, his Life, his Doctrine, and his Order. Translated by Dr. Wm. Hoey, B.C.S. 8vo. 18s.

—— vide Vinaya Pitakam.

Pali Miscellany, by V. Trenckner. Part I. The Introductory Part of the Milinda Panho, with an English Translation and Notes. 8vo. 4s.

Peill (Rev. George) The Threefold Basis of Universal Restitution. Crown 8vo, cloth. 3s.

Pennethorne (John) The Geometry and Optics of Ancient Architecture, illustrated by Examples from Thebes, Athens and Rome. Folio, with 56 Plates, some in colours. Half morocco. £7. 7s.

Perrin (R. S.) The Religion of Philosophy; or, the Unification of Knowledge. A Comparison of the chief Philosophical and Religious Systems of the World, made with a view to reducing the Categories of Thought, or the most general Terms of Existence, to a single Principle, thereby establishing a true Conception of God. 8vo, cloth. 16s.

Pfleiderer (O.) Paulinism: a Contribution to the History of Primitive Christian Theology. Translated by E. Peters. 2 vols. 8vo. 21s.

—— The Teaching of the Apostle Paul and its Influence on the Development of Christianity. (Hibbert Lectures, 1885.) 8vo, cloth. 10s. 6d.

—— Philosophy of Religion. Translated by the Rev. Alexander Stewart, of Dundee. Vol. I. 8vo. 10s. 6d. Vol. II. shortly.

Platonis Philebus, with Introduction, Notes and Appendix; together with a Critical Letter on the "Laws" of Plato, and a Chapter of Palæographical Remarks, by the Rev. Dr. Chas. Badham, D.D. 2nd Edition, enlarged. 8vo, cloth. 4s.

Platonis Euthydemus et Laches, with Critical Notes and "Epistola critica" to the Senate of the Leyden University, by the Rev. C. Badham, D.D. 8vo, cl. 4s.

—— Convivium (Symposium), with Critical Notes and an Epistola (de Platonis Legibus) to Dr. Thompson, Master of Trinity College, Cambridge, by the Rev. C. Badham, D.D. 8vo, cloth. 4s.

Poole (Reg. L.) Illustrations of the History of Medieval Thought in the Departments of Theology and Ecclesiastical Politics. 8vo, cloth. 10s. 6d.

Protestant Commentary, A Short, on the Books of the New Testament: with general and special Introductions. Edited by Professors P. W. Schmidt and F. von Holzendorff. Translated from the Third German Edition, by the Rev. F. H. Jones, B.A. 3 vols. 8vo, cloth. Each 10s. 6d.

Quarry (Rev. J.) Genesis and its Authorship. Two Dissertations. 2nd Edition, with Notice of Animadversions of the Bishop of Natal. 8vo. 12s.

Reliquiæ Aquitanicæ; being Contributions to the Archæology and Palæontology of Périgord and the adjoining Provinces of Southern France. By Lartet and Christy. Edited by T. Rupert Jones, F.R.S., F.G.S. 87 Plates, 3 Maps, and 130 Wood Engravings. Royal 4to, cloth. £3. 3s.

Renan (E.) On the Influence of the Institutions, Thought and Culture of Rome on Christianity and the Development of the Catholic Church. (Hibbert Lectures, 1880.) 8vo, cloth. 10s. 6d.

Renouf (P. le Page) Lectures on the Origin and Growth of Religion as illustrated by the Religion of Ancient Egypt. (Hibbert Lectures, 1879.) 8vo, cloth. 10s. 6d.

Reville (Dr. Alb.) Prolegomena of the History of Religions. By Albert Réville, D.D., Professor in the Collége de France, and Hibbert Lecturer. With an Introduction by Professor F. Max Müller. 8vo, cloth. 10s. 6d.

Reville (Rev. Dr. A.) On the Native Religions of Mexico and Peru. Translated by the Rev. P. H. Wicksteed. (Hibbert Lectures, 1884.) 8vo, cl. 10s. 6d.

—— The Song of Songs, commonly called the Song of Solomon, or the Canticle. Crown 8vo, cloth. 1s. 6d.

Sadi. The Gulistan (Rose-Garden) of Shaik Sadi of Shiraz. A new Edition of the Persian Text, with a Vocabulary, by F. Johnson. Square royal 8vo, cloth. 15s.

Samuelson (James) Views of the Deity, Traditional and Scientific: a Contribution to the Study of Theological Science. Crown 8vo, cloth. 4s. 6d.

Savage (Rev. M. J.) Beliefs about the Bible. By the Rev. M. J. Savage, of the Unity Church, Boston, Mass., Author of "Belief in God," "Beliefs about Man," &c. 8vo, cloth. 7s. 6d.

Schmidt (A.) Shakespeare Lexicon. A complete Dictionary of all the English Words, Phrases, and Constructions in the Works of the Poet. 2 vols. Imp. 8vo, cloth. 34s.

Schrader (Prof. E.) The Cuneiform Inscriptions and the Old Testament. Translated by the Rev. O. C. Whitehouse. Vol. I. With a Map. 8vo, cl. 10s. 6d. Vol. II. shortly.

Schurman (J. G.) Kantian Ethics and the Ethics of Evolution. A Critical Study. (Published by the Hibbert Trustees.) 8vo, cloth. 5s.

Seth (A.) The Development from Kant to Hegel, with Chapters on the Philosophy of Religion. (Published by the Hibbert Trustees.) 8vo, cloth. 5s.

Sharpe (Samuel) History of the Hebrew Nation and its Literature. With an Appendix on the Hebrew Chronology. 4th Edition, 487 pp. 8vo, cl. 7s. 6d.

—— Hebrew Inscriptions from the Valleys between Egypt and Mount Sinai, in their Original Characters, with Translations and an Alphabet. 2 Parts. 20 Plates. 8vo, cloth. 7s. 6d.

—— vide also Bible, and Testament.

Smith (Rev. J. F.) **Studies in Religion under German Masters.** Essays on Herder, Goethe, Lessing, Frank, and Lang. Crown 8vo, cloth. 5s.
—— vide Ewald's Prophets and Job.
Sophocles. The Greek Text critically revised, with the aid of MSS., newly collated and explained. By Rev. F. H. M. Blaydes. I. Philoctetes. II. Trachiniæ. III. Electra. IV. Ajax. 8vo, cloth. Each 6s.
Spencer (Herbert) First Principles. 5th Thousand, with an Appendix. 8vo. 16s.
—— **The Principles of Biology.** 2 vols. 8vo. 34s.
—— **The Principles of Psychology.** 4th Thousand. 2 vols. 8vo. 36s.
—— **The Principles of Sociology.** Vol. I. 21s.
—— **Ceremonial Institutions.** (Principles of Sociology, Vol. II. Part 1.) 8vo. 7s.
—— **Political Institutions.** (Principles of Sociology, Vol. II. Part 2.) 8vo. 12s.
—— **Ecclesiastical Institutions.** (Principles of Sociology, Vol. II. Part 3.) 5s.
—— **The Data of Ethics.** Being the First Portion of the Principles of Ethics. 8vo, cloth. 8s.
—— **The Study of Sociology.** Library Edition (being the 9th), with a Postscript. 8vo, cloth. 10s. 6d.
—— **Education:** Intellectual, Moral, and Physical. 8vo, cloth. 6s.
—— The same, cheaper Edition, 4th Thousand. 12mo, cloth. 2s. 6d.
—— **Essays:** Scientific, Political, and Speculative. (Being the First and Second Series re-arranged, and containing an additional Essay.) 2 vols. 4th Thousand. 8vo, cloth. 16s.
—— **Essays.** (Third Series.) Including the Classification of the Sciences. 3rd Edition. 8vo. 8s.
—— **The Man versus the State.** Paper covers, 1s.; better paper, cloth, 2s. 6d.
—— **The Philosophy of M. Comte**—Reasons for Dissenting from it. 6d.
—— **Descriptive Sociology,** or Groups of Sociological Facts. Compiled and abstracted by Professor D. Duncan, of Madras, Dr. Richard Sheppig, and James Collier. Folio, boards. No. 1.

English, 18s. No. 2. Ancient American Races, 16s. No. 3. Lowest Races, Negritto Races, Polynesians, 18s. No. 4. African Races, 16s. No. 5. Asiatic Races, 18s. No. 6. American Races, 18s. No. 7. Hebrews and Phœnicians, 21s. No. 8. The French Civilization, 30s.
Spinoza. Four Essays by Professors Land, Van Vloten, and Kuno Fischer, and by E. Renan. Edited by Professor Knight, of St. Andrews. Crown 8vo, cloth. 5s.
Stephens (George) Old Northern Runic Monuments of Scandinavia and England, now first collected and deciphered. Numerous Engravings on Wood and 15 Plates. Vols. I.—III. Folio. Each 50s.
—— **Handbook of old Northern Runic Monuments of Scandinavia and England.** Abridged from the larger Work, retaining all the Illustrations. Royal 4to. 40s.
—— **Thunor the Thunderer,** carved on a Scandinavian Font about the year 1000. 4to. 6s.
Stokes (Geo. J.) The Objectivity of Truth. 8vo, cloth. 5s.
Stokes (Whitley) Old Irish Glossaries. Cormac's Glossary. O'Davoran's Glossary. A Glossary to the Calendar of Oingus the Culdee. Edited, with an Introduction and Index. 8vo, cloth. 10s. 6d.
—— **Middle-Breton Hours.** Edited, with a Translation and Glossary. 8vo, boards. 6s.
—— **The Creation of the World.** A Mystery in Ancient Cornish. Edited, with Translations and Notes. 8vo, cloth. 6s.
Strauss (Dr. D. F.) Life of Jesus for the People. The Authorized English Edition. 2 vols. 8vo, cloth. 24s.
Sullivan (W. K.) Celtic Studies, from the German of Dr. Hermann Ebel, with an Introduction on the Roots, Stems and Derivatives, and on Case-endings of Nouns in the Indo-European Languages. 8vo, cloth. 10s.

Williams and Norgate's Catalogue.

Taine (H.) English Positivism. A Study of John Stuart Mill. Translated by T. D. Haye. Crown 8vo, cloth. 3s.

Tayler (Rev. John James) An Attempt to ascertain the Character of the Fourth Gospel, especially in its relation to the first Three. 2nd Edition. 8vo, cl. 5s.

Testament, The New. Translated by S. Sharpe, Author of "The History of Egypt," &c. 14th Thousand. Fcap. 8vo, cloth. 1s. 6d.

Thoughts (365) for Every Day in the Year. Selected from the Writings of Spiritually-minded Persons. By the Author of "Visiting my Relations." Printed with red lines. Crown 8vo, cl. 2s. 6d.

Turpie (Dr. D. McC.) The Old Testament in the New. The Quotations from the Old Testament in the New classified according to their Agreement with or Variation from the Original : the various Readings and Versions of the Passages, Critical Notes. Royal 8vo, cloth. 12s.

—— Manual of the Chaldee Language : containing Grammar of the Biblical Chaldee and of the Targums, a Chrestomathy, Selections from the Targums, with a Vocabulary. Square 8vo, cl. 7s.

Vinaya Pitakam : one of the principal Buddhist Holy Scriptures. Edited in Pali by Dr. H. Oldenberg. In 5 vols. 8vo. Each 21s.

Williams (Rev. Dr. Rowland) The Hebrew Prophets, during the Assyrian and Babylonian Empires. Translated afresh from the Original, with regard to the Anglican Version, with Illustrations for English Readers. 2 vols. 8vo, cloth. 22s. 6d.

—— Psalms and Litanies, Counsels and Collects, for Devout Persons. Edited by his Widow. Fcap. 4to, cloth extra. 12s. 6d.

—— Broadchalke Sermon-Essays on Nature, Mediation, Atonement, Absolution, &c. Crown 8vo, cloth. 7s. 6d.

Wright (G. H. B.) The Book of Job. A new critically revised Translation, with Essays on Scansion, Date, &c. By G. H. Bateson Wright, M.A., Queen's Coll., Oxford, Head Master of the Government Central School, Hong Kong. 8vo, cloth. 6s.

Zeller (Dr. E.) The Contents and Origin of the Acts of the Apostles critically investigated. Preceded by Dr. Fr. Overbeck's Introduction to the Acts of the Apostles from De Wette's Handbook. Translated by Joseph Dare. 2 vols. 8vo, cloth. 21s.

WILLIAMS & NORGATE have published the following Catalogues of their Stock.

1. CLASSICAL CATALOGUE. Greek and Latin Classics.
2. THEOLOGICAL CATALOGUE. Including Philosophy and Metaphysics.
3. FRENCH CATALOGUE. General Literature, History, Travels, &c.
4. GERMAN CATALOGUE. General Literature.
   * MAP CATALOGUE. Foreign Maps and Atlases.
5. LINGUISTIC CATALOGUE. European Languages.
   * ITALIAN CATALOGUE.
   * SPANISH CATALOGUE.
6. ORIENTAL CATALOGUE. Oriental Languages and Literature.
7. MEDICAL CATALOGUE. Medicine, Surgery, &c.
8. NATURAL HISTORY CATALOGUE. Zoology, Botany, Geology, Palæontology.
9. NATURAL SCIENCE CATALOGUE. Mathematics, Astronomy, Physics, Mechanics, Chemistry, &c.
10. ART CATALOGUE. Architecture, Painting, Sculpture and Engraving. Books illustrated by Artists.
11. SCHOOL CATALOGUE. Elementary Books, Maps, &c.